IMAGES of America

AROUND THE VILLAGE OF CHATHAM

I0809013

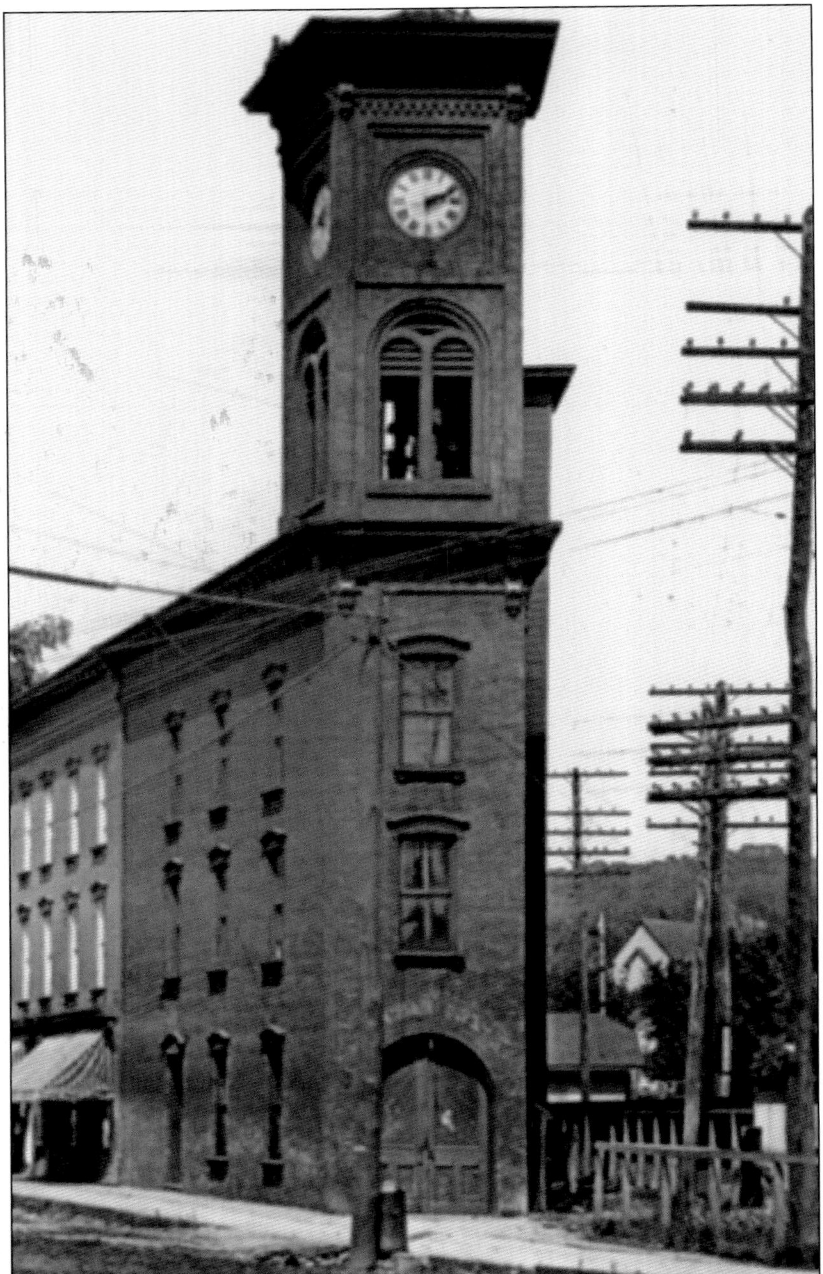

The tower at 1 Main Street stands above the first village hall. Its bell sounded the alarm for the fire department that was housed below. The clock was purchased from the Howard Clock Company of Boston in 1873. O. M. Whyland and Son, local businessmen, gilded the weather vane and repainted the clock face in 1909. When the village government removed to the Tracy Village Hall, it retained ownership of the tower. (Courtesy of Jon Meredith.)

On the cover: Please see page 68. (Courtesy of Ralph Blass family.)

IMAGES
of America

AROUND THE VILLAGE OF CHATHAM

Gail Blass Wolczanski

ARCADIA
PUBLISHING

Copyright © 2009 by Gail Blass Wolczanski
ISBN 978-0-7385-6591-0

Published by Arcadia Publishing
Charleston, South Carolina

Printed in the United States of America

Library of Congress Control Number: 2009921635

For all general information contact Arcadia Publishing at:
Telephone 843-853-2070
Fax 843-853-0044
E-mail sales@arcadiapublishing.com
For customer service and orders:
Toll-Free 1-888-313-2665

Visit us on the Internet at www.arcadiapublishing.com

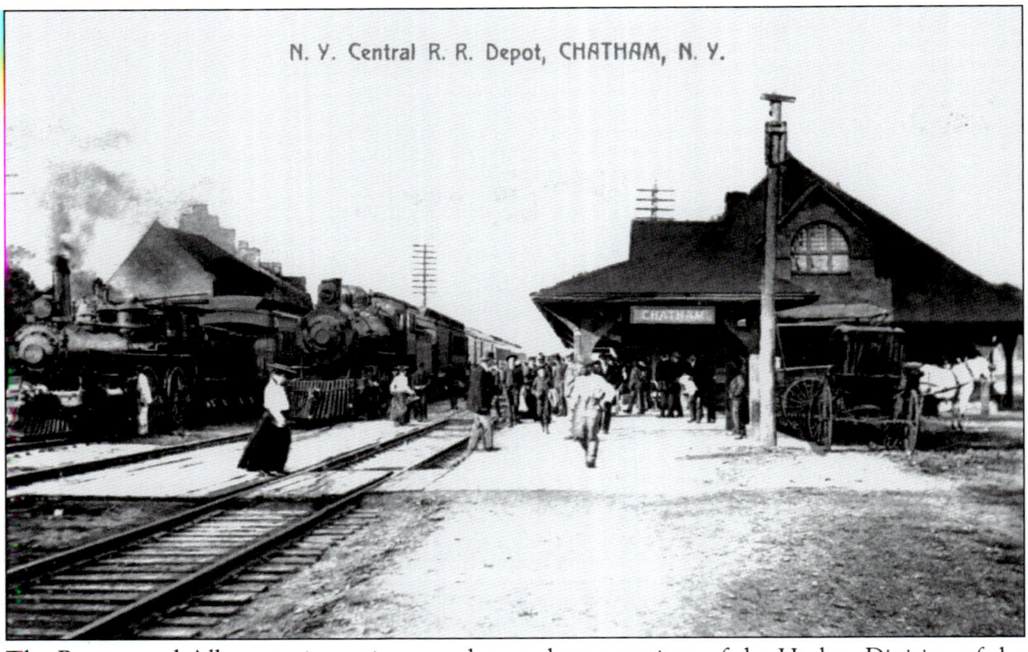

The Boston and Albany train station was the northern terminus of the Harlem Division of the New York Central and Hudson River Railroad, the Hudson Division of the Boston and Albany, and the southern terminus of the Lebanon Springs, later the Rutland Railroad. This moment in time was captured in 1916. (Courtesy of Chatham Village Historical Society.)

Contents

ACKNOWLEDGMENTS

A deadline was the line on the perimeter of a prisoner of war camp where, if you crossed it, you would be shot dead. Under the pressure of my self-imposed publishing deadline my thoughts kept running back to my fear of forgetting to acknowledge an individual who may have saved my life to meet the publication deadline through sharing their time, thoughts, or collections. I hope I was transparently grateful when we met to compensate for your absence from my acknowledgments, should you be the one I sadly overlook.

Throughout this journalistic adventure I have been blessed to work closely with several friends, renewed and freshly formed. None of them were hard to find because the knowledge that I would attempt to capture the history of our village for everyone to read drew strong support from everyone. Their sacrifices of personal and work time to help me accomplish this goal will never be forgotten.

The historic photographs and ephemera depicted throughout this publication come to you through the kindness of Dwight and Mace Sawyer, Jon and April Meredith, Bill Wood, Frank Cappozzo, Julia and Bob Gross, Cal Pitcher, Roberta Eigenbrodt, George Hughes, Dave Chapman, Murray and Julia Rosen, Ike Harvey, Lou Grogan, Molly Harding, and Rich Kraham. The professional and personal interest in helping me cannot be overstated about the staff at the Chatham Public Library (CPL), history teacher John Gould, the Columbia County Agricultural Society (CCAS), the Columbia County Historical Society (CCHS), the Hudson Public Library's History Room (HLHR), the New York State Library (NYSL), and of course, the Chatham Village Historical Society (CVHS). You can appreciate their contributions by reading the initials or names following each caption.

Not to be overlooked is the emotional and educational support that no words can describe. That support has come from my comrades, the Chatham Village Historical Society Board of Trustees, Rich Kraham and his staff at the Chatham Press, Virginia Balfour and friends, and all those who continually support me in the effort to "Save the Charm That's Chatham" in my capacity as president of the village historical society.

This acknowledgment would be woefully amiss if I did not recognize how important das Design Studio has been to this effort sacrificing business and personal time, contributing financially and emotionally to make this book happen; Debi Giardino and especially Len MacDonald deserve my undying appreciation.

This book is dedicated to my mother and father whose deep love for Chatham must have passed to me through their genes, high school sweethearts Louise M. Strever and Ralph C. Blass.

INTRODUCTION

I was surprised when my Fredonia State college professor told me he knew where Chatham, New York, was. When pressed, he related that he had taken a train north from New York City with the intention of getting off along the line but fell asleep, waking up at the Chatham Union Station.

The Dutch called the area Douve Vlacht (Dove Plain), the Native Americans' pathway for horses and wagons to pass through from north to south or east to west. The rich farmland and running water did not entice many to settle in the village until the Thomas family settled here. William Thomas created a stagecoach stop when he built a tavern on the central square in 1811. Stagecoach companies used the early-19th-century turnpikes to carry passengers to and from Albany, New York City, Hartford, Lebanon Springs, and elsewhere.

Retailers found customers in the travelers at the Stanwix or the Park House. Farms sprang up on either end of the Union Turnpike, and those families frequented the small village for supplies. The most important boost to business and industry, immensely increasing the population, was the advent of railroads as early as 1838. The Hudson and Berkshire Railroad Company pulled into the village in September of that year, followed in December 1841 by the Western Railroad. Agriculture and transportation were an unbeatable team for well over a century. Retail and wholesale businesses expanded exponentially, so much so that in the 1930s Adolf Hitler targeted the village of Chatham. A strike against this transportation hub would help cripple the economy of the United States.

The Columbia County Agricultural Society established itself at Chatham Four Corners in the 1850s to educate and perpetuate the agricultural industry. The Columbia County Fair increased railroad business and local commerce with its highly anticipated sulky races, floral parades, and thrill rides. Local agriculture, livestock, and manufacturing were promoted strongly to visitors who came from near and far.

Wealth was accrued in the agricultural and transportation venues. The railroad tie between New York City and the upstate village was mutually beneficial economically and culturally. The Chatham Village Board of Trade posted notice at train depots that there was free land for anyone who established a business enterprise. New York City investors came and built second homes. Daily trains from New York brought news of timely world events, the latest fashion, and performers. Cady Hall and the New Columbia Theatre provided continual entertainment. In the 1930s, the village embraced moving pictures, hosting established movie companies and founding ones of its own. Filming was done on Main Street, at the Old Pond, and elsewhere around town.

Individuals whose lives were enriched by living in the community of Chatham gave back proportionally what they had achieved. Firefighters' devotion to the welfare of their neighbors was held in equal esteem to the financial institution leaders. Businessmen balanced profit with philanthropy. That pattern of mutual respect set a precedent for generations to come. Monuments to generosity and philanthropy can be seen today in the Tracy Memorial Village Hall, the Morris Memorial Community Center, and the Louis F. Payn Foundation Retirement Home. The union depot, the former Stanwix Hotel, the wood framed houses on Kinderhook Street, and the Victorian homes of Hudson Avenue retain an image of the village history.

Although preferred photographs may not have met the publisher's standards for your viewing, I believe this book provides to people already familiar with the area, newcomers, and visitors a glimpse into the charm that is Chatham.

One

At a Crossroads

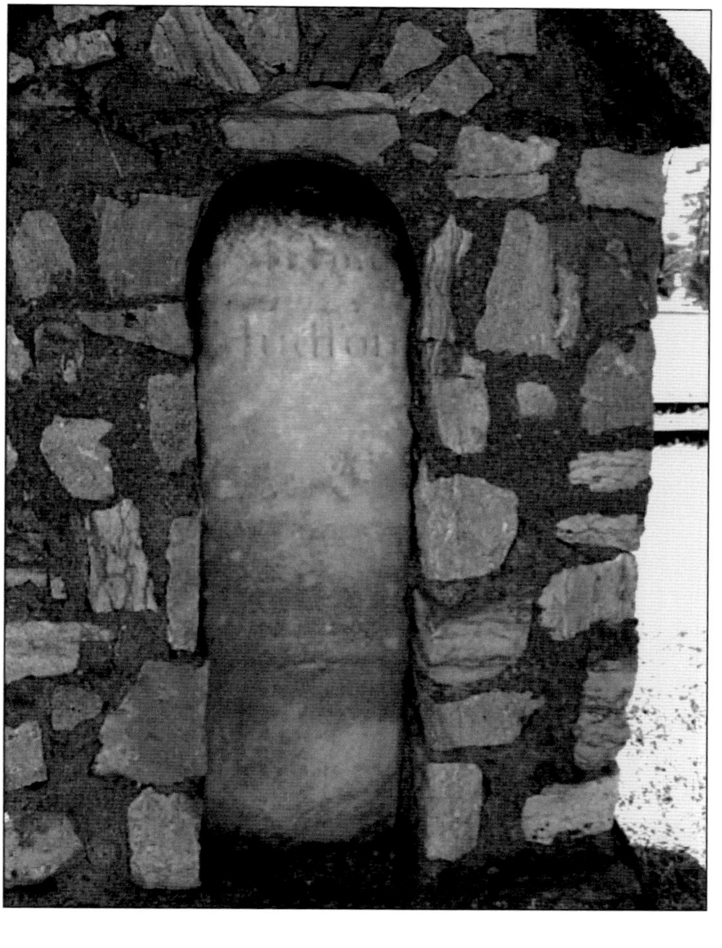

Grain, potatoes, and hay raised by the early settlers were carted down the Union Turnpike to the Hudson River and then shipped to New York City. Cattle and turkeys were also driven to the docks for sale. Ice was harvested in the winter to preserve butter, eggs, and milk transported from Chatham area farms to New York City stores. Agricultural and grazing interests were most prosperous through the 1850s, hence the local reference of Union Turnpike as the "Farmers' Turnpike." This Farmers' Turnpike marker was posted on Hudson Avenue in the village near Church Street. (Courtesy of CVHS.)

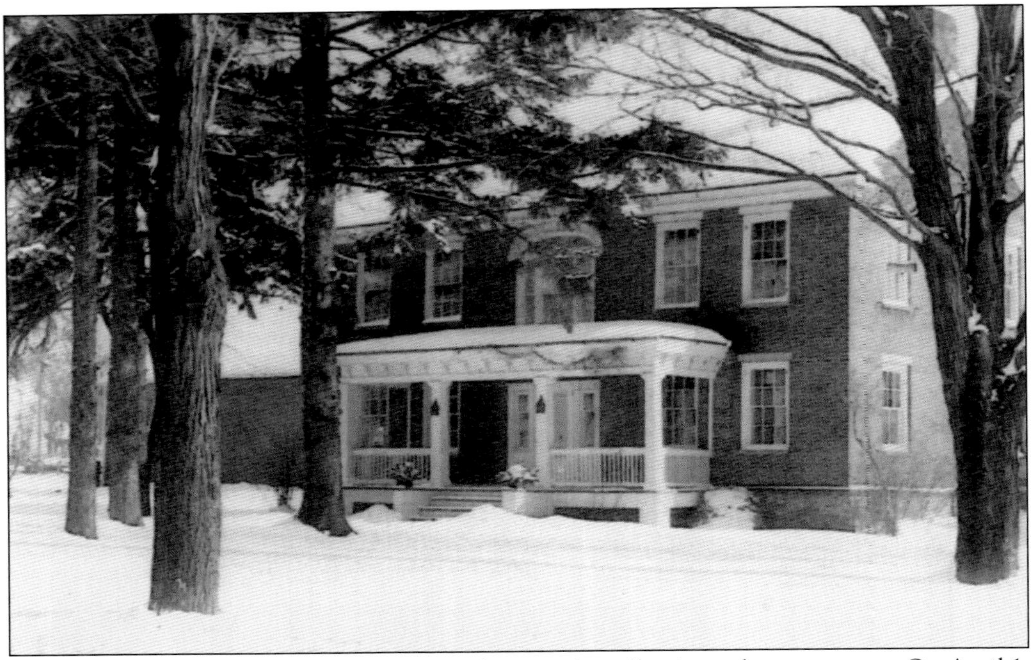

The Union Turnpike intersected a 182-acre farm on the village's southern entrance. On April 1, 1853, William Groat (son of Capt. Peter Groat) and his wife, Augusta, purchased that property and agreed to keep open "a road or street not less than two rods in width" that ran north to south just yards from their front door. The brick residence was built at the same time as Peter Groat's tavern. (Courtesy of CPL, Dardess Collection.)

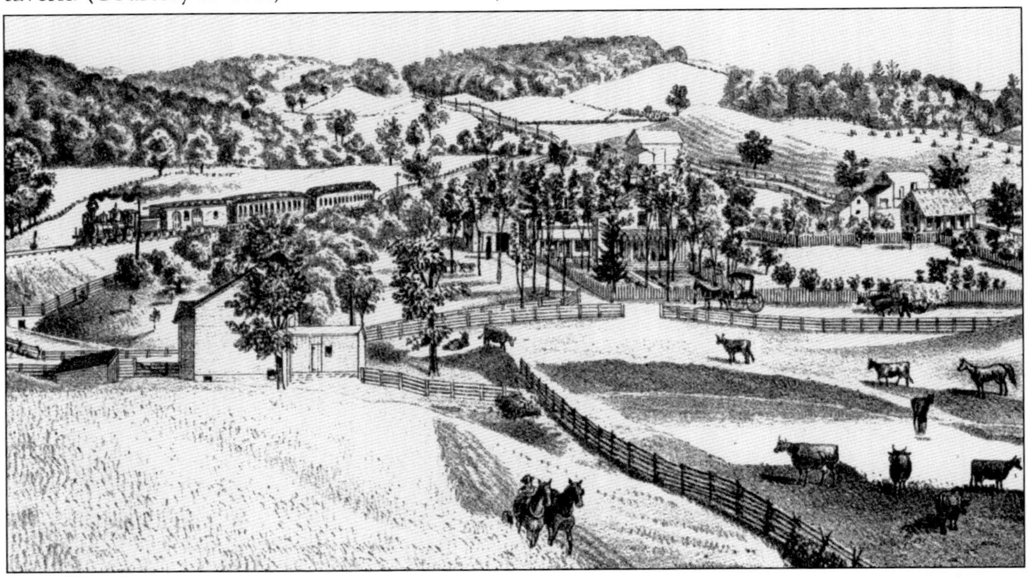

More large farms were established on Union Turnpike, west from the central square. The largest land owner was the Hogeboon family. John B. Strever moved north from Ancram, erecting a farmhouse and barns with the help of his sons. Joel H. Angell, a descendant of Quakers, was raised on his father's farm. The sale of his 112-acre farm, pictured here, would lead him to a comfortable village retirement. (Courtesy of CVHS.)

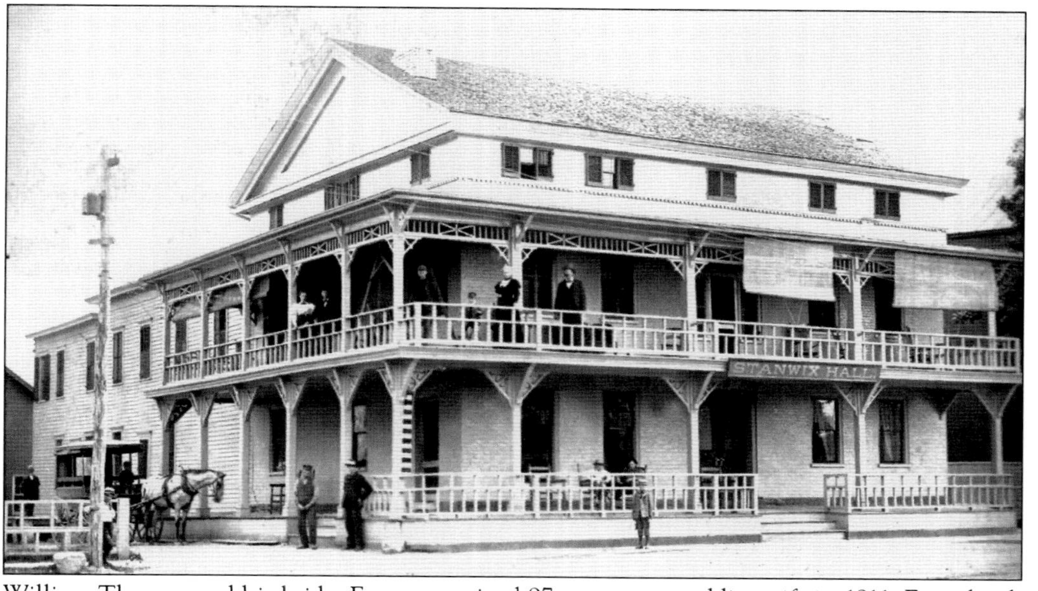

William Thomas and his bride, Emma, received 97 acres as a wedding gift in 1811. From brick formed at the brick kiln near the future Boston and Albany depot, Thomas built a tavern next to the only village house, opened it to the public on January 1, 1812, and catered to turnpike stagecoach passengers whose routes crisscrossed the front yard. (Courtesy of Chatham Press.)

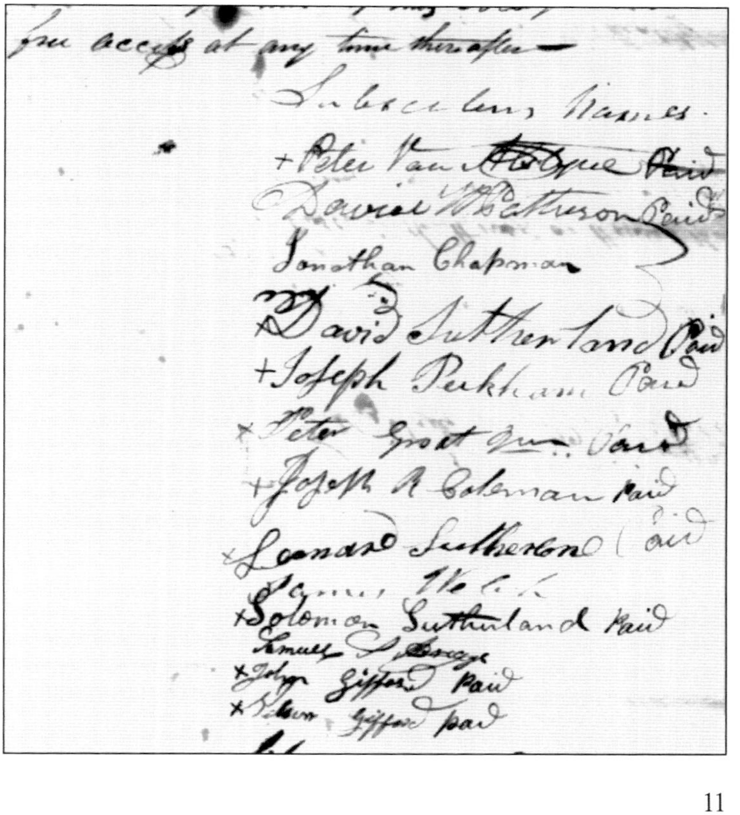

free access at any time thereafter—

Subscribers Names.

+Peter Van [illegible] Paid

Daniel W. Patterson Paid

Jonathan Chapman

David Sutherland Paid

+Joseph Peckham Paid

+Peter Groat Jun. Paid

+Joseph A Coleman Paid

+Leonard Sutherland Paid

[illegible]

+Solomon Sutherland Paid

Samuel [illegible]

+John Gifford Paid

+[illegible] Gifford paid

Pres. Martin Van Buren frequented Chatham Four Corners on horseback to visit friends. Peter Groat Jr., a friend of Van Buren's, paid his annual $1 fee and signed a pledge on July 12, 1822, along with other inhabitants of the town of Chatham who "voluntarily associated together for the purpose of detecting Thieves of all description and more perticulerly [sic] for Pursuing and taking Horse thieves and bringing them to Justice." (Courtesy of CVHS.)

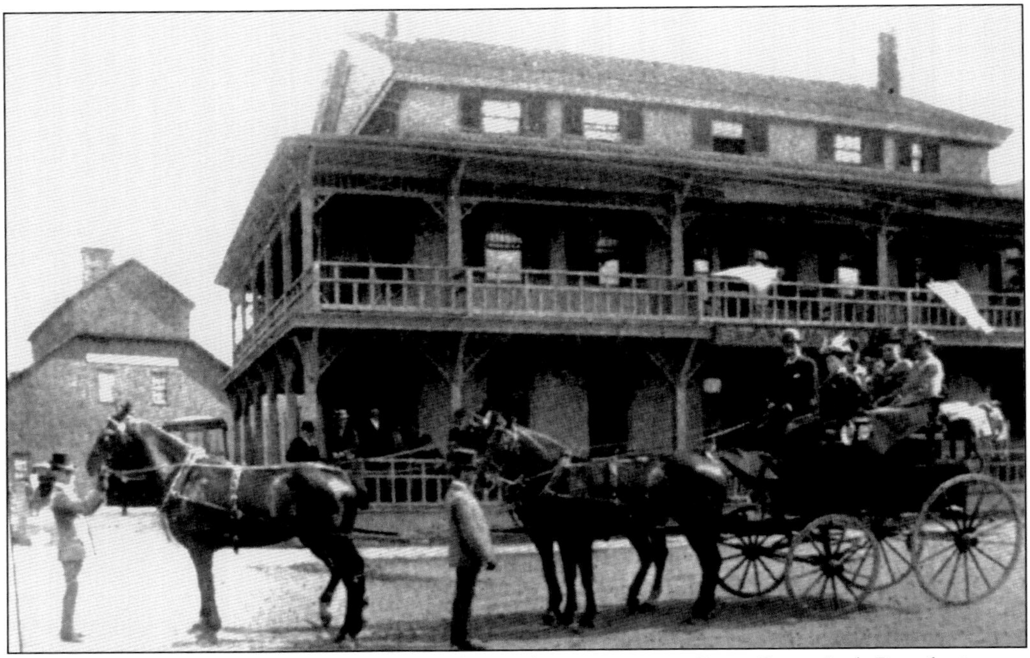

Stagecoach driver George Bain bought William Thomas's tavern. Peter Groat Jr. (a Revolutionary War captain) ran a blacksmith shop on the central square opposite Bain's. In 1815, Peter Groat bought the tavern, created a stagecoach line, and ran the post office from Groat's Corners. A young lad, Louis Payn, held former president Van Buren's horse on one visit and later described him as a "round little Dutchman." (Courtesy of Jon Meredith.)

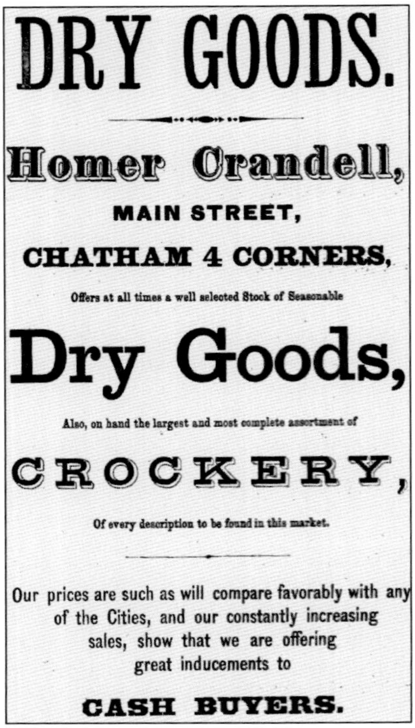

DRY GOODS.

Homer Crandell,

MAIN STREET,

CHATHAM 4 CORNERS,

Offers at all times a well selected Stock of Seasonable

Dry Goods,

Also, on hand the largest and most complete assortment of

CROCKERY,

Of every description to be found in this market.

Our prices are such as will compare favorably with any of the Cities, and our constantly increasing sales, show that we are offering great inducements to

CASH BUYERS.

William Thomas had built a store on the central square and Austeritz Street in addition to the tavern. Ebenezer Crocker became its owner, making it a tavern. Solomon Crandell's store, just north of Groat's Tavern, had been Dr. Edward Dorr's office. Crandell's 1829–1855 account book lists prime sale items as hay, eggs, and potatoes. Hens sold for 30¢ to customers like the Ostranders, Bassets, and VanAlstynes. Homer Crandell continued the family business. (Courtesy of CPL.)

Solomon Crandell moved to the main street and bought the corner lot on the square to build the corner store around 1838. The Hudson and Berkshire Railroad made Crandell's former store its rail station. A law was passed on March 23, 1840, ordering licensing permits to control the many peddlers frequenting the village. By the 1850s, commercial areas were the central square and a small rail yard business. (Courtesy of Jon Meredith.)

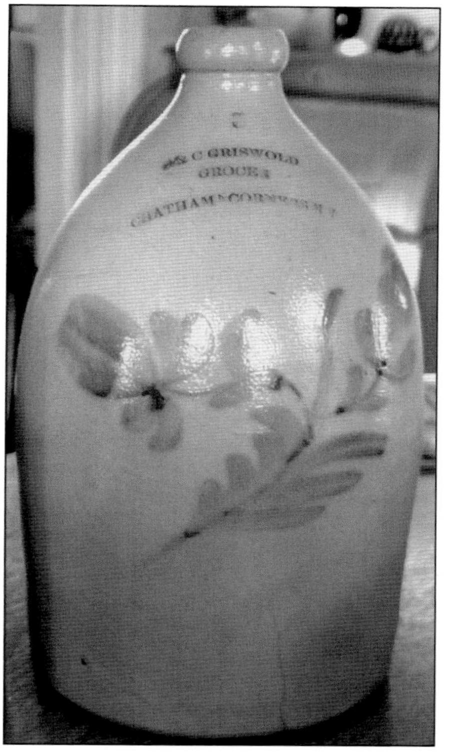

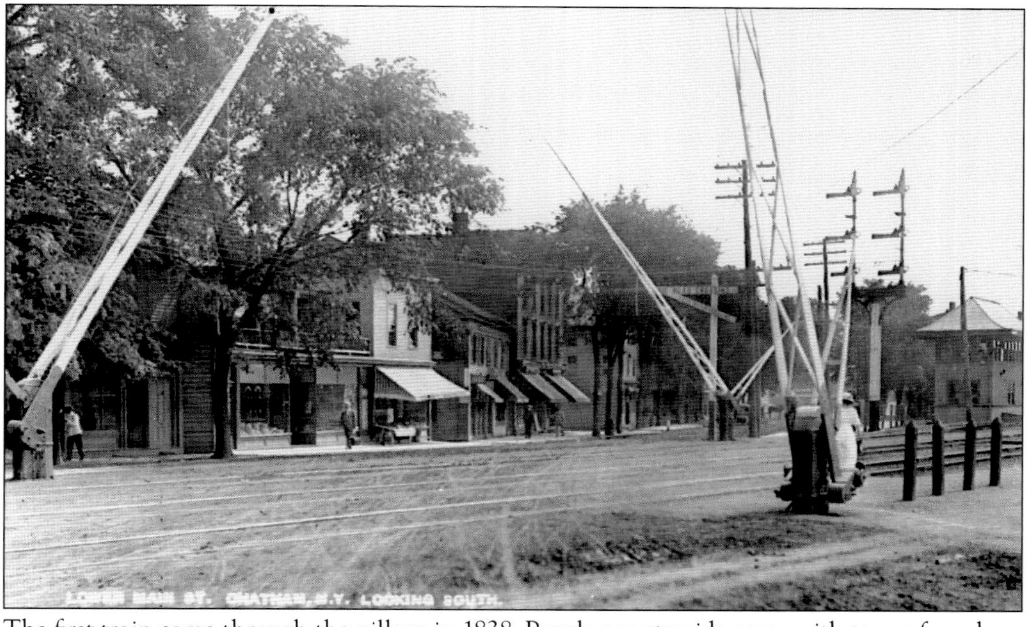

The first train came through the village in 1838. People countywide came with teams from long distances to observe the occasion as a holiday. They took the precaution to leave their horses at least half a mile from the track. The Western Railroad came in 1840, and the village grew with great rapidity. By 1860, Main Street and Lower Main Street (Hudson Avenue) merged commercially. (Courtesy of CCHS, Monthie Collection.)

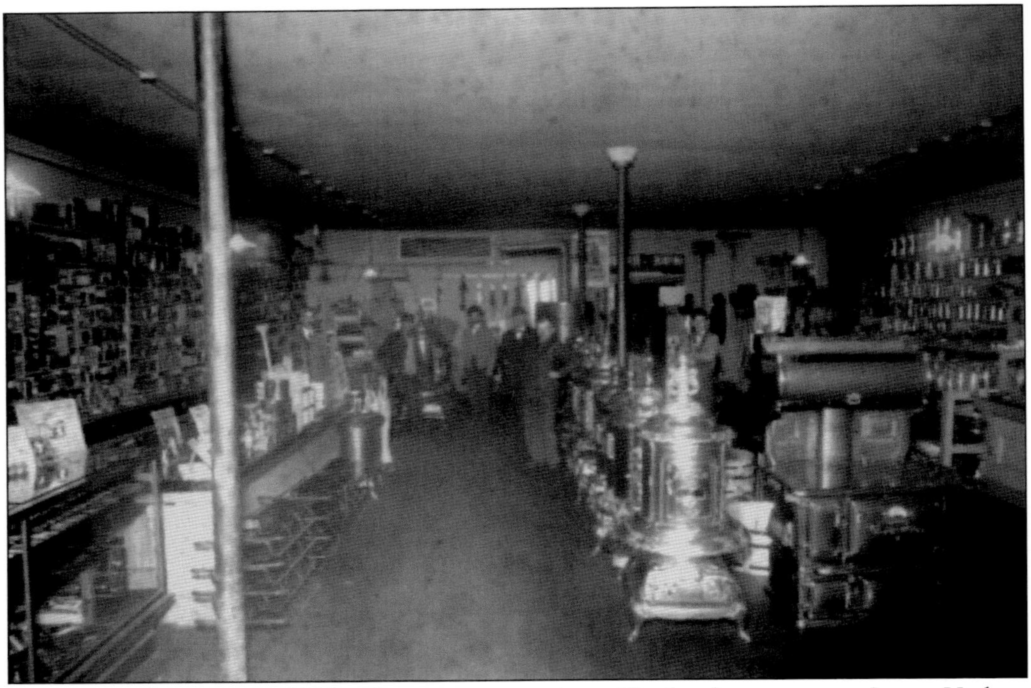

"Tinman" Allen was an 1870 hardware store proprietor. The hardware store on Lower Hudson Avenue carried Glenwood ranges and heaters. The Chatham Fruit Store located at its right would become Maddelena Cappozzo's confectionery store. In the future, her store would move into the larger hardware store location on Lower Main Street. (Courtesy of Frank Cappozzo.)

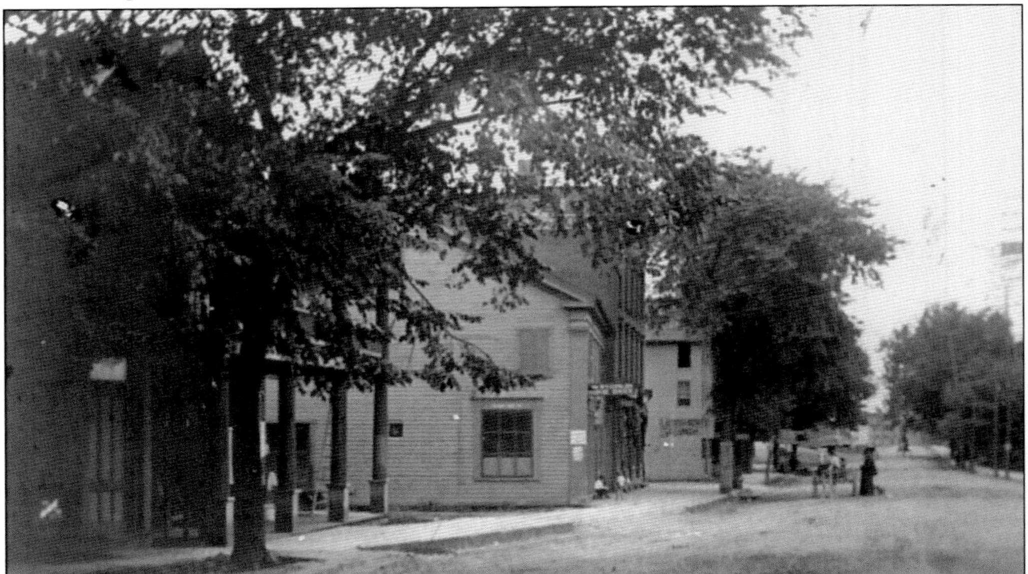

Contemporaries of William Thomas and Peter Groat Jr. were John L. Sharp, a cabinetmaker; Hezekiah Hulbert, a wagoner; Joseph R. Coleman, a miller; Simeon VanAlstyne, a lawyer; and Edward Dorr, a physician. Looking south on Lower Main Street one can read a sign that offered "Ladies and Gents 5¢ Lunch" and the services of a horseshoer. (Courtesy of CPL.)

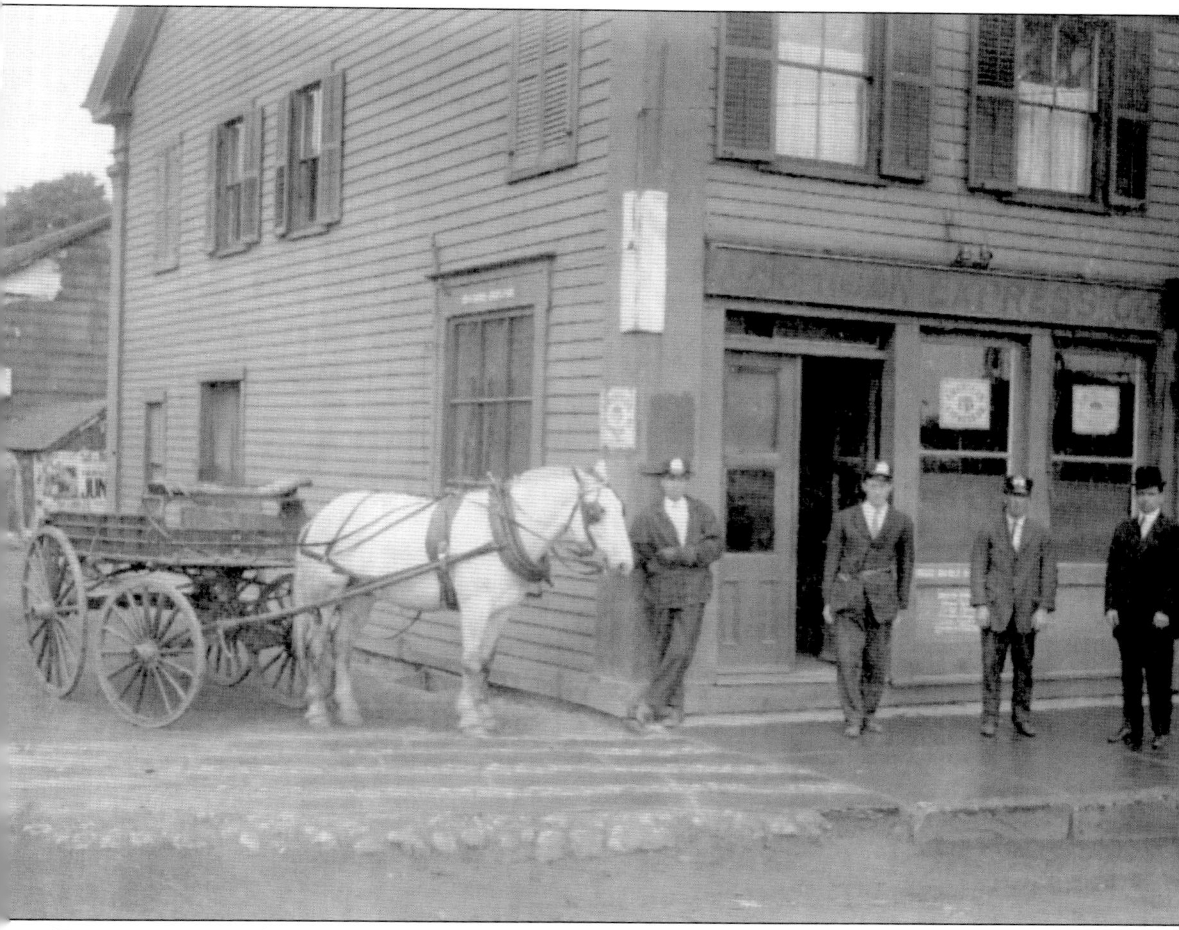

Transportation and communication went hand and hand in the growing village. Chatham Four Corners was host to three railroads, an American Express terminal, and a Western Union Telegraph office. In 1911, the American Express office was on Lower Main Street, shown here. Village wagoner Peter Hobel built wagons for the great American Express Company. (Courtesy of CPL.)

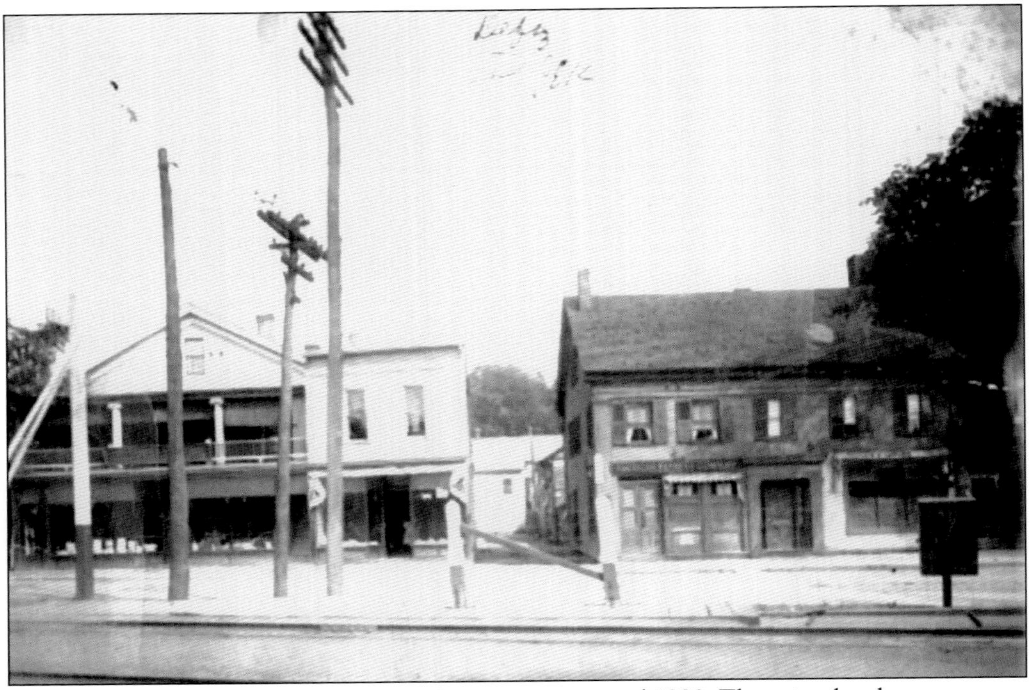

This photograph captures Lower Main Street stores around 1880. There is a hardware store on the left. Contratto's Chatham Fruit Store has its striped awning rolled up. The American Express Company, to the right of the alley, shared the same building with B. F. Sawyer's establishment. These businesses sat directly across from the Boston and Albany train station. (Courtesy of Frank Cappozzo.)

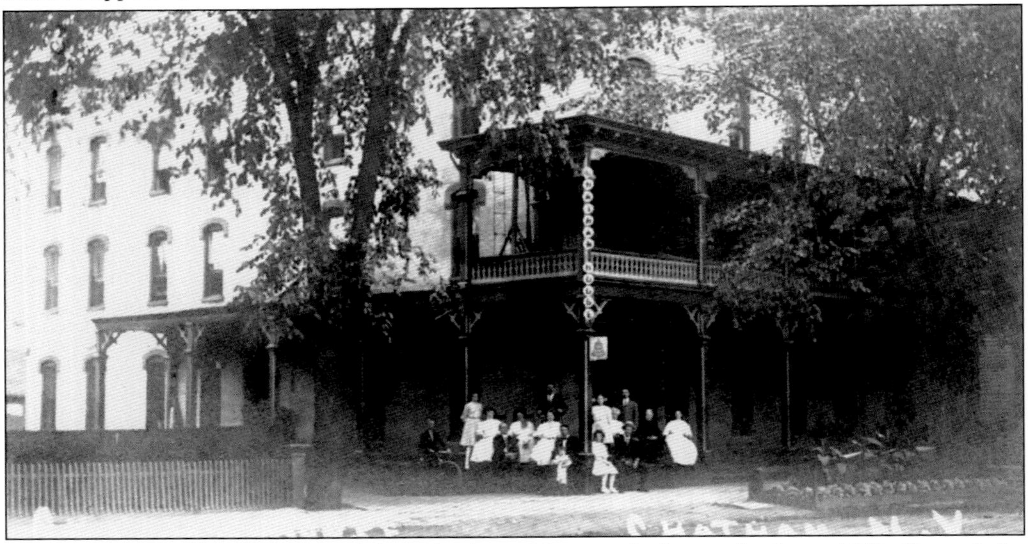

Patrons pose on the veranda of the Chatham House, which was built in 1859. One of the best-known hostelries in the Hudson River tier, it was frequently patronized by Cornelius Vanderbilt. In 1902, John B. Sinclair was the proprietor and manager. It boasted steam heat, hot and cold water, electric lights, a livery, and box stalls. Landlord Sinclair reportedly made his fortune, retired, and left the hostelry to Mr. Gorman's ownership in 1906. (Courtesy of Jon Meredith.)

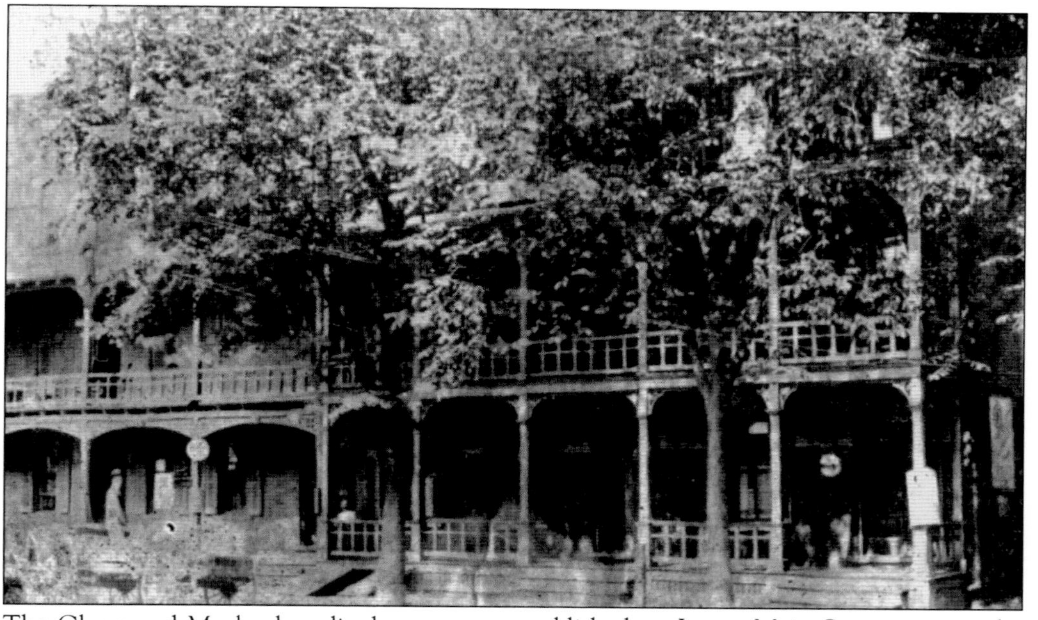

The Glynn and Mealey boardinghouses were established on Lower Main Street next to the railroad tracks. The Mealey House, in business since 1853, offered 20 boarding rooms and a well-stocked bar. It was a family-run establishment handed down to George Mealey when his father and brother passed away. Mealey was a member of the Chatham Board of Directors for the board of trade. (Courtesy of CVHS.)

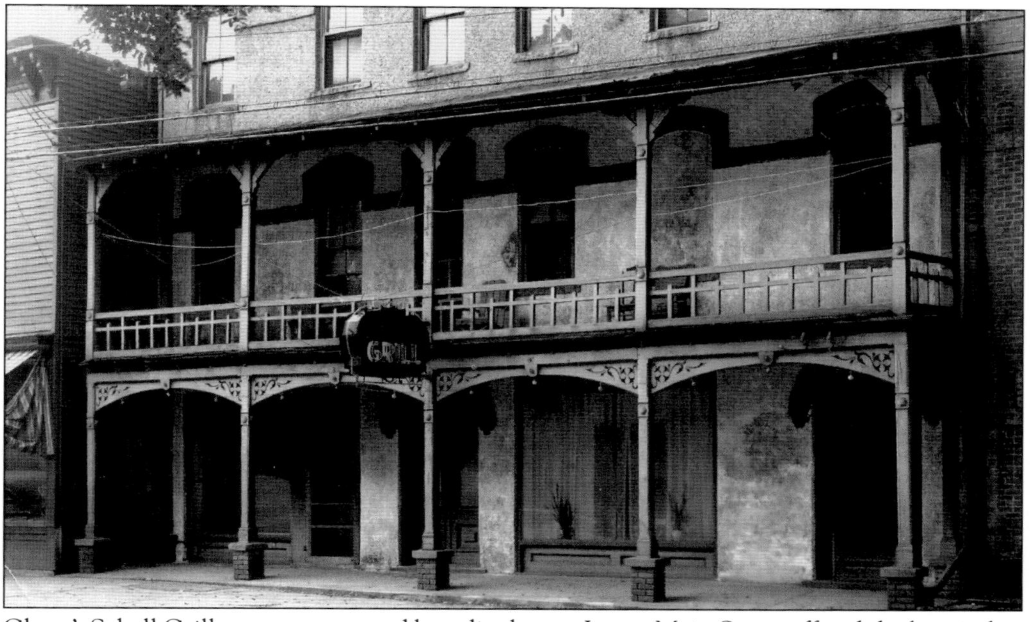

Glynn's Schell Grill was an eatery and boardinghouse. Lower Main Street offered the hospitality of several saloons to thirsty villagers and indigent travelers. Spencertown was a temperance village in 1897 when young Lee Palmer's father jested that they tell their family "something real devilish that we stopped at Callahan's on Hudson Avenue and had a beer together." (Courtesy of Chatham Press, photograph by Savastano.)

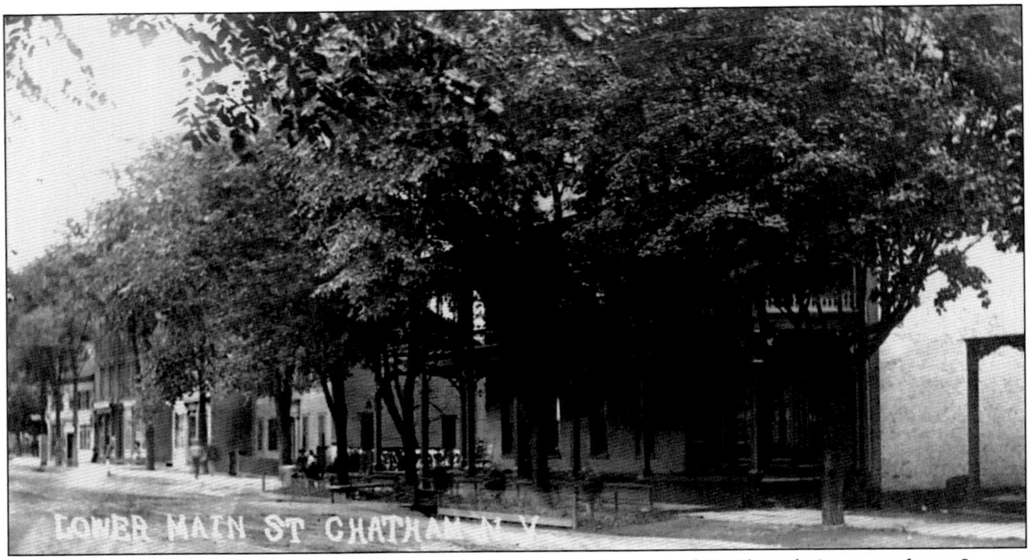

This 1909 photograph captures the view looking north toward Railroad Avenue from Lower Main Street. The Chatham House is visible in the foreground on the right. In back of the photographer would be the hill to the village cemetery. At the end of this view, Lower Main Street connected with Railroad Avenue at the Western Railroad crossing, where the village Main Street was accessed through depot square. (Courtesy of CCHS, Monthie Collection.)

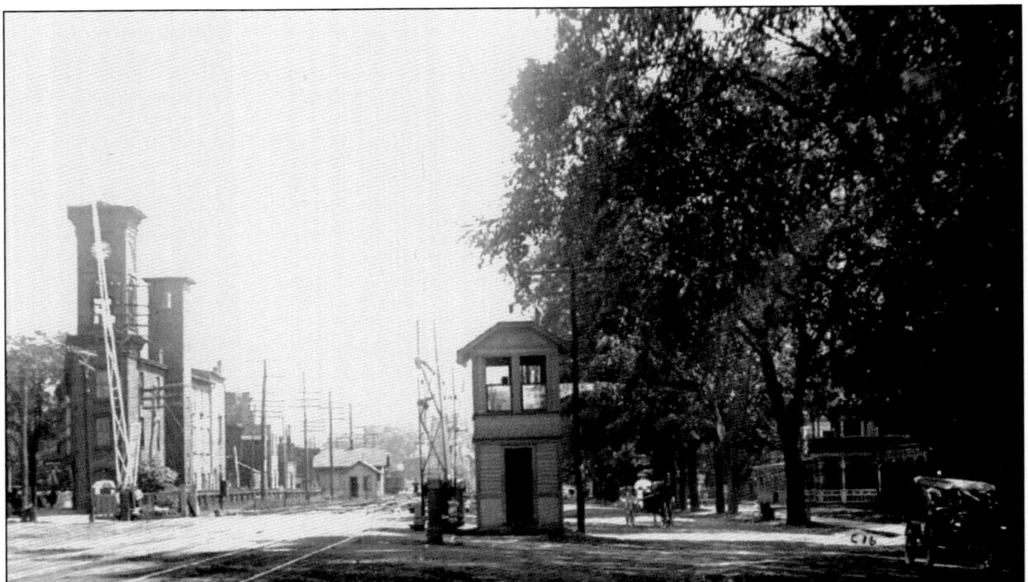

Railroad Avenue paralleled the Western, then later the Harlem railroad tracks. At this site Main Street was on the left. Railroad Avenue connected north with Spring Street where Austerlitz Street intersects the next railway crossing. The prized mare of Dr. Martin E. Williams was stabled in the barn at 7 Railroad Avenue across from the gates. A painting by Dr. Edward Dorr captured its unusual record-breaking, beautiful, lengthy mane and tail. (Courtesy of CCHS, Monthie Collection.)

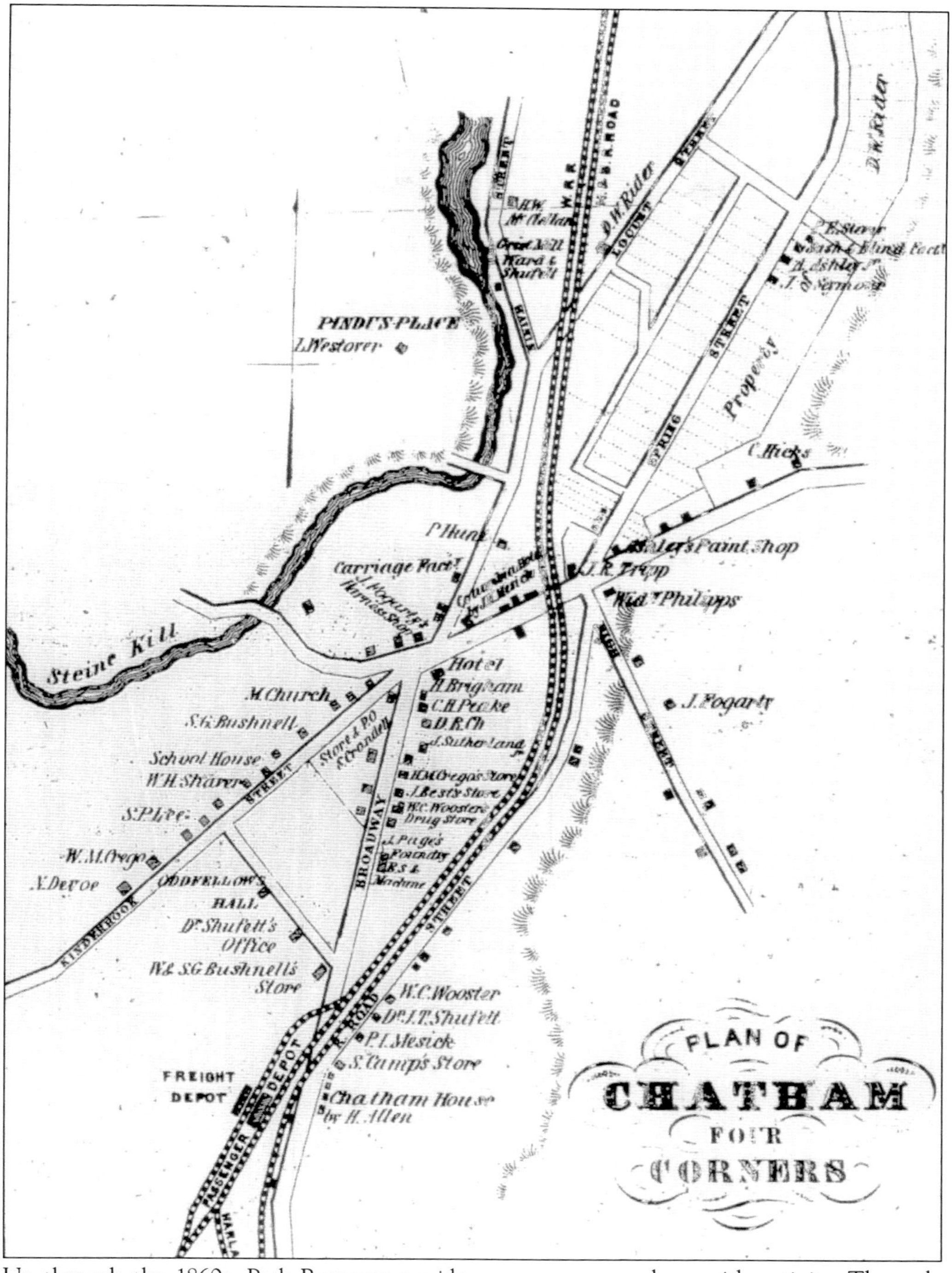

Up through the 1860s, Park Row was a wide-open grassy area busy with activity. The only buildings were on the south side of the green. They included the home and watch and jewelry business of Talcott Burrows, brother Charles Burrows's grocery store, and his close friend A. J. Fellows's drugstore. Notice that Main Street has been identified as Broadway on this c. 1861 map. (Courtesy of NYSL.)

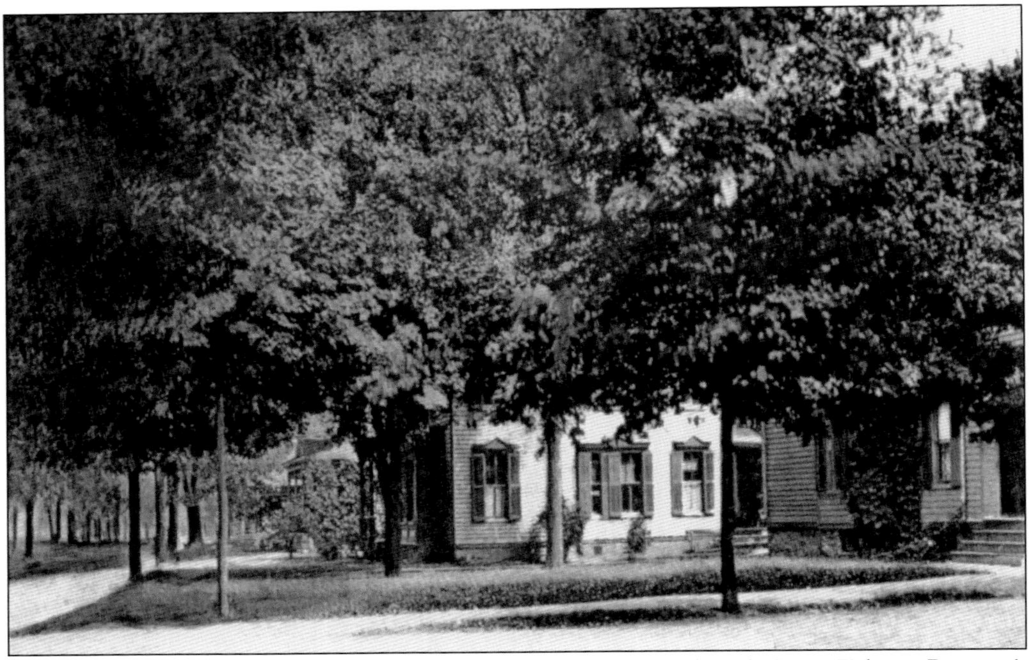

This photograph shows the corner of Kinderhook Street and Park Row. Talcott Burrows's daughter, Dora, viewed the earliest events on the town green, that of militia practicing in front of her father's Park Row business during the Civil War. Circuses came later, setting up colorful tents. Most exciting were the baseball games in which her uncle Charlie played. In 1865, Chatham had its first baseball team made up of young men in their 30s. (Courtesy of CVHS.)

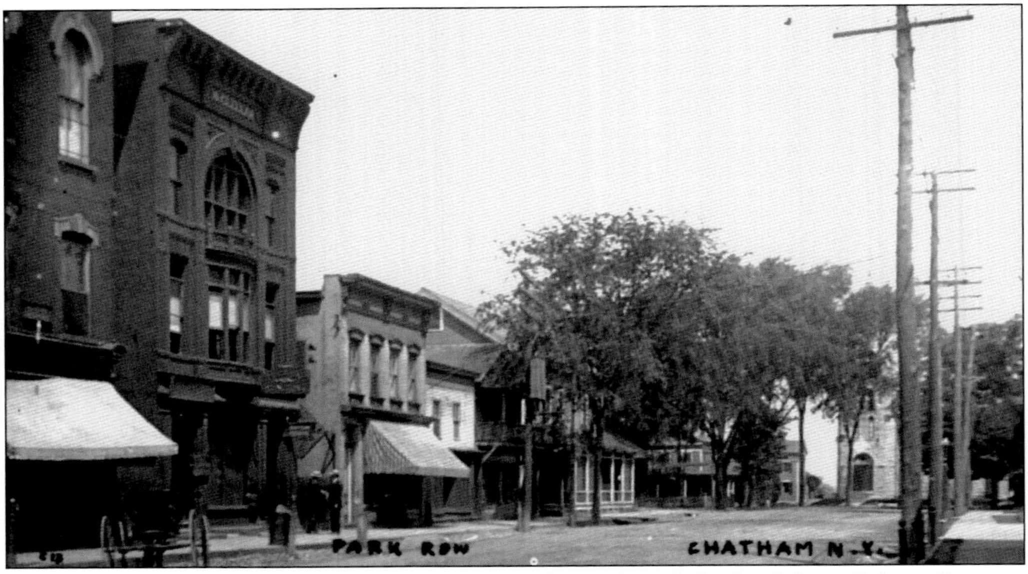

Park activities dwindled when the Columbia Bank purchased the land from Talcott Burrows on the corner of Park Row and Main Street. Dr. W. E. Walker's Park Row dental parlors offered these services: 22-karat-gold caps $5, fillings $1.50 and up, and porcelain crowns $3. The post office and law offices occupied the McClellan building constructed alongside Burrows's business in 1887. (Courtesy of Jon Meredith.)

Two

WITH HOPE AND FAITH

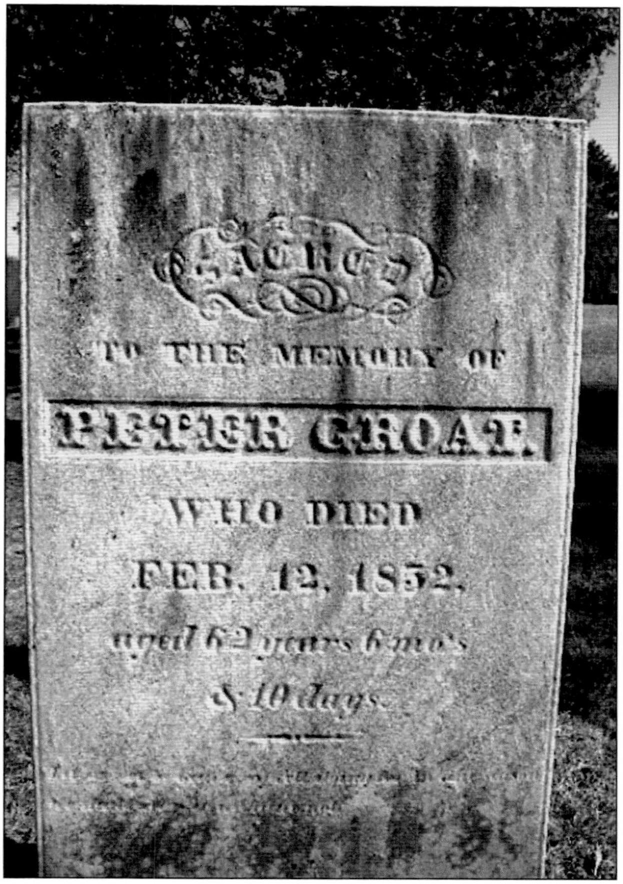

Young Mervale Burlugh Westover was buried on the hillside overlooking Stein Kill by his nurse governess. His parents, associated with the local iron industry, were out west when he passed away. They erected a granite shaft on his grave when they returned. The Hogeboon and Strever families laid their loved ones to rest on a hillside overlooking their farms. Revolutionary War soldier Maj. Ebenezer Bassett was buried in White Mills Methodist Cemetery, but Capt. Peter Groat Jr.'s epitaph could be found on Cemetery Hill. (Courtesy of CVHS.)

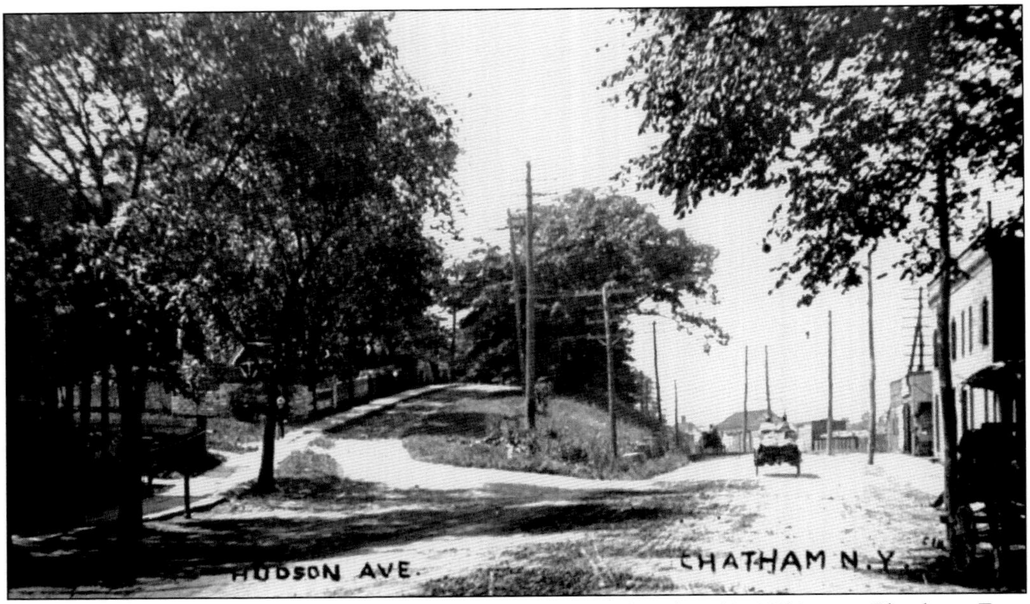

The Chatham Rural Cemetery Association first met on October 21, 1856, at a Chatham Four Corners' office. The members stated that they were "desirous to form an association for the purpose of procuring and holding lands to be used exclusively for a Cemetery or place for the Burial of the Dead." The location was on acreage donated in part from J. Browning's farm and accessed from lower Hudson Avenue through Cemetery Avenue. Its elevated location gave it the name of Cemetery Hill. (Courtesy of CCHS.)

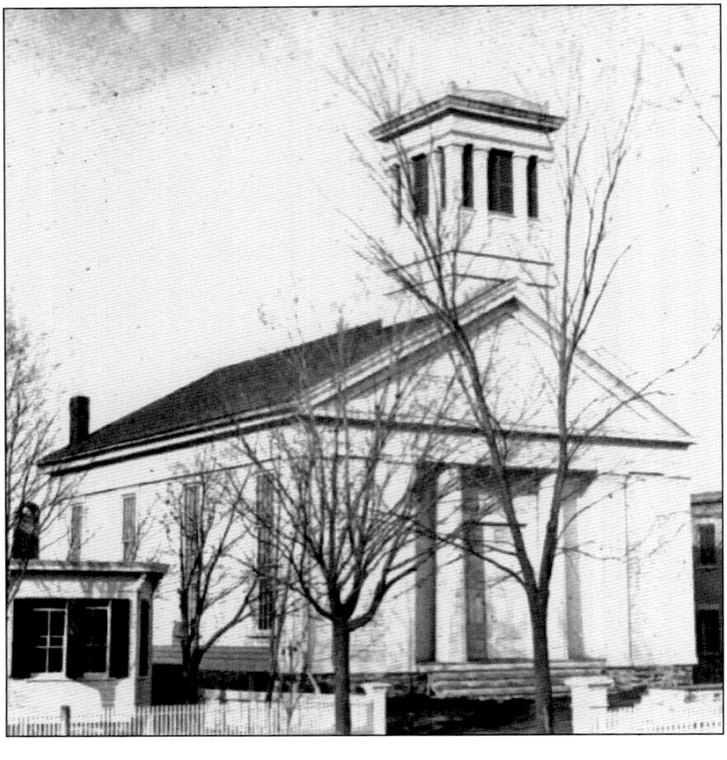

Methodist Episcopal religious meetings were held in barns before the two-story White Mills meetinghouse was constructed in June 1835. Among its trustees were Cornelius Shufelt, Mark K. Crandell, Jehoikim Blass, and James Van Valkenburgh. Despite the concern that the growing Chatham Four Corners perpetuated vice and corruption, the congregation moved to a new church at 13 Kinderhook Street that burned in 1853. It was replaced by the wooden church shown here. (Courtesy of CPL.)

Hailstones reportedly as large as hens eggs or bigger heavily damaged the second church constructed on the Kinderhook Street site. A third Methodist Episcopal church was built of stone and brick in 1886 and dedicated on November 3, 1887. There were 420 members in the church at that time, of which 350 were residents in the village. The Methodist Episcopal church was designed by Jacob Snyder, an Akron, Ohio, architect. (Courtesy of Jon Meredith.)

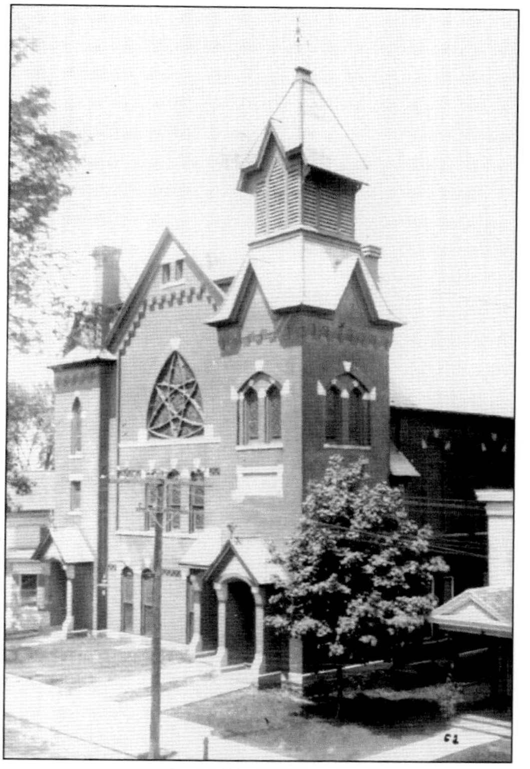

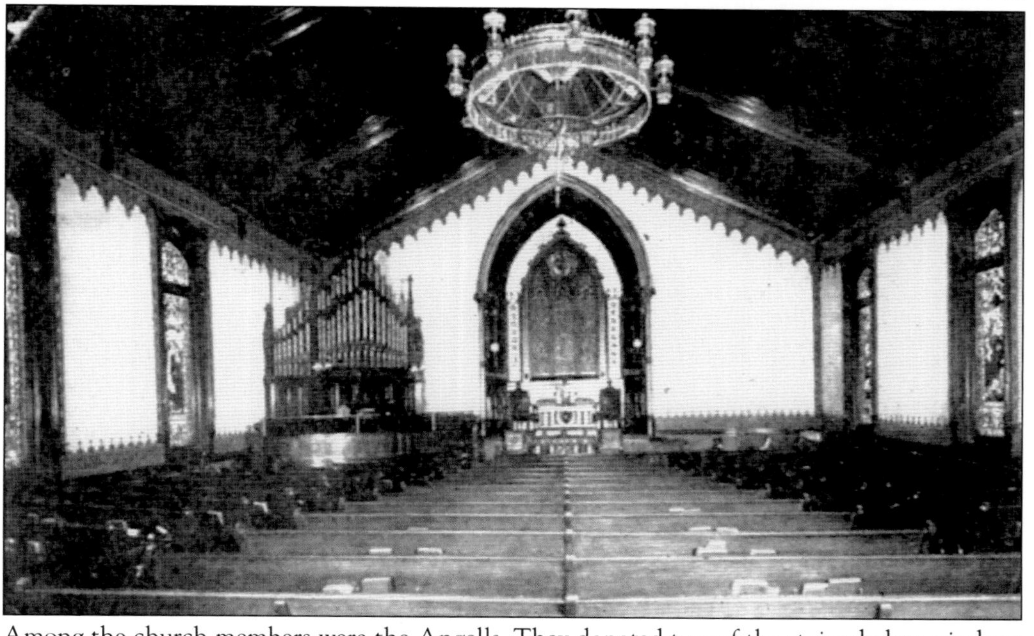

Among the church members were the Angells. They donated two of the stained-glass windows that were made in London, England. One was framed in back of the altar and the other to the left of the pipe organ. Edward Seymour of Chatham did the interior decoration, detailed frescoes, and dadoes. (Courtesy of CPL.)

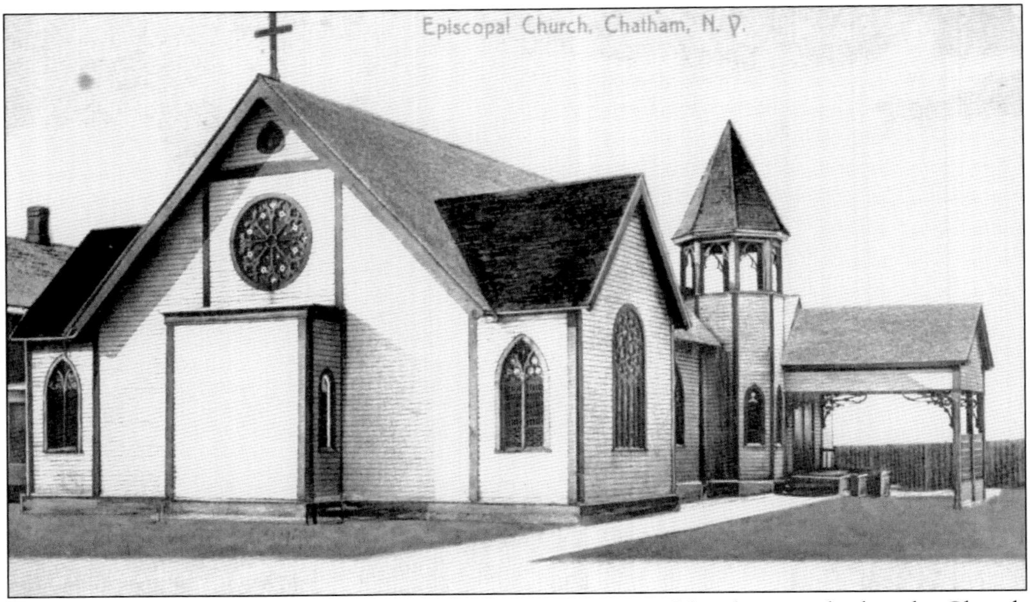

St. Luke's Episcopal Church began with an area community of families attached to the Church of England. In 1851, Chatham Episcopal Church members attended service at St. Paul's Church in Kinderhook. Reverend Smith and his congregation held services in Cady Hall in 1875. Other facilities were utilized until 1892, when the cornerstone was laid for the church on Woodbridge Avenue. St. Luke's church opened for divine service on Easter Day in 1893. (Courtesy of CPL.)

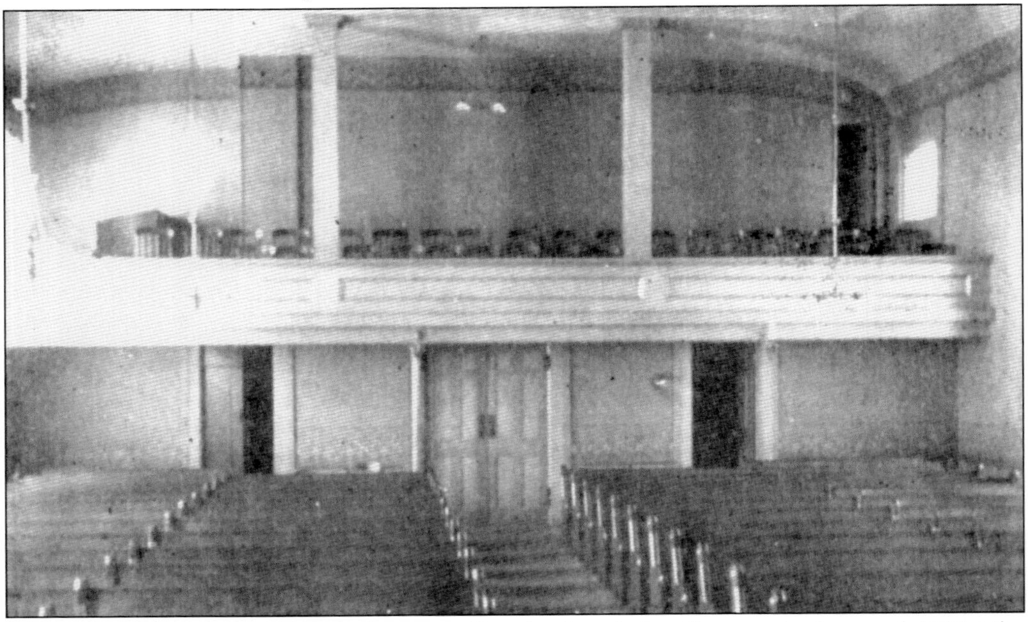

Followers of the First Reformed Protestant Dutch Church locally organized around 1800. The small wooden schoolhouse on Kinderhook Street on the village green (see page 19) served as their place of worship. The congregation built its first church in 1843 on Union Turnpike, the main street, when there were fewer than 12 houses in the village. Services were held inside that wooden church (shown in the photograph) until November 20, 1902. (Courtesy of CPL.)

Rev. William J. Leggett, Ph.D., was pastor when the Vermont white marble church was dedicated on November 20, 1902. It was constructed on Kinderhook Street opposite Park Row. Prices were affixed to each pew so the congregation would know what to pay for the pew they selected to rent. Items brought from the old church included the Bible, the baptismal font, the organ, the bell, and the memorial windows. (Courtesy of Jon Meredith.)

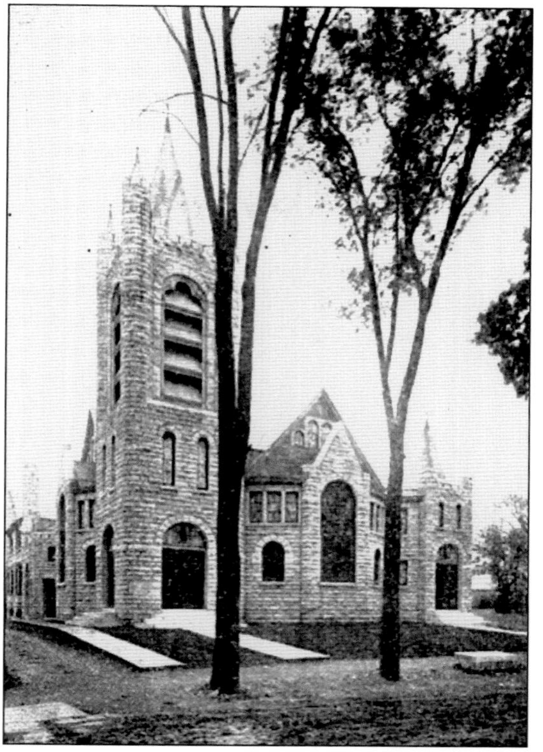

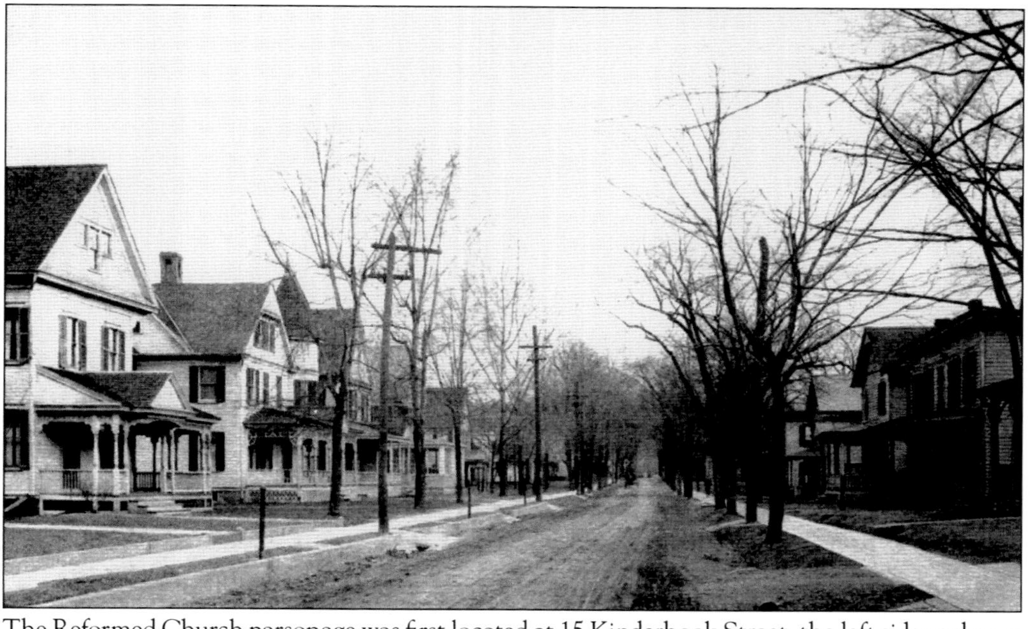

The Reformed Church parsonage was first located at 15 Kinderhook Street, the left side as shown in photograph. The Rutland railroad crossing sign, in the distant background, was originally an archway crossing the street where the white signpost is shown at Park Row. In 1896, a new parsonage was built at 66 Kinderhook Street that had many interior characteristics of the new church. (Courtesy of Jon Meredith.)

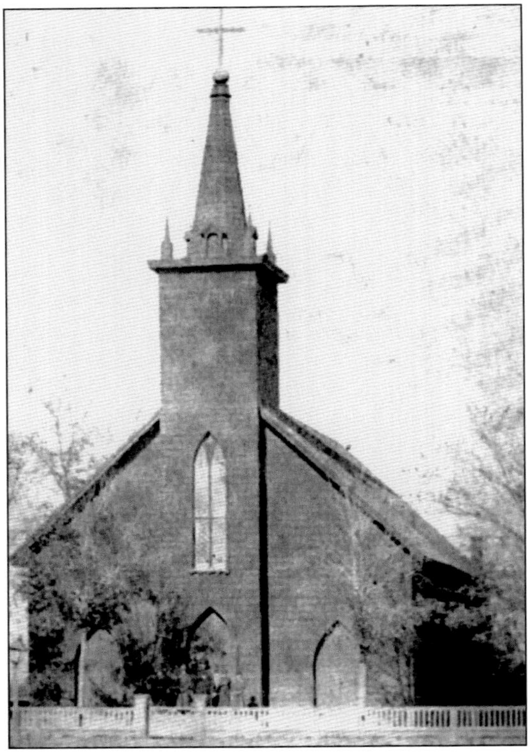

Catholic residents in Chatham's village received occasional missionary work from the pastor of St. Mary's in Hudson around 1850. Rev. James O'Sullivan began providing service with regular visits in 1855. The following year, St. Patrick's Church was constructed on Church Street across from what would be the Columbia County Fairgrounds. Fr. James Moriarty is pictured here with two altar boys. (Courtesy of Chatham Press.)

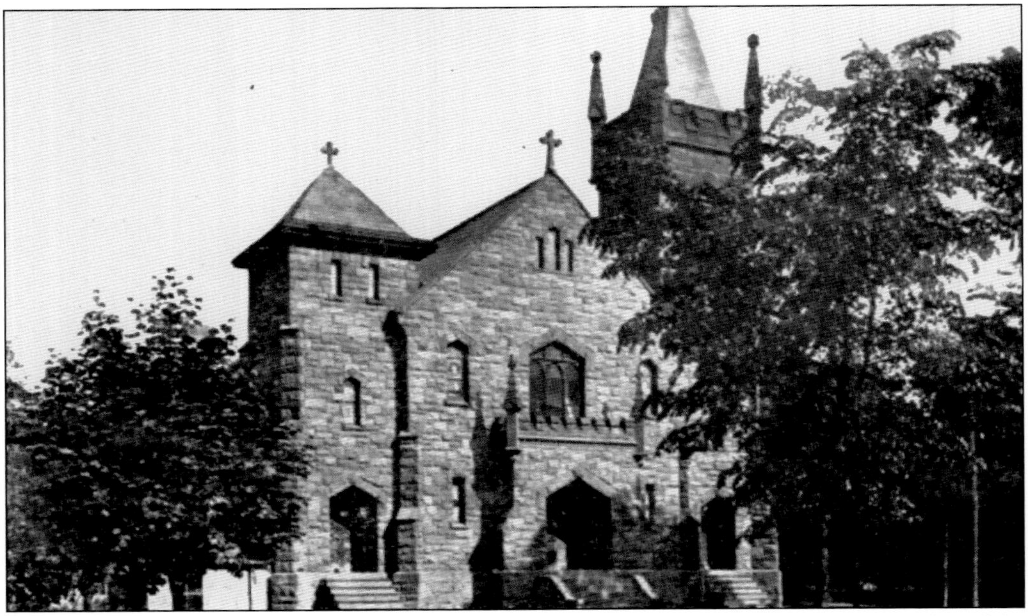

Rev. James L. Walsh served the Catholic community from 1892 to 1905. Land was purchased for St. James Church on Hudson Avenue and a cemetery in Ghent. Services were held at Cady Hall during church construction. When the basement of the new church was completed, services were held there. In 1905, Rev. Cornelius Lineman acquired the Hudson Avenue rectory and completed the decoration of the church. (Courtesy of CPL.)

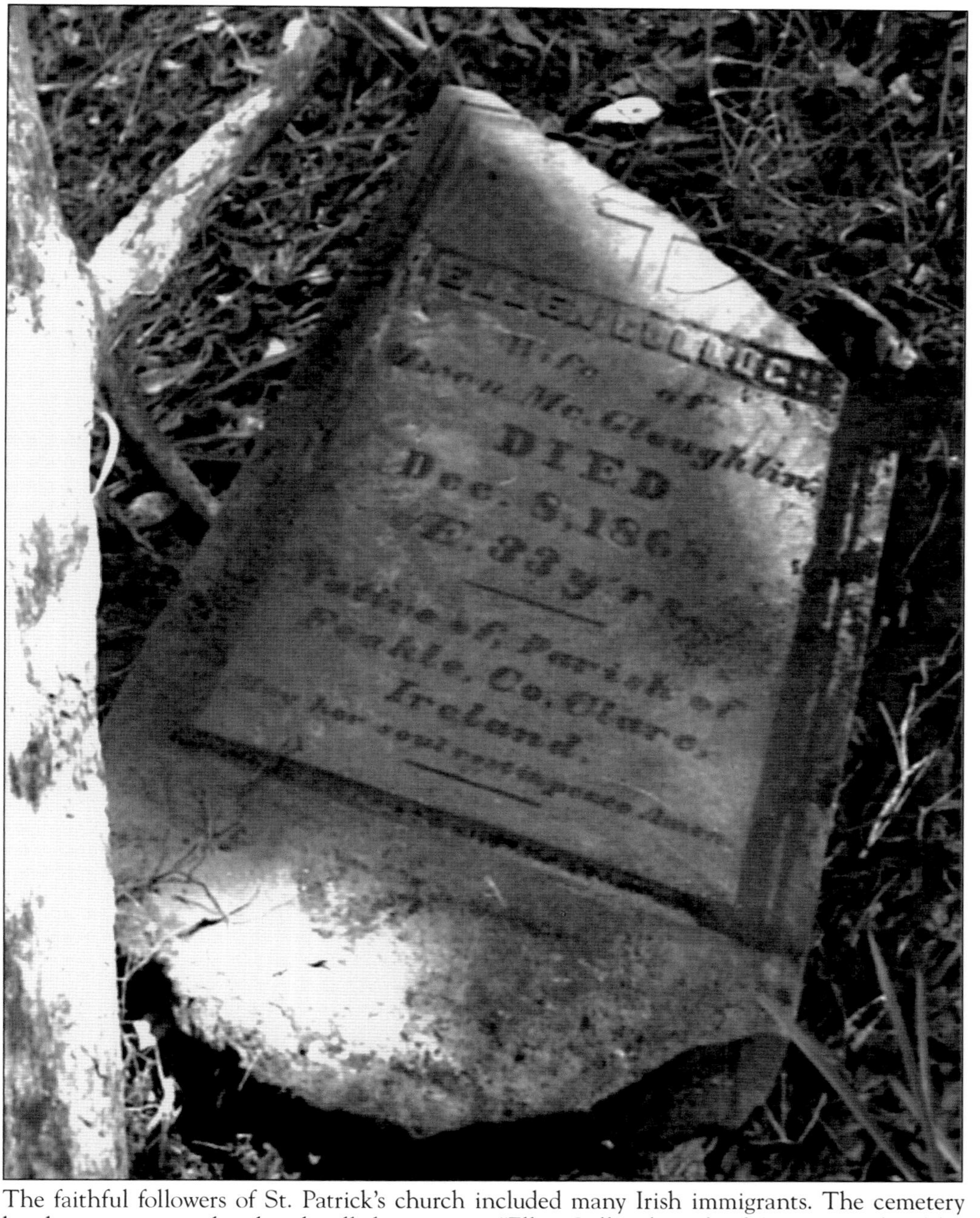

The faithful followers of St. Patrick's church included many Irish immigrants. The cemetery headstones next to the church tell their stories: "Ellen Cullough, wife of Aaron McGloughlin died December 8, 1868, age 33 years. Native of Parish Feakle County Clare, Ireland. May her soul rest in peace. Amen." Rose Ann McBride from the parish of Donegal, Meva County, Ireland died at 11 years, 9 months in Chatham. (Courtesy of Chatham Press.)

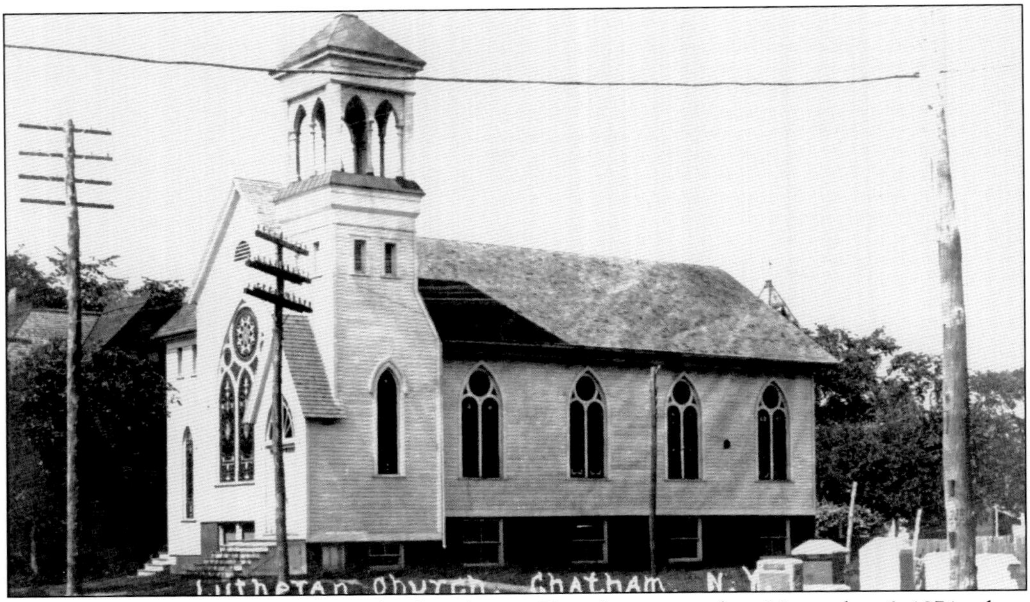

The Christ and Emmanuel Evangelical Lutheran Church organized on November 6, 1874, when J. G. Griffith was pastor. The congregation first met at Bullis Temperance Hall on Park Row. A small-framed chapel was built across from the hall in 1875 but remained incomplete. On November 6, 1897, the cornerstone for the permanent church was laid with its dedication held on March 23, 1898. The steeple bell was a gift in 1920. (Courtesy of CPL.)

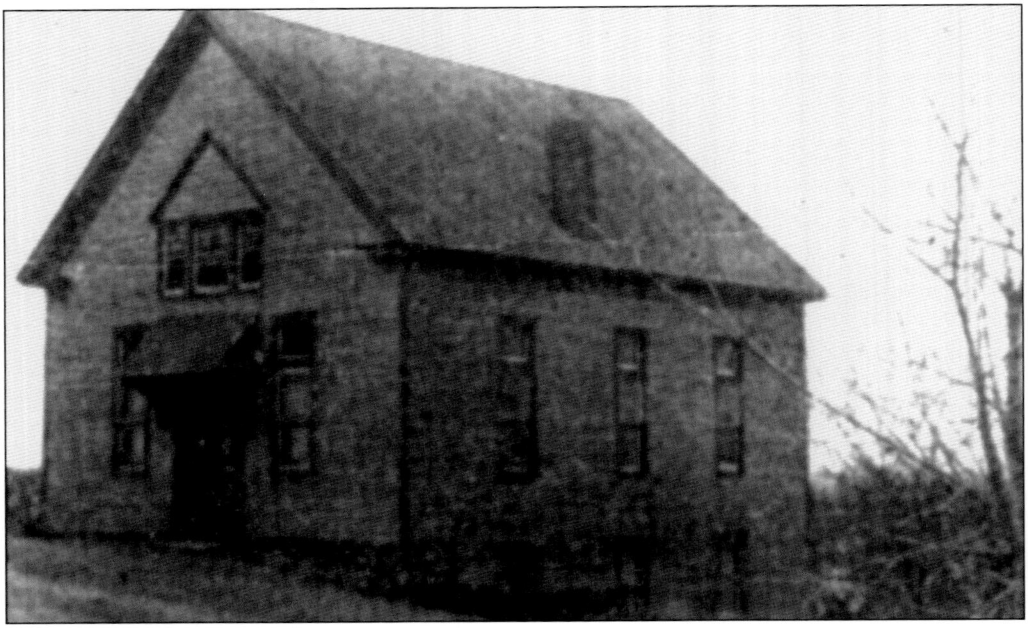

The first African Methodist Episcopal services were held in Chatham in 1856. Reverend Jenkins had originally planned for a church on lower Hudson Avenue, but it was Rev. Charles N. Gibbons's efforts that succeeded. The African Methodist Episcopal church was built on High Street in 1892. For years it was referred to as the Payn African Methodist Episcopal Church for Louis F. Payn, who contributed to its construction. (Courtesy of CVHS.)

Three

The Community Grows

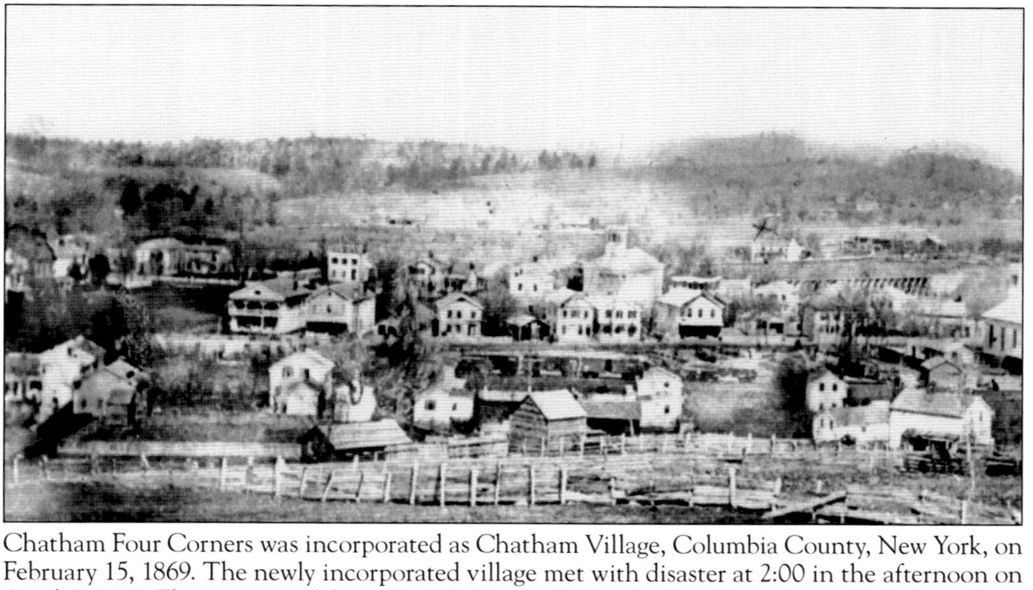

Chatham Four Corners was incorporated as Chatham Village, Columbia County, New York, on February 15, 1869. The newly incorporated village met with disaster at 2:00 in the afternoon on April 5, 1869. Flames erupted from the Stickler and Wheeler Iron Foundry and Machine shop, the second floor of its wooden structure at 1 Main Street. This daguerreotype was taken from a High Street location looking west after the fire. Looking closely one can view a train moving alongside the destruction. (Courtesy of CPL.)

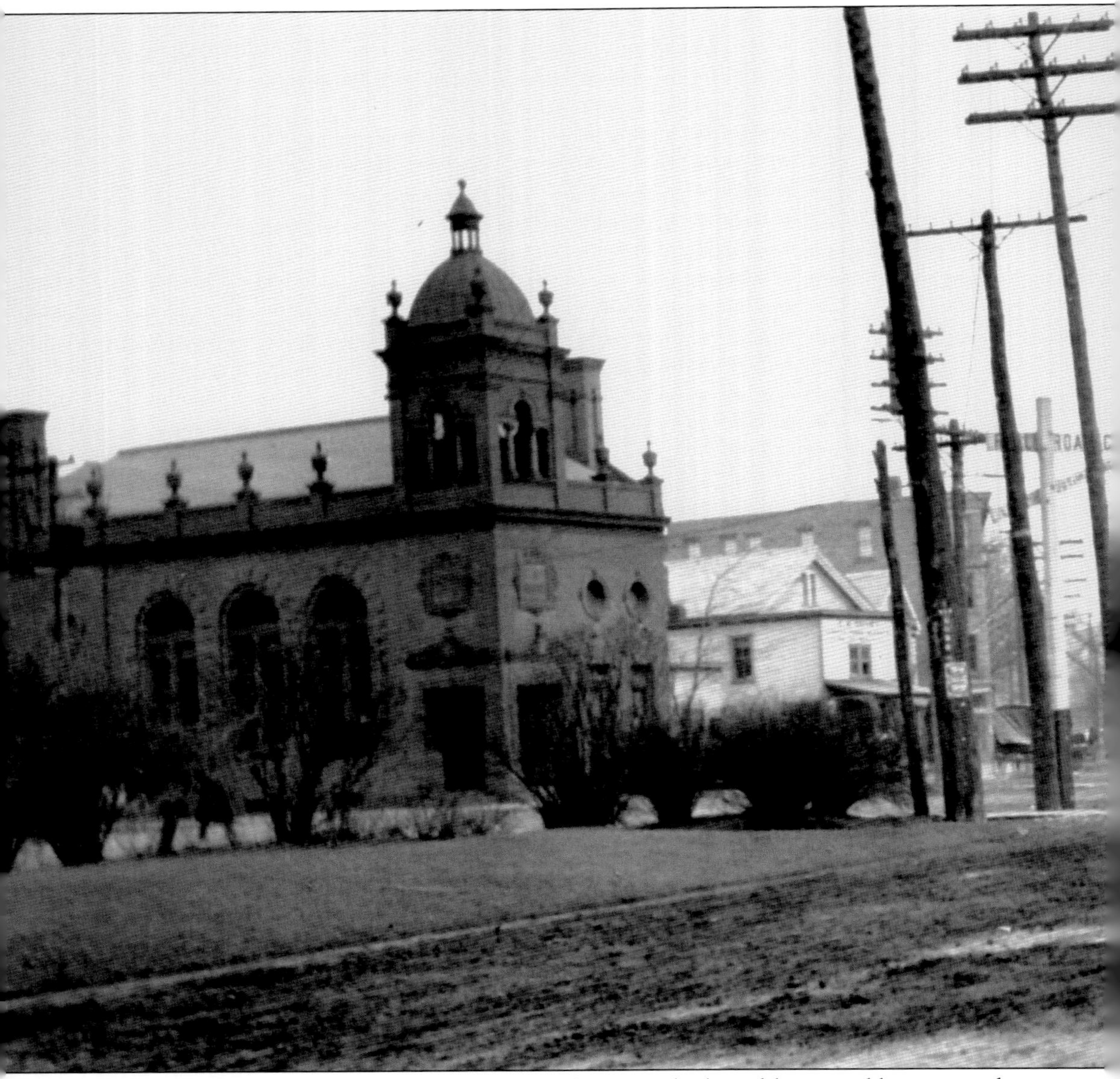

On page 29, at the extreme right are the Park House sheds and livery stable, next is the rear view of Stanwix Hall and then Krafts meat market on the central square. At the extreme rear in the fields is a barn and to its left a residence and barns then owned by S. B. Noble then Mrs. P. A. Shufelt on Fairview Avenue. The wooden trestle for the Lebanon Springs (later Rutland) railroad may also be seen. Main Street's eastern side (closest to the camera) was razed from the rear view of the Reformed church and John Cadman's house remnants all the way left

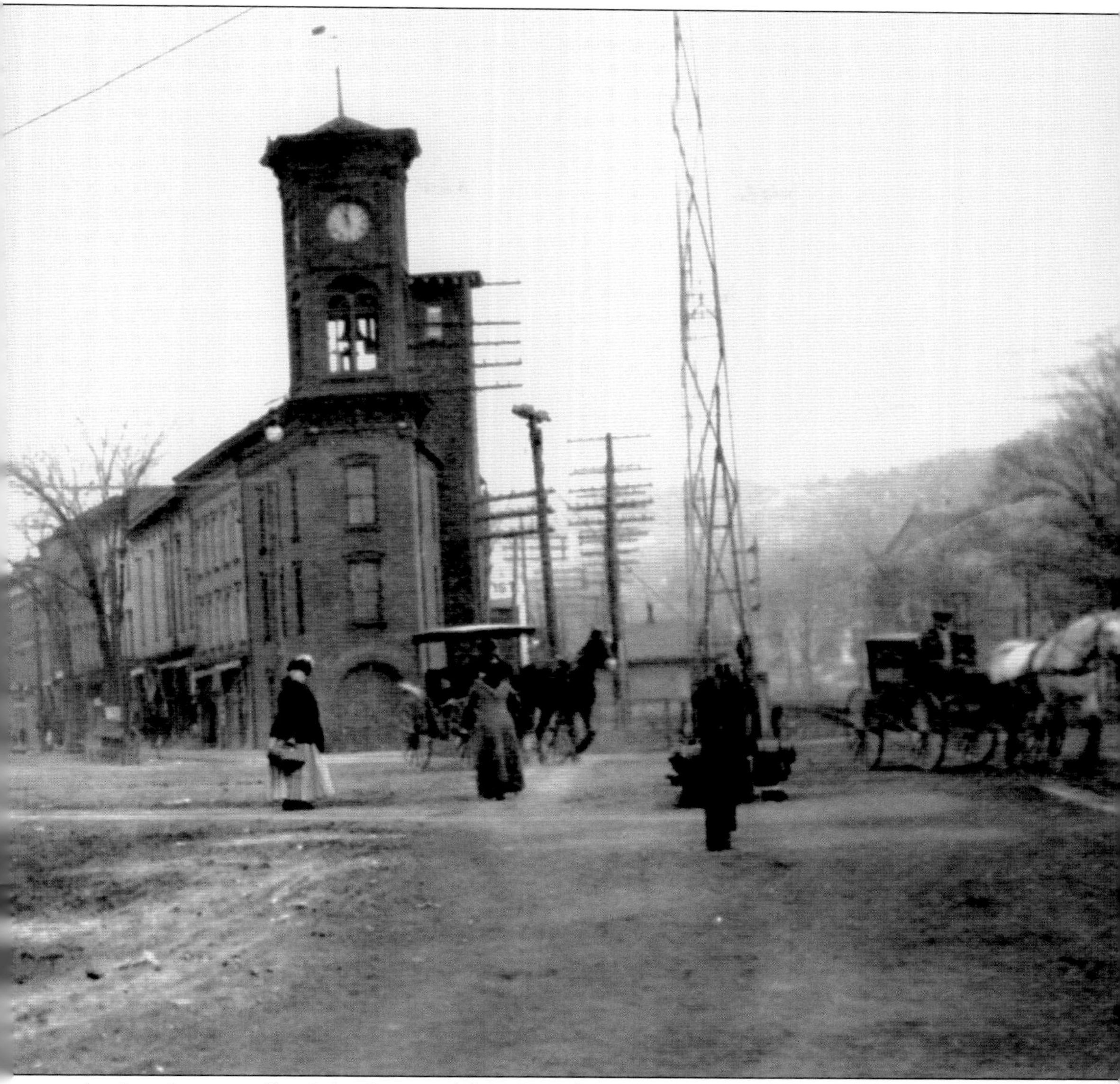

to the foundation walls of the destroyed foundry. This successful agricultural community with its efficient turnpike and railroad transportation systems incorporated with 852 acres and was home to 1,355 residents. April elections in 1869 appointed William A. Woodbridge presiding officer and trustee. William Trowbridge would be elected Chatham Village president. This image from the depot square shows the restored eastern Main Street. (Courtesy of Dwight Sawyer, Miller collection.)

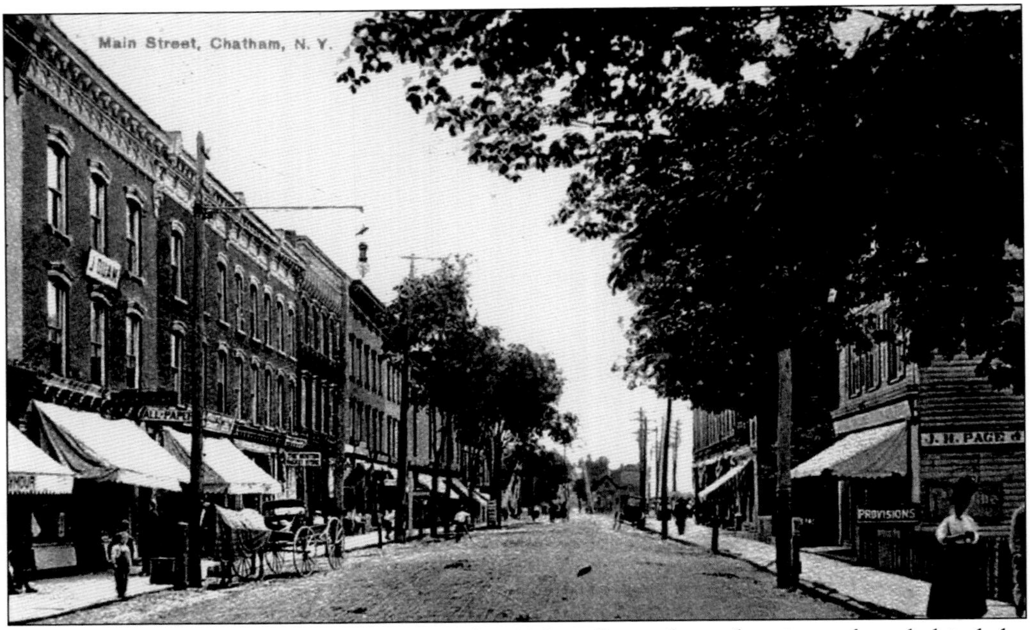

Homer Crandell's residence on the west side of Main Street faces the viewer from behind the trees at the right of this photograph. Crandell's former store, occupied by J. H. Page, is at the left of his residence. The small home of Catharine Tompkins, then occupied by Wilson Terry, was next on the left followed by the Kane building occupied by surrogate H. W. McClellan before it was remodeled. (Courtesy of CCHS.)

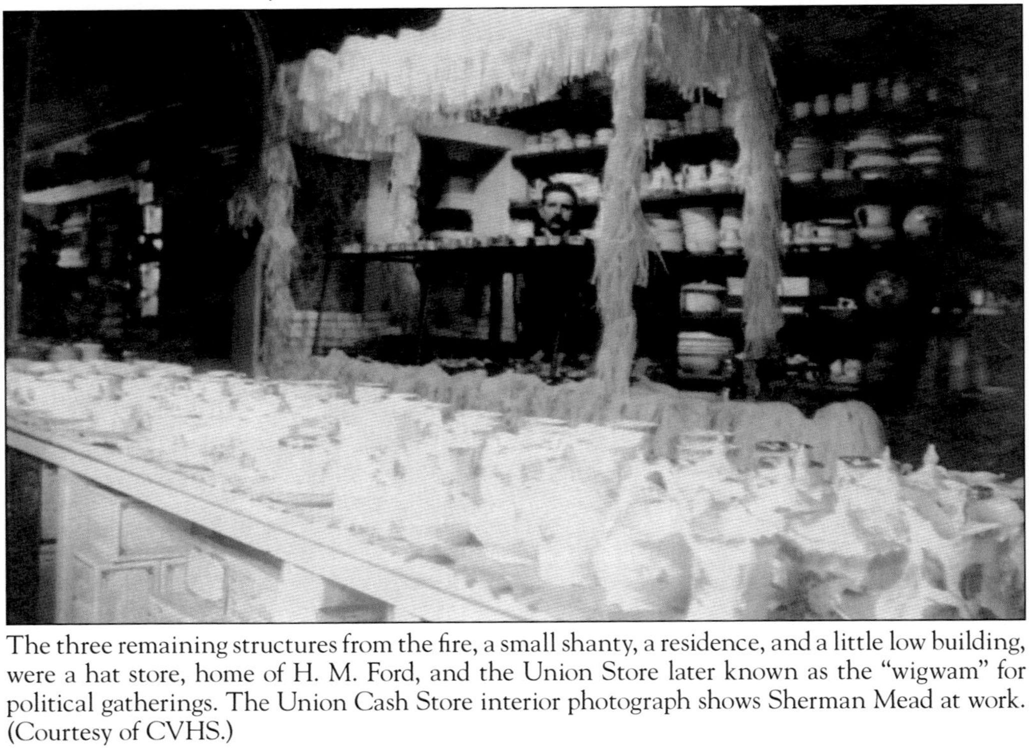

The three remaining structures from the fire, a small shanty, a residence, and a little low building, were a hat store, home of H. M. Ford, and the Union Store later known as the "wigwam" for political gatherings. The Union Cash Store interior photograph shows Sherman Mead at work. (Courtesy of CVHS.)

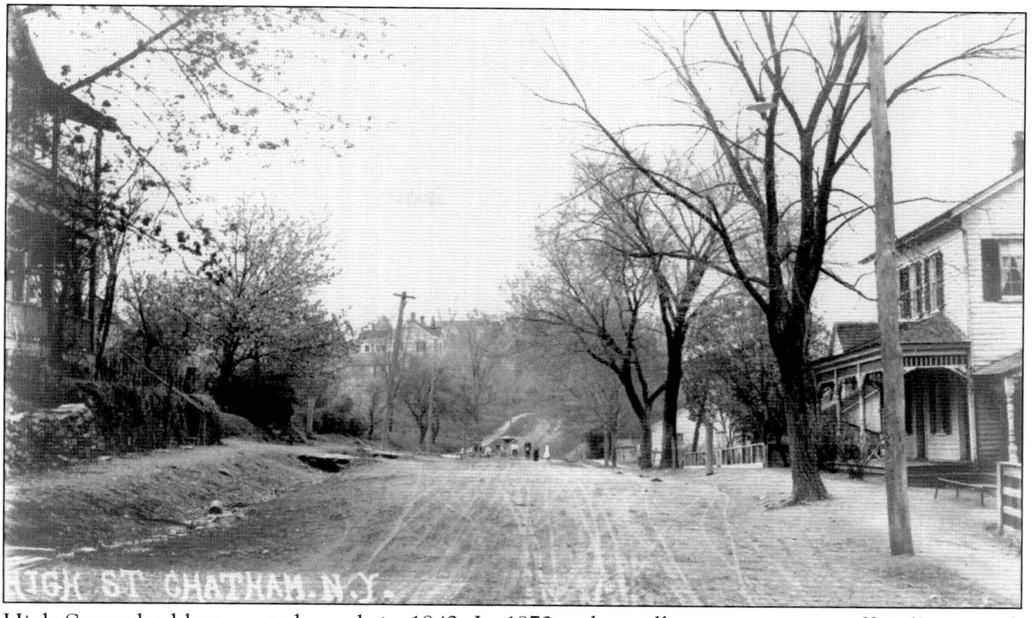

High Street had been cut through in 1842. In 1872, other village streets were officially named. Village officers included Abram B. Pugsley, John Wing, Mark Mealey, and George L. Morris, trustees; Abram Ashley Jr., clerk; Richard H. Bump, Joseph P. Hogeboom, and Samuel Jerkowski, assessors; Enos Peake, collector; and James T. Shufelt, treasurer and health officer. Police justice W. C. Daley with constables George C. Burrows and George E. Kenworthy were assigned to keep the peace. (Courtesy of CPL.)

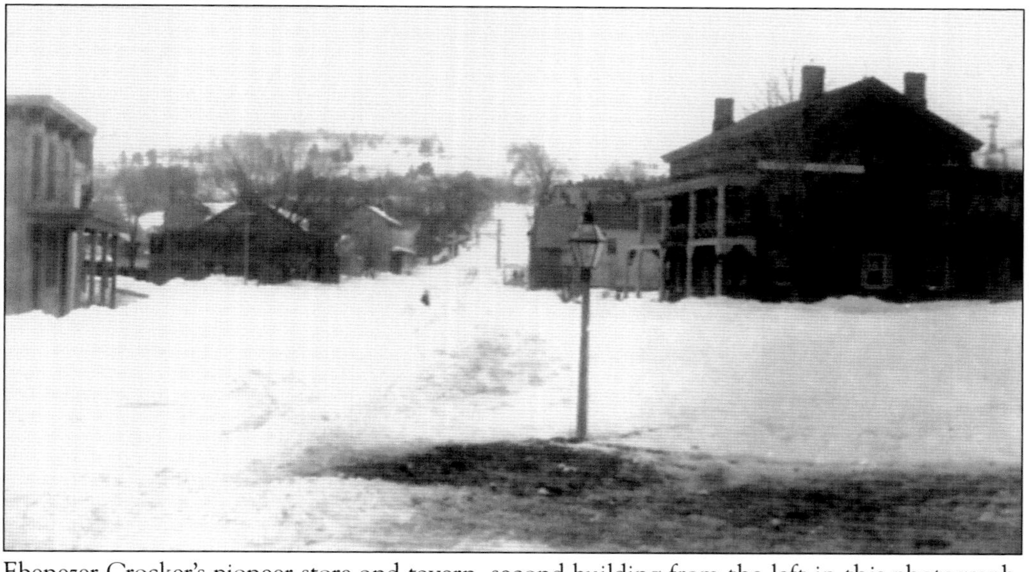

Ebenezer Crocker's pioneer store and tavern, second building from the left in this photograph, became the Columbia Hotel, as indicated on an 1851 map. By 1871, the name changed to the Park House where Charles Childs had a livery. The hostelry claimed to have the first electric lights. On June 18, 1879, the Park House offered its weekly Wednesday open-air concert by the Citizen's Band from its balcony. Some time before 1890, the structure was dismantled and removed, in part becoming a residence on River Street. (Courtesy of CPL.)

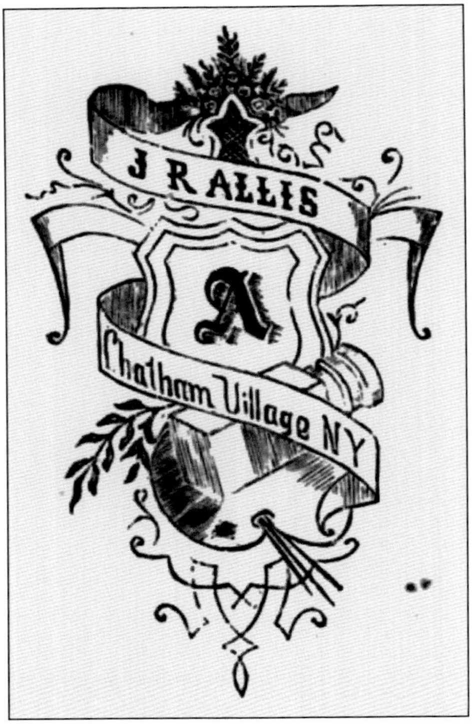

In 1877, S. Allis purchased the building lot on the central square where the very first farmhouse had stood. There he erected a three-story wooden structure with three or four living rooms on the third floor, a public gathering room on the second floor, and a variety of retail stores on the first floor (see page 35). He had his photography studio there. (Courtesy of CPL.)

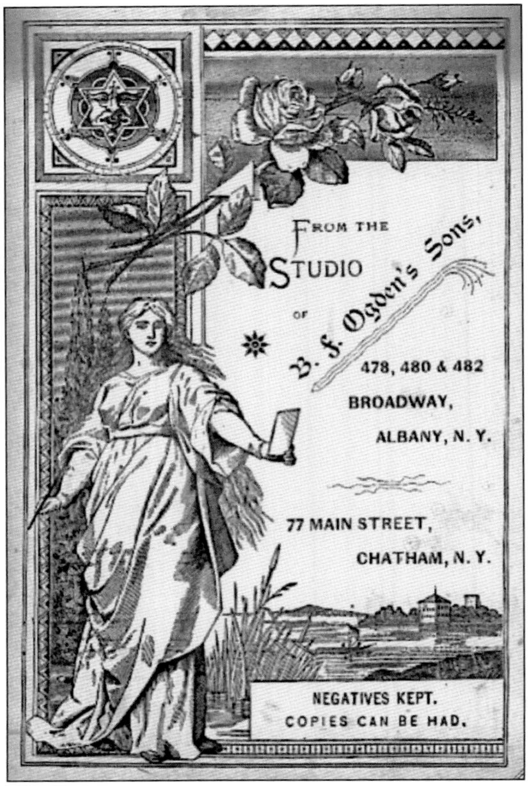

J. R. Allis's photograph gallery first occupied an Allis Building storefront. Ogden Photograph Gallery followed. George Tompkins's Paper Store also occupied the Allis Building. As shown in the bottom photograph on page 35, the prominent building was the largest business building in the village. To the right stood Alex Hulbert's residence and shop. (Courtesy of CVHS.)

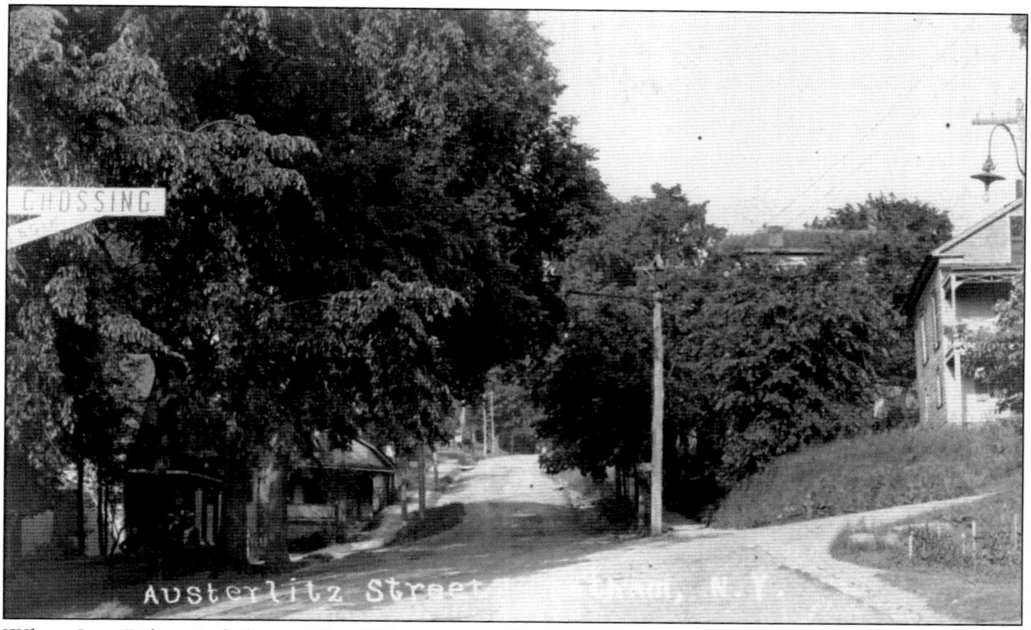

When Lee Palmer's father said to "Harness up the mare, we're going over to Chatham," for him it was the biggest moment of the year 1897. Spencertown was considerably rural compared to the bustling Chatham Four Corners. He recalled trotting over the flats to Hogle Hill, witnessing the Catskills, and close at hand the village of Chatham. At the junction of Jones Avenue and Austerlitz Street they trotted past the lone old brown house of Eunice Bunker then across the Western Railroad tracks to enter the central square. (Courtesy of CPL.)

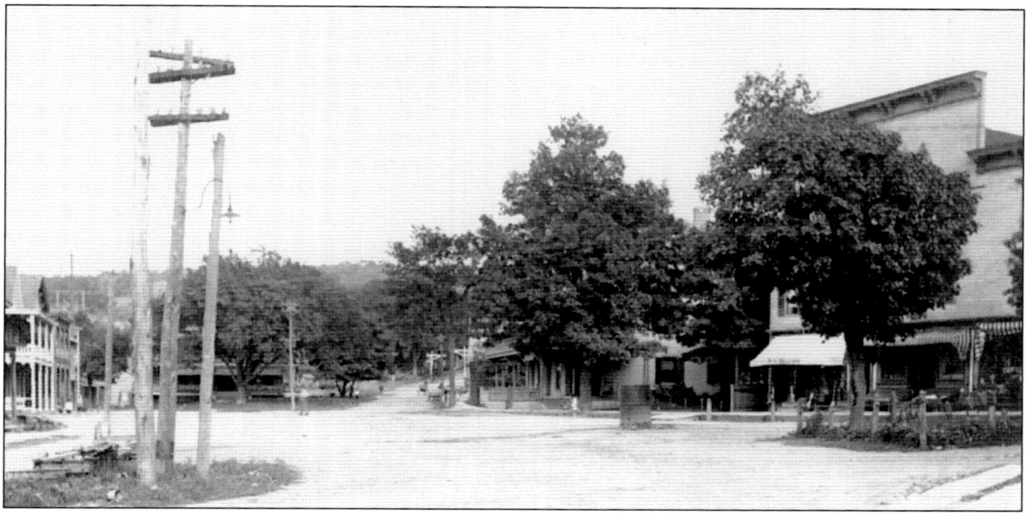

What a thrill it was for a Spencertown boy to pass "the mammoth Windsor Hotel" on their way to the watering trough on the central square so their mare Nellie could get a drink. C. H. Mason, M.D., and his brother, Abbott M. Mason, M.D., known for the Vegetable Cancer Cure (VCC) treatment, were proprietors of the sanitarium hotel built on the Park House site, obscured by the utility pole and mature tree. Austerlitz Street is in the center of the central square photograph. (Courtesy of Jon Meredith.)

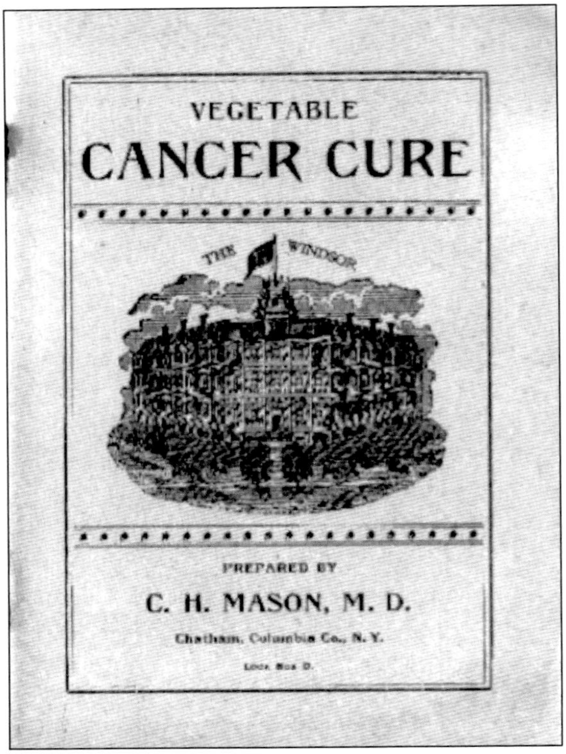

The undated VCC and promotional sanitarium booklet recorded that "the new structure has all modern improvements as to comfort and sanitation. 'The Windsor' Sanitarium, at Chatham, N.Y. is one of the finest institutions of its kind ever erected" with 50 large and commodious rooms all facing the front for $2 or $3 a day. (Courtesy of Jon Meredith.)

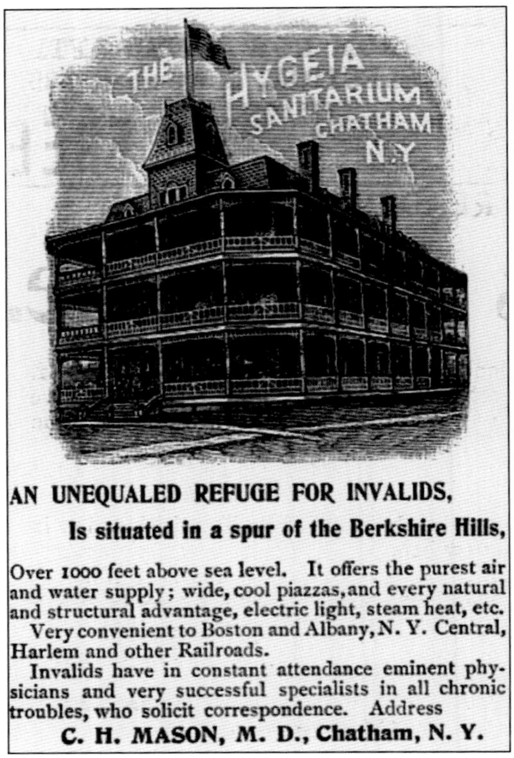

Dr. Charles Mason was his own architect, and the building was constructed under his personal supervision, and everything to make it comfortable and homelike was considered. "Friends can be accommodated at the Windsor at all times at reasonable rates." Indeed, the sanitarium hotel accommodated staff and boarders, chambermaids, and railroad station agents, with the convenience of the Western Union Telegraph and a telephone (number 17-4) with long-distance service. (Courtesy of Scott Wood.)

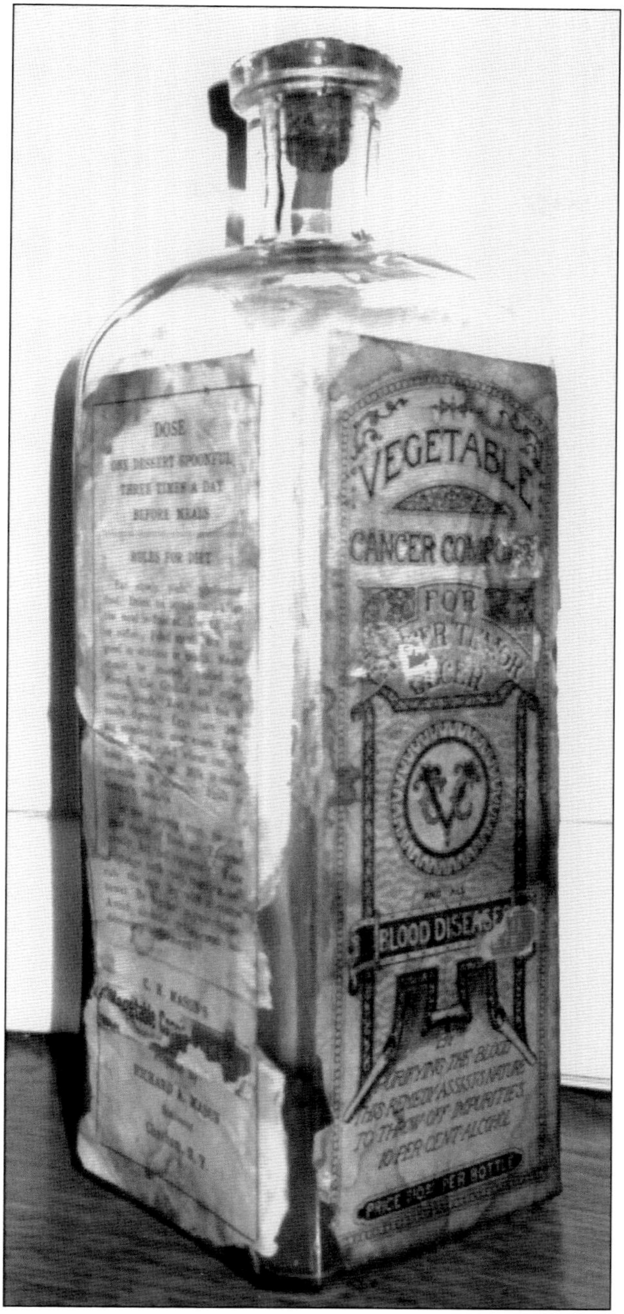

"A purely Vegetable Compound of roots, herbs, and barks, containing no minerals or poisons" was promised as the only remedy to cure cancers, tumors, and ulcers "unaided by knife or plaster." Barbara B. Hansberger, a young nursing mother from Germantown, Pennsylvania, attended the sanitarium on April 26, 1896, after finding a tumor in her breast. She remained under treatment in Chatham for one month and continued with the VCC medicine and lotion for six months after returning home. Hansberger wrote a testimonial for Dr. C. H. Mason stating that she was entirely cured under his care. (Courtesy of Jon Meredith.)

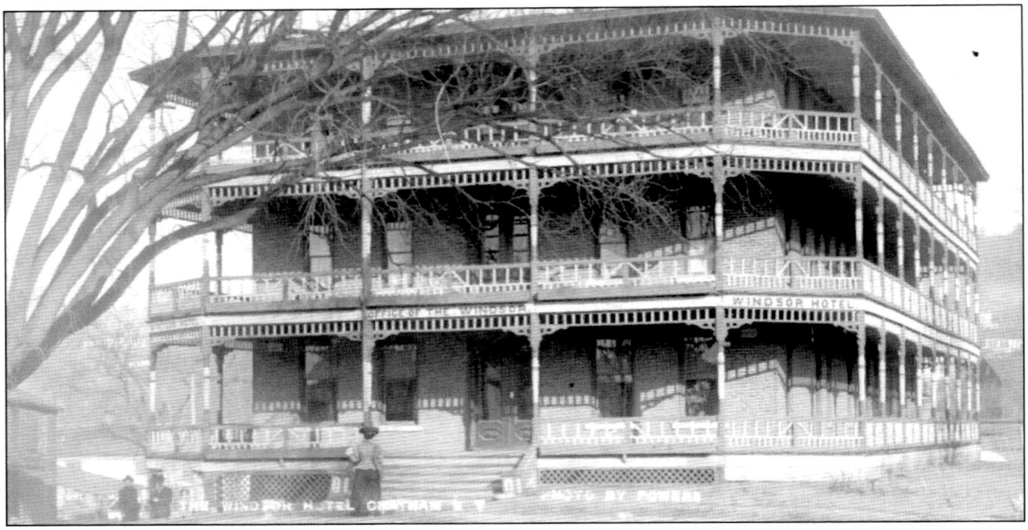

In 1891 or 1892, the hotel laboratory and residence of the Mason doctors caught fire. In 1899, the Windsor fire would be the first in the village history to take a human life. In October, the hotel chef, Christopher Sheppard, weighing some 300 pounds and with slight paralysis, aroused 27 "inmates" who found their only means of escape was from the piazzas. Mr. Wallace, an out-of-town guest, was aiding a lady to an escape window when he screamed and collapsed. His body was found where he had fallen, reported the *Chatham Courier*. (Courtesy of CPL.)

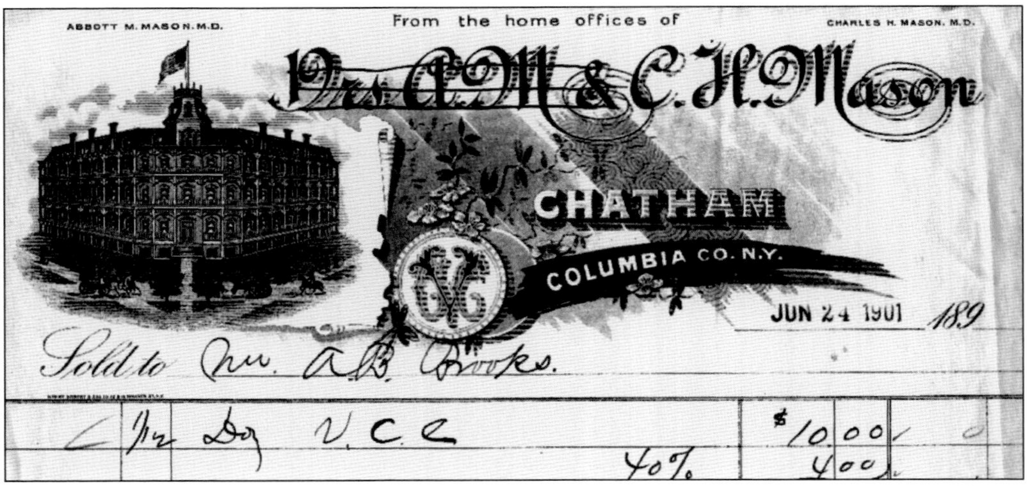
ABBOTT M. MASON, M.D.   From the home offices of   CHARLES H. MASON, M.D.

Drs. A. M. & C. H. Mason

CHATHAM

COLUMBIA CO. N.Y.

JUN 24 1901 189

Sold to Mr. A. B. Brooks.

½ Doz V.C.C			$10.00	
		40%	4.00	

By 1898, C. H. Mason had constructed a beautiful Victorian residence he called Echo Villa "in the most approved modern style" two and a half miles from the village. After the 1899 Windsor fire, he rebuilt and managed the hotel. In 1902, a Christmas dinner fare was offered at the New Windsor. Echo Villa's 140 acres also continued to grow the vegetables for his VCC medicine and hotel meals. This receipt offered Mr. Brooks, a customer, a 40 percent discount for the VCC. (Courtesy of CVHS.)

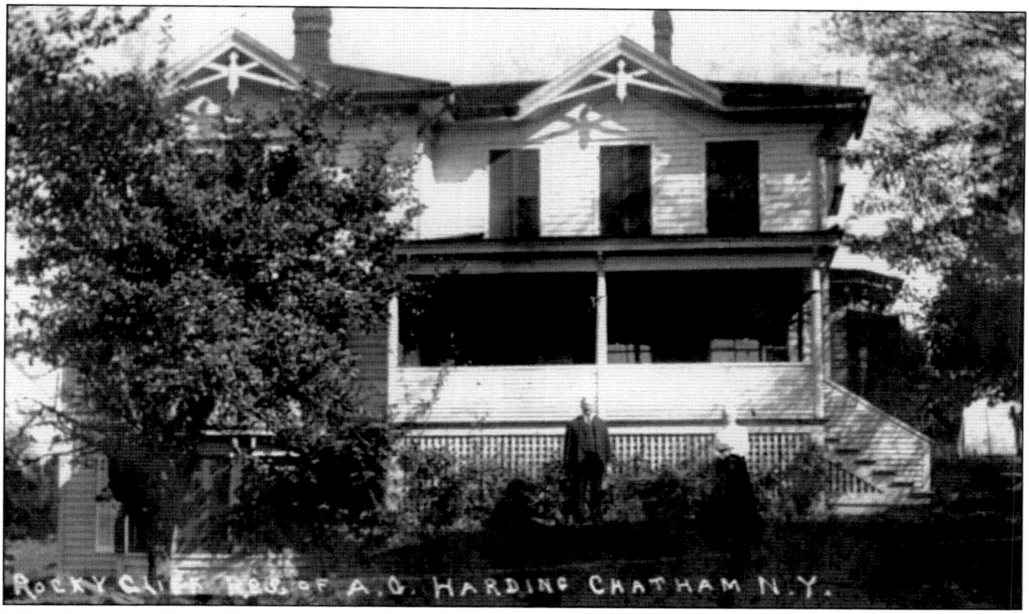

The Stanwix, formerly Groat's Tavern, had a fire at its livery and stable in 1884. Albert and Mary Harding may have been its proprietors at that time. They chose to live in their home called Rocky Cliffs located on Prospect Street in the village instead of in the tavern. (Courtesy of Molly Harding.)

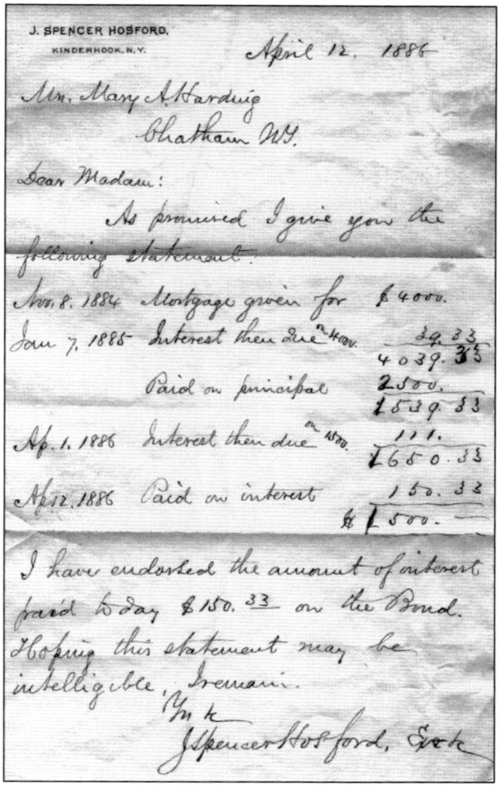

J. SPENCER HOSFORD,
KINDERHOOK, N.Y.

April 12, 1886

Mrs. Mary A. Harding
Chatham N.Y.

Dear Madam:

As promised I give you the following statement:

Nov. 8. 1884	Mortgage given for	$4000.
Jan 7, 1885	Interest then due on 4000.	39.33
		4039.33
	Paid on principal	2500.
		1539.33
Ap. 1. 1886	Interest then due on 1500.	111.
		1650.33
Ap. 12. 1886	Paid on interest	150.33
		$1500.

I have endorsed the amount of interest paid today $150.33 on the Bond. Hoping this statement may be intelligible, I remain.

Yrs &c

J. Spencer Hosford, Exr.

In 1886, Mary Harding had to assume responsibility for the Stanwix Hotel and tavern when her husband passed away. In the correspondence received at the hotel, her lawyer delineates the financial obligations remaining for her as sole proprietor. (Courtesy of Molly Harding.)

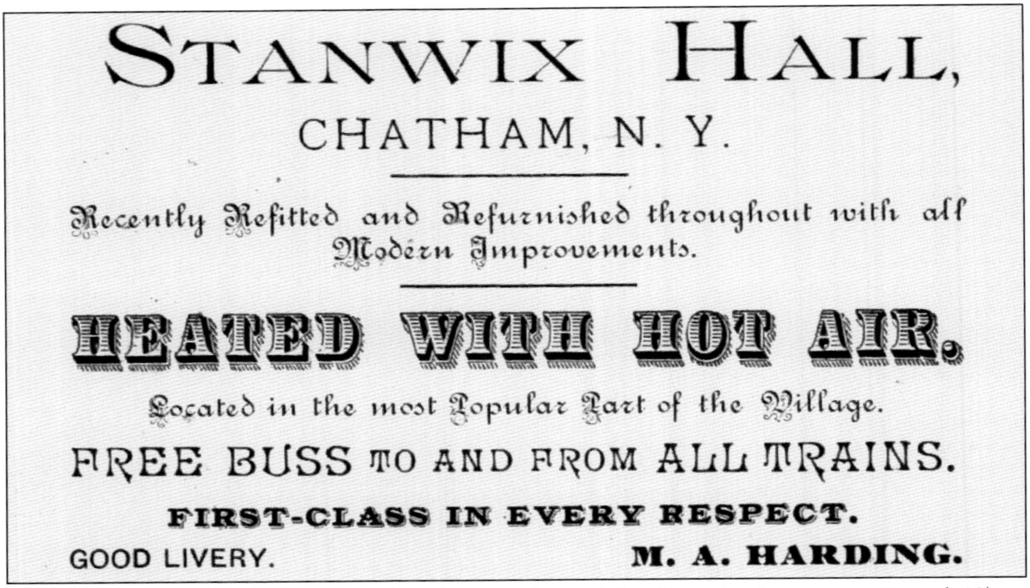

In May 1897, Mary Harding transferred ownership of the Stanwix (see pages 11 and 12) to A. B. Francisco. It boasted 40 guest rooms, a parlor, office, ladies' parlor, reading room, and bar. Conveniences included electric lights, steam heat, telephone service, electric call and return bells, water and sewer connections, and baths. Special rates were given to families on the American plan. (Courtesy of Molly Harding.)

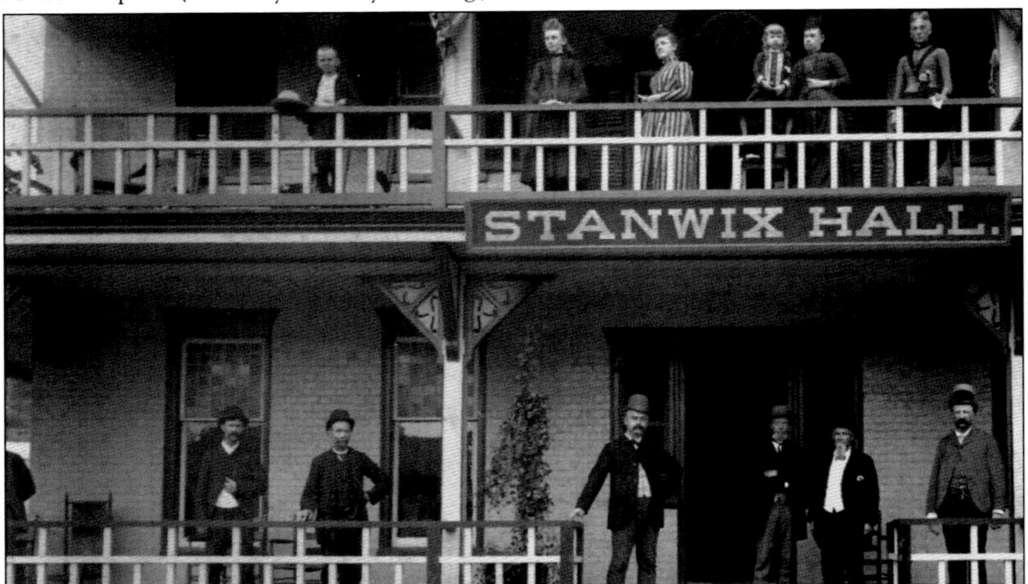

From lower Austerlitz Street, young Lee Palmer recorded this reaction to the oldest hotel on the central square, the former Groat's Tavern, in 1897: "On the left was the Stanwix Hotel, a large mysterious building which we children were told not to get very close to. It had a big livery stable in the rear yard and several important looking men, who father called 'politicians,' were holding head to head conversations on the front porch, between puffs of cigar smoke." (Courtesy of CPL.)

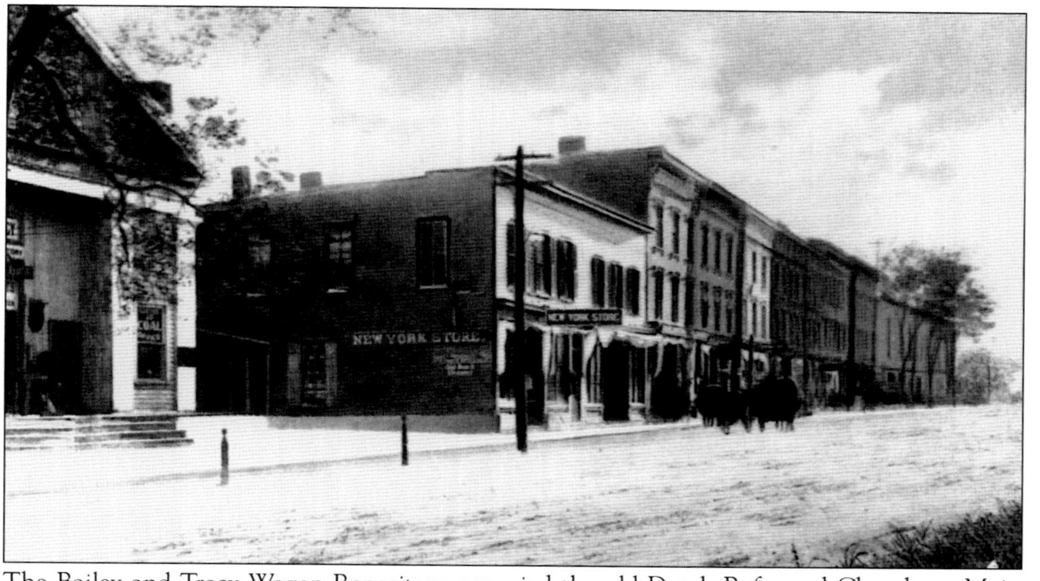

The Bailey and Tracy Wagon Repository occupied the old Dutch Reformed Church on Main Street (formerly Halstead and Pierson's). They carried manufactured wagons, featuring Empire State wagons. American fencing, Lister fertilizers, and agricultural implements were also sold. Their trade reached far outside the village. The former Reformed church, shown on the far left, was saved when Judge John Cadman blew up his home that stood in the space in the photograph. (Courtesy of CPL.)

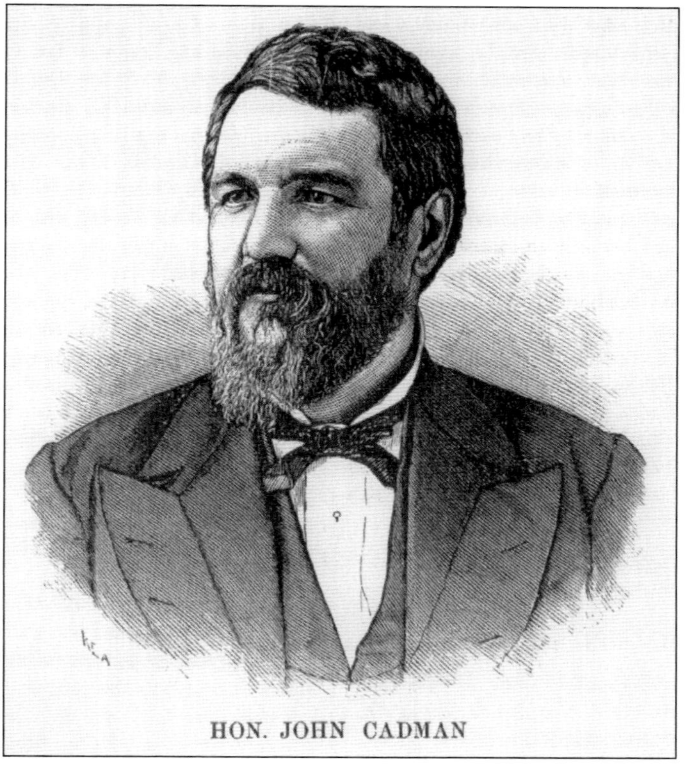

The following notice appeared in the April 21, 1869, edition of the *Chatham Courier*: "During the fire April 5th books and papers from Cadman & Daley [attorneys] tumbled. The docket of Justices record was removed. It is in the shape of a common accounts book. Liberal reward." John Cadman would help rebuild Main Street with the Cadman Building and investing in the State Bank of Chatham. (Courtesy of CVHS.)

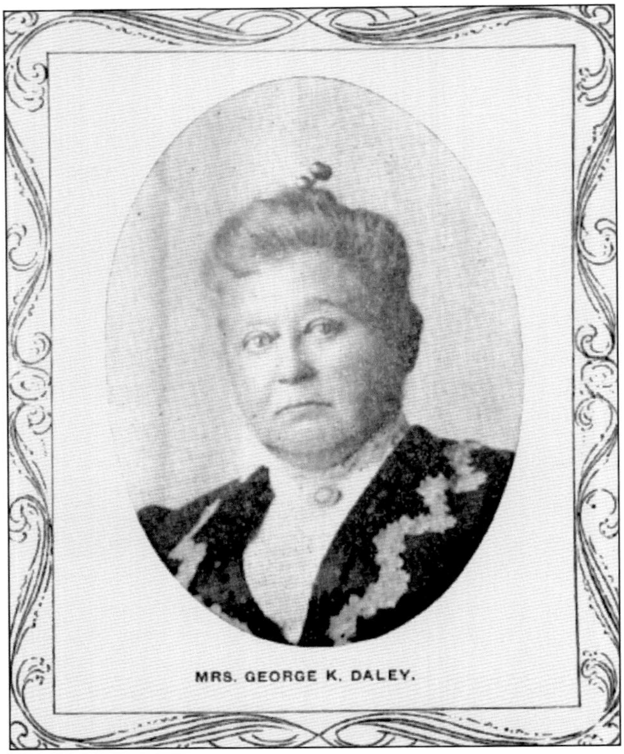

Mrs. Daley (shown), George Daley's wife and legal assistant, received a commendation from the U. S. attorney general of the United States for compiling a 50-volume digest of U.S. Supreme Court reports. (Courtesy of CVHS.)

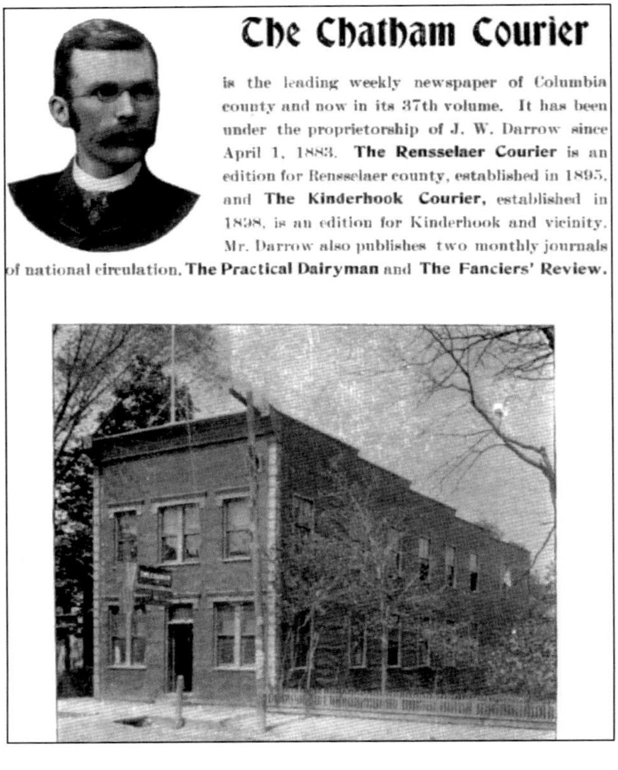

The Chatham Courier

is the leading weekly newspaper of Columbia county and now in its 37th volume. It has been under the proprietorship of J. W. Darrow since April 1, 1883. **The Rensselaer Courier** is an edition for Rensselaer county, established in 1895, and **The Kinderhook Courier,** established in 1898, is an edition for Kinderhook and vicinity. Mr. Darrow also publishes two monthly journals of national circulation, **The Practical Dairyman** and **The Fanciers' Review.**

Heading down Main Street from the central square, Charlie McKern's market was on the right, also the brick building of the *Chatham Courier*, whose harried editor was Harry Doty. J. Wallace Darrow, the *Courier*'s publisher, might be seen bicycling his way to the depot for the latest news in 1898. (Courtesy of CVHS.)

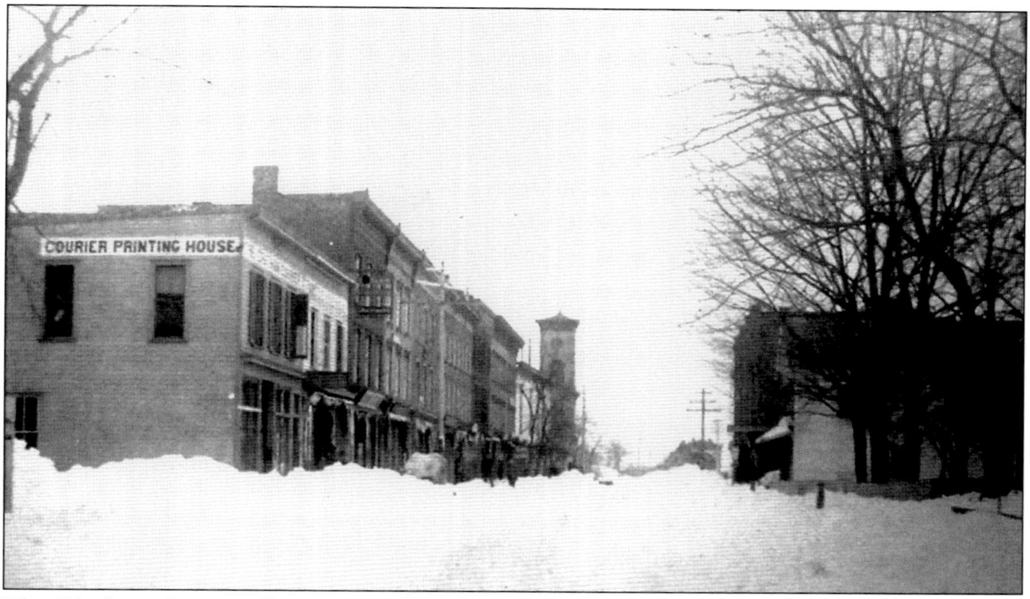

The *Chatham Courier* office was on the east side of Main Street in this 1888 photograph. The *Courier* had begun in a barn on Kinderhook Street in 1862 when Delos Sutherland put out a four-page paper issued every Thursday. The business was moved to a place across from the Stanwix Hall then to the Cadman Building, shown here. J. Wallace Darrow purchased the publication in 1883. (Courtesy of CPL.)

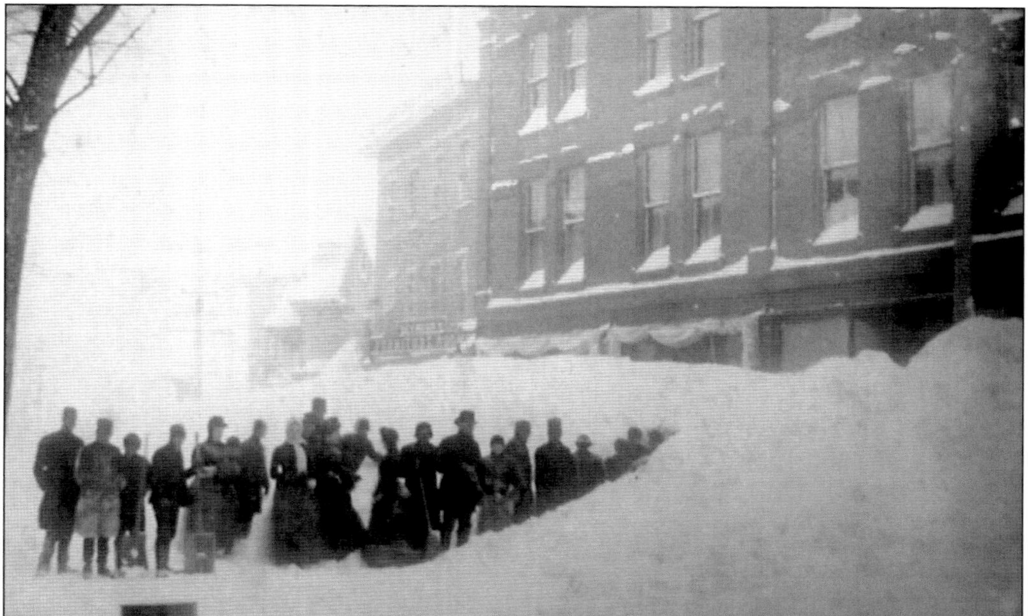

This 1888 snowstorm photograph shows that Rogowski's new business block was an immense establishment for its time. It began on the eastern side of Main Street as the Ladies' Bazaar (see page 49). Comparatively, Rogowski's had Wanamaker's and Macy's beat with its variety of stock from horse liniment to soapstone bed warmers. (Courtesy of Chatham Village Hall.)

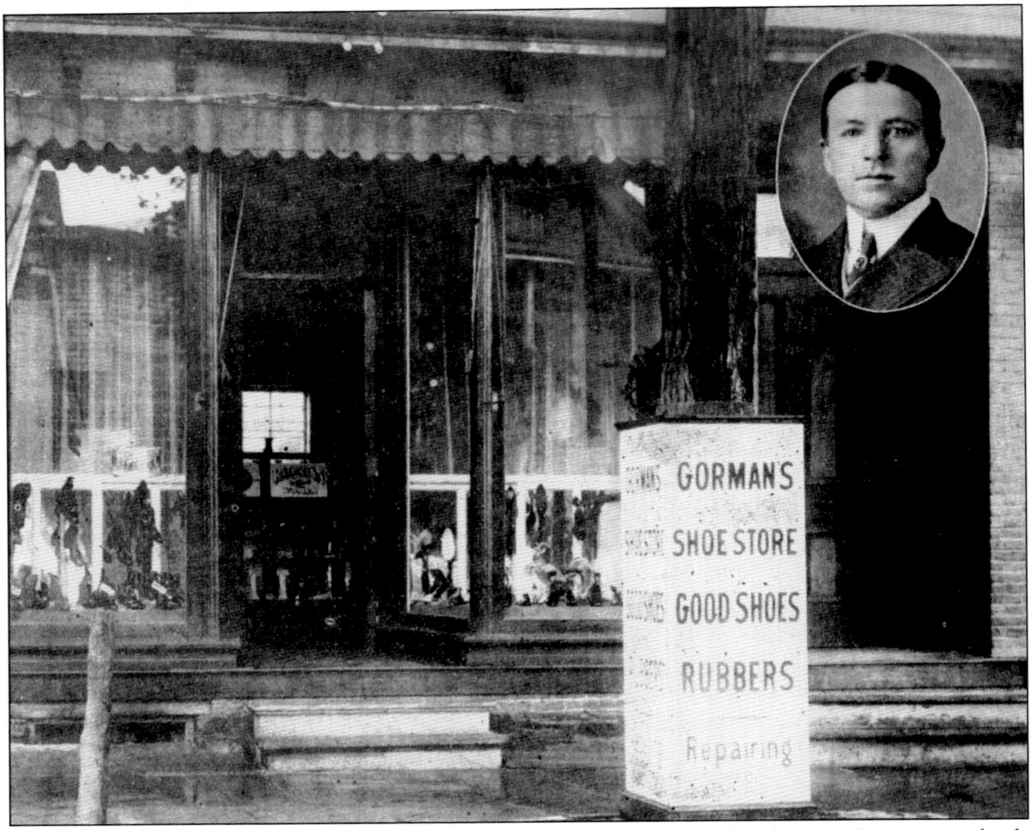

Due to the 1869 fire, many retailers relocated on the western side of Main Street or rebuilt fire-safe establishments. The eastern side of the street became almost uniformly brick two- and three-story structures. Many retailers have occupied these storefronts over the decades. (Courtesy of CPL.)

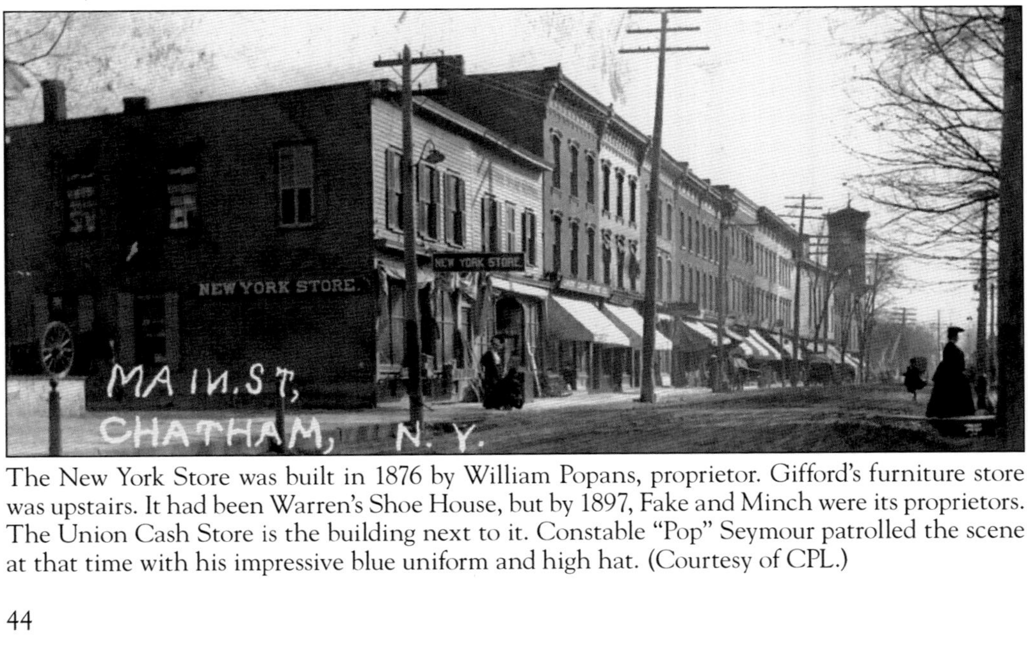

The New York Store was built in 1876 by William Popans, proprietor. Gifford's furniture store was upstairs. It had been Warren's Shoe House, but by 1897, Fake and Minch were its proprietors. The Union Cash Store is the building next to it. Constable "Pop" Seymour patrolled the scene at that time with his impressive blue uniform and high hat. (Courtesy of CPL.)

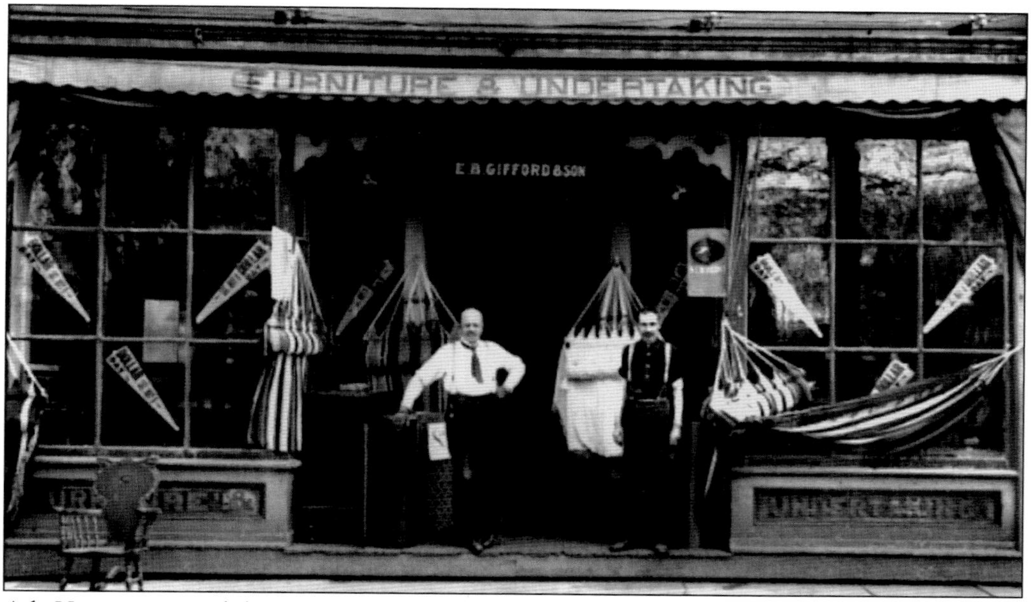

Ada Hamm accepted the proprietorship of Hamm Furniture following the death of her husband. The Main Street store was considered very large and offered a wide variety of furniture. Her associate, E. B. Gifford, was also located in the building and was responsible for the undertaking business. Gifford would later partner with his son and remain the village undertakers for generations. (Courtesy of CVHS.)

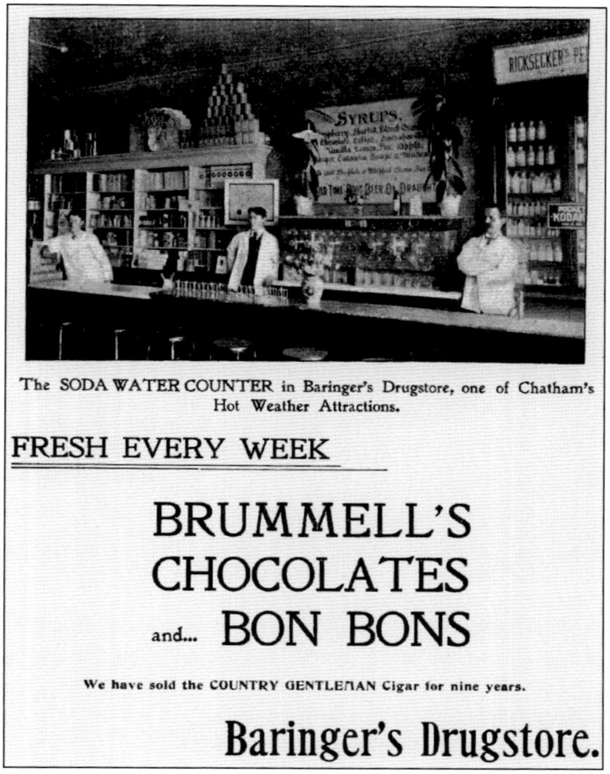

Baringer's Drugstore's soda fountain was considered one of Chatham's hot weather attractions. Cigars sold included Country Gentleman, Thoroughbred, and General Greene brands. Their advertisement appeared in *Picturesque Chatham* in 1898. (Courtesy of CVHS.)

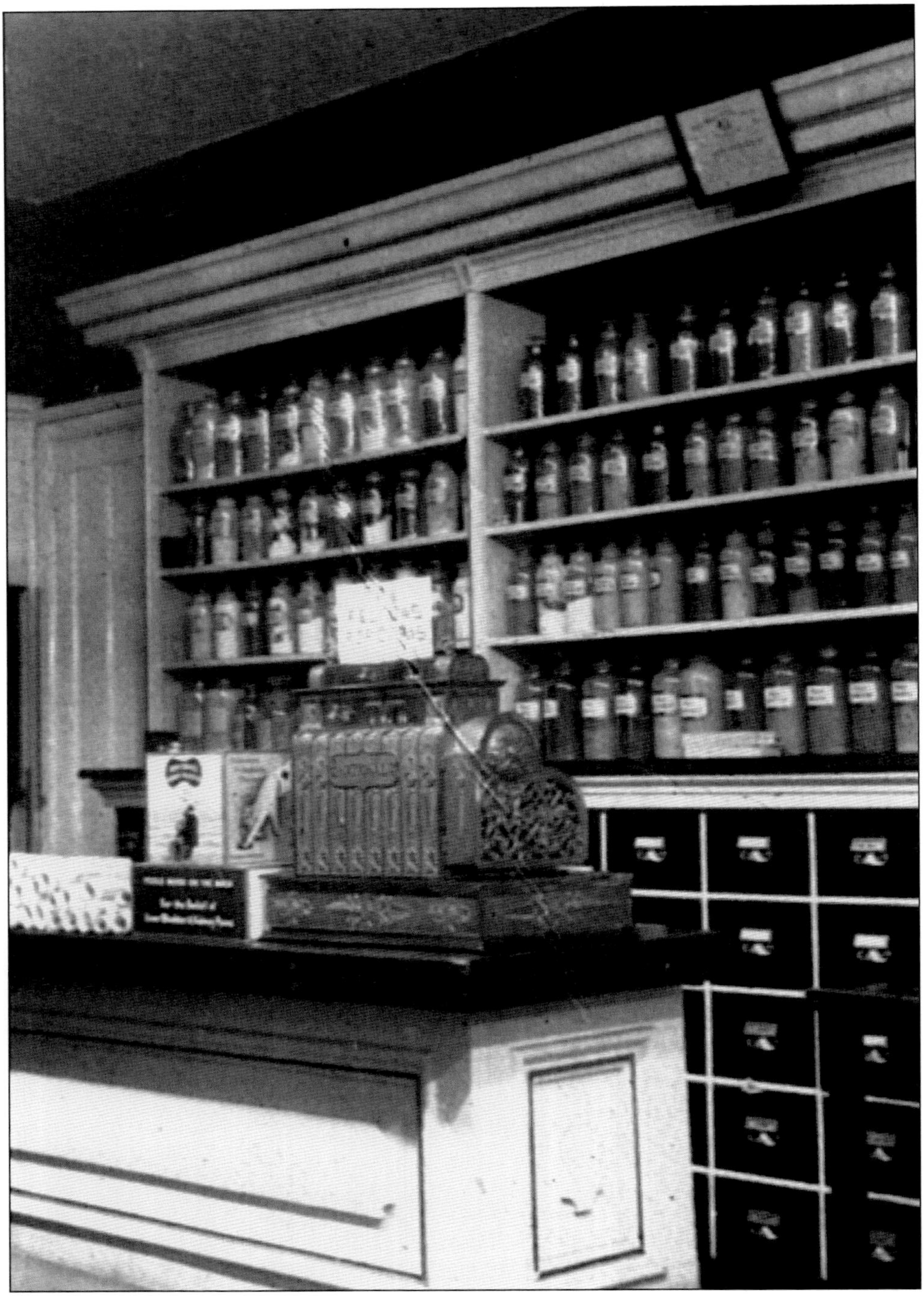

Fellow's Pharmacy was in the Masonic building at the corner of Park Row and the depot square. The old Civil War veteran prescribed medication for 50 years and gathered the news in the community while dealing reliably with his customers. His pharmacy is pictured. Contemporary drugstores were Branion's, Barnes, and Vincent's. The latter served Borden's malted milk. (Courtesy of Dwight Sawyer, Miller Collection.)

Reuben W. Seymour acquired Dr. Barnes's drugstore in 1890 and the same year was elected town clerk. Dr. I. C. Washburn became his partner. (Courtesy of CVHS.)

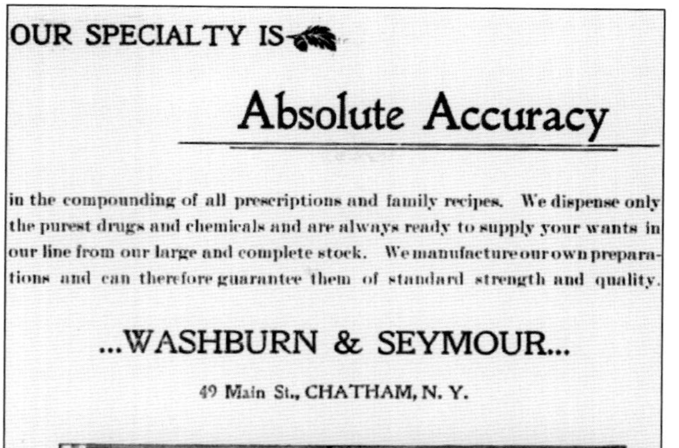
OUR SPECIALTY IS

Absolute Accuracy

in the compounding of all prescriptions and family recipes. We dispense only the purest drugs and chemicals and are always ready to supply your wants in our line from our large and complete stock. We manufacture our own preparations and can therefore guarantee them of standard strength and quality.

...WASHBURN & SEYMOUR...

49 Main St., CHATHAM, N. Y.

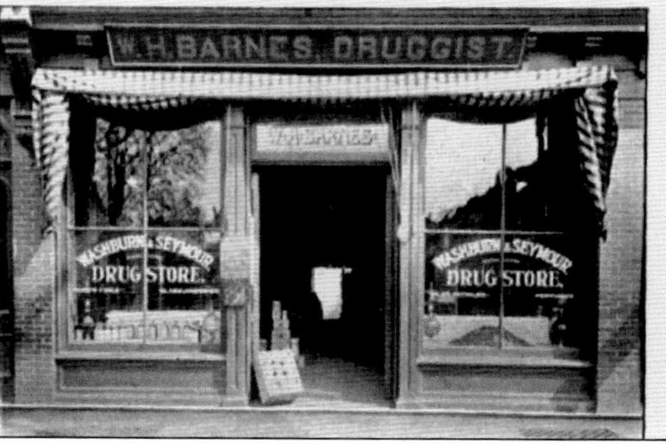

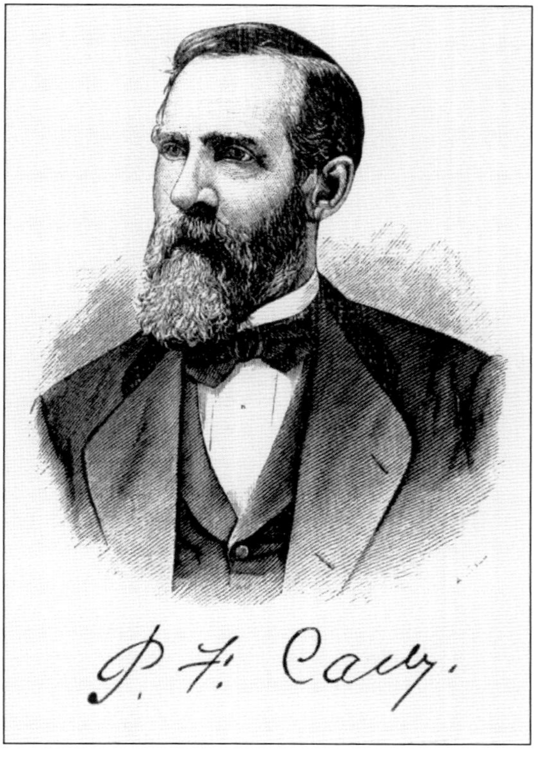

Cady Hall opened in 1871, the village's first opera house. The 1872 *Chatham Courier* reported, "Mr. Cady's Hall is just what had been needed for the village. Being well arranged for any entertainment with stage, gallerie, anteroom, and ticket office." Ocean Fire Company No. 1's banquet was the first event held in the highly decorated hall complete with stage and beautiful chandeliers. (Courtesy of CVHS.)

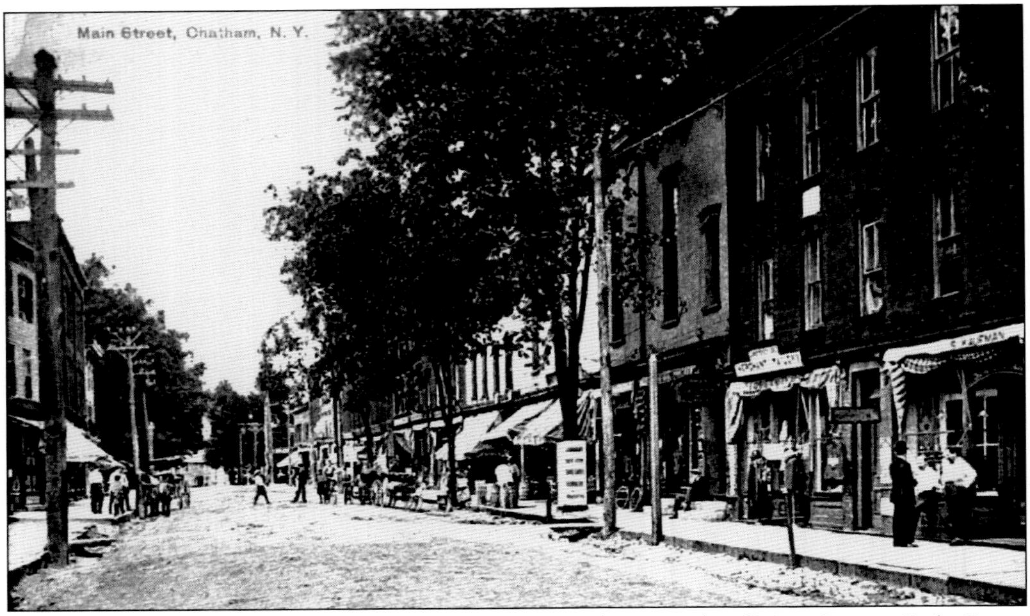

This view is facing toward the central square showing the east side of Main Street. Cady Opera Hall on the right has the long slender windows and trees in front of it. Gorman's shoe store advertisement is wrapped around one of those trees. To its right is Christensen Brothers clothier and S. Kaufman's. The clock tower over village hall would be at the southern end of that line of businesses. (Courtesy of CPL.)

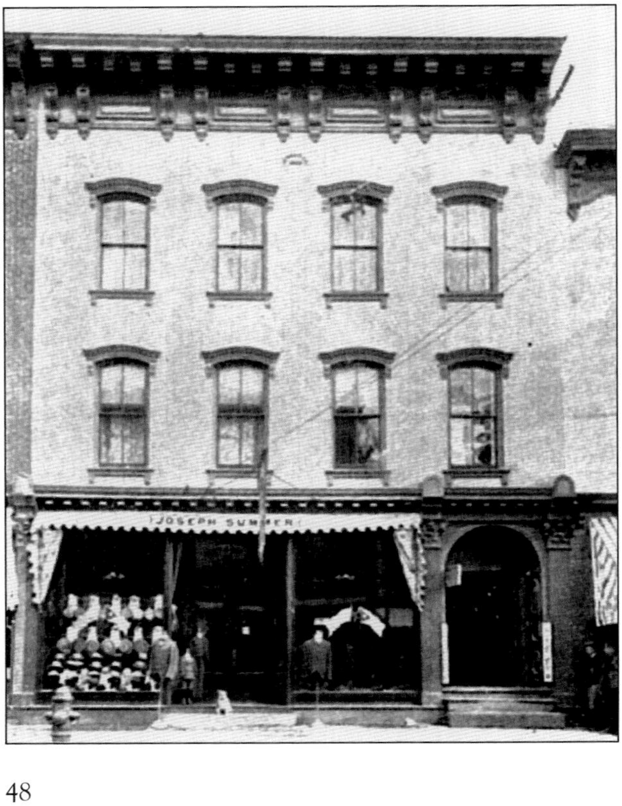

In 1893, Joseph Summers clothing store occupied the Jerkowski Building. He was a gents' tailor. Upstairs Dr. Harmon performed dentistry with a portable drill operated by a foot pedal. When the cavity was extremely deep the extra friction on the drill would cause the foot-powered belt to slip and the drill to stop. The Independent Order of Good Templars held their meetings there. (Courtesy of CVHS.)

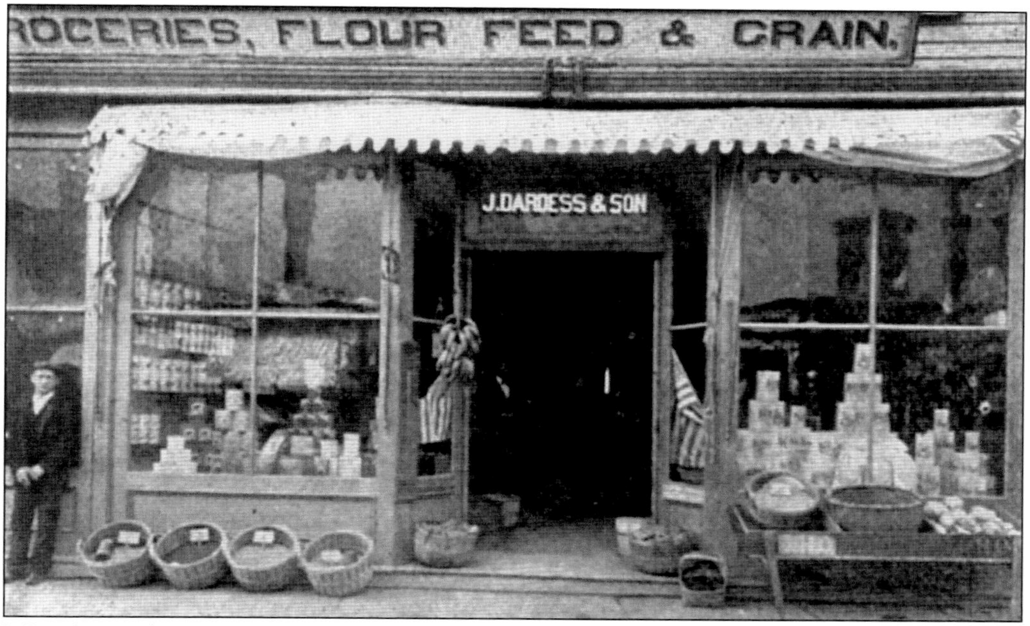

J. Dardess and Son was established in 1883 on the west side of Main Street. The store provided its customers with groceries, flour, and provisions. Fruits and vegetables were seasonal. Their specialty products were "Chace and Sanborn's coffees" and Ferris's hams and bacon. The village hall clock tower has its reflection captured in the right storefront window. (Courtesy of CVHS.)

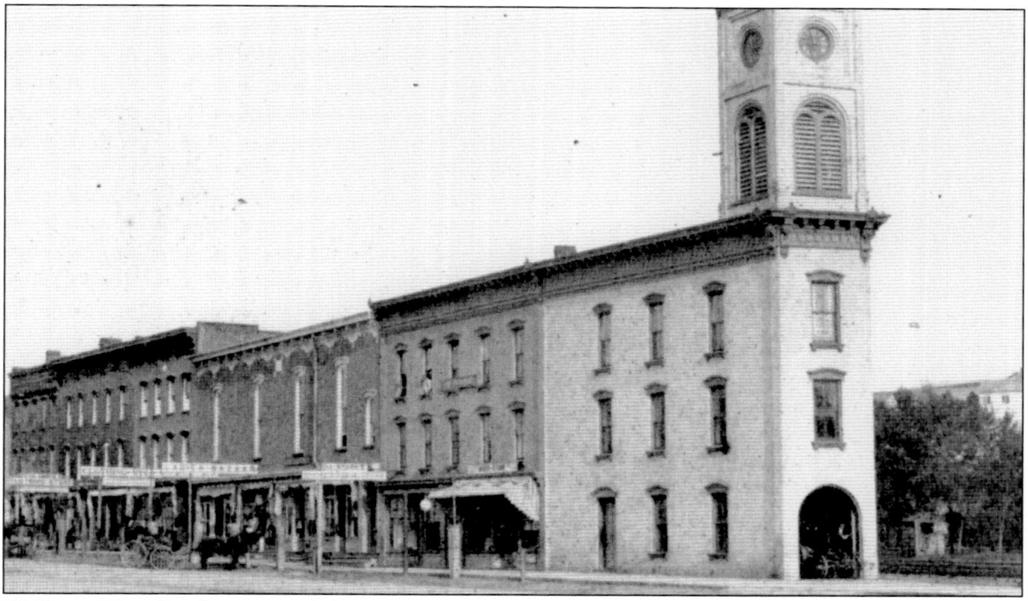

William Woodbridge erected the triangular brick Italianate structure in 1872. It had been the site of the foundry where three years earlier flames ignited half of Main Street. Woodbridge had presided over the first village election in 1863 and sold this building to the village of Chatham for $5,500. It housed the village offices, the police court, and the firemen's hall for Ocean Fire Company No. 1. (Courtesy of CVHS.)

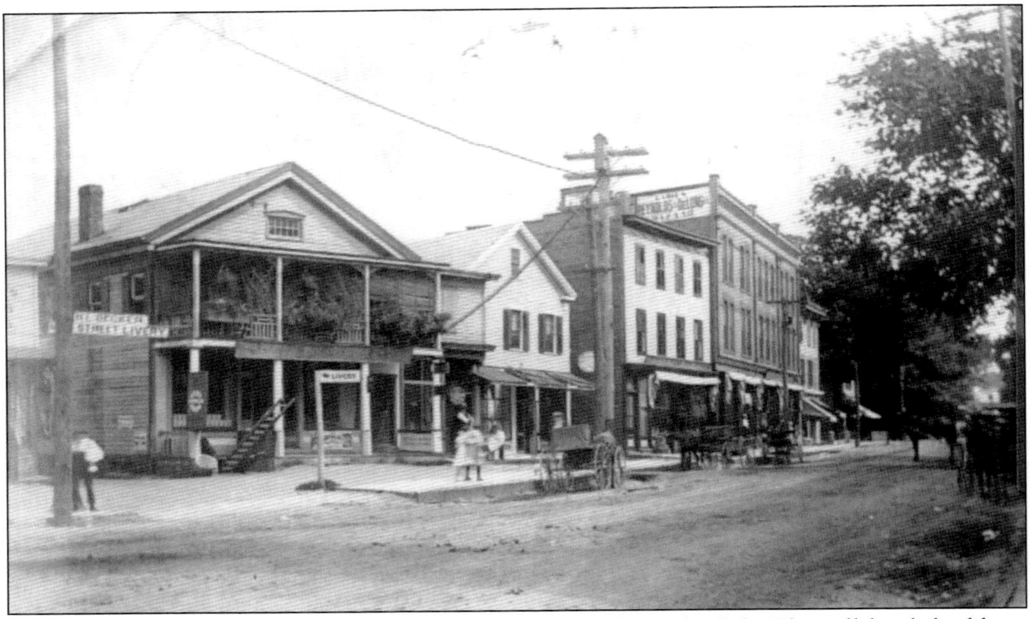

H. L. Decker's street livery sign hangs from a utility pole at the left. The tall brick building, built by the Rogowskis, was under the ownership of E. B. Reynolds and Harry J. DeLong at this photograph moment. E. B. Reynolds had been a cash boy for William Rogowski in the 1870s. Reynolds was a hometown boy. His partner, DeLong, had business experience with Albany's John G. Myers Company. (Courtesy of CCHS.)

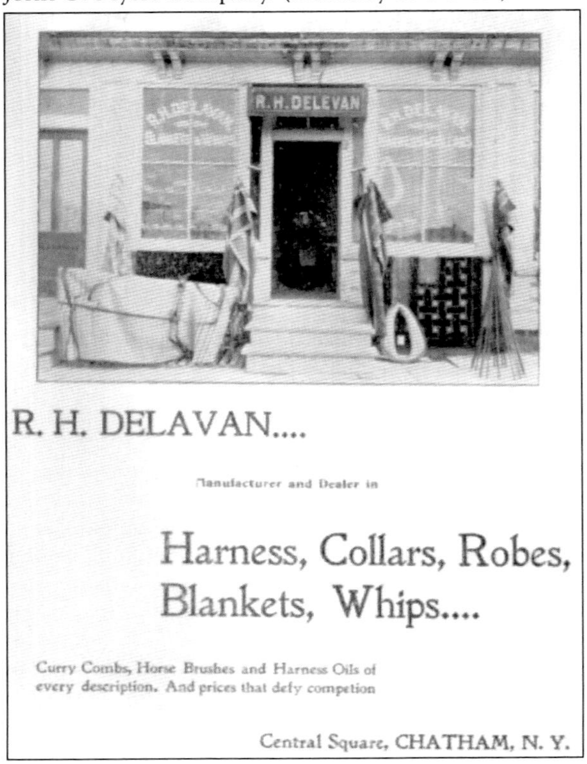

R. H. Delavan's or Delevan's harness shop was between the Stanwix Hall and Allis Building. The business manufactured and dealt in collars, robes, blankets, whips, curry combs, horse brushes, and harness oils of every description with prices that defied competition (see page 35). Covey's store, on the southwest end of Main Street near the State Bank, carried high-quality handmade tack and everything anyone needed for a well-appointed stable. (Courtesy of CVHS.)

Grange No. 900 Patrons of Husbandry organized in 1901. Officers included master J. W. Darrow, assistant steward F. B. Pratt, secretary Harry M. Doty, and treasurer William H. Housman. Housman moved to the village in 1899 and labored for Ephraim G. Palmer, owner of a flour and grain business. Housman later acquired the business, was financially successful, and gave away land to encourage further local industry. (Courtesy of CVHS.)

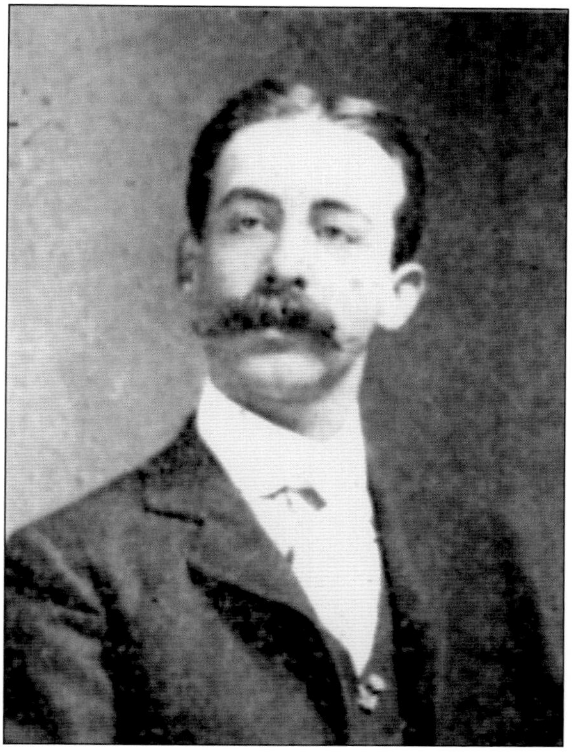

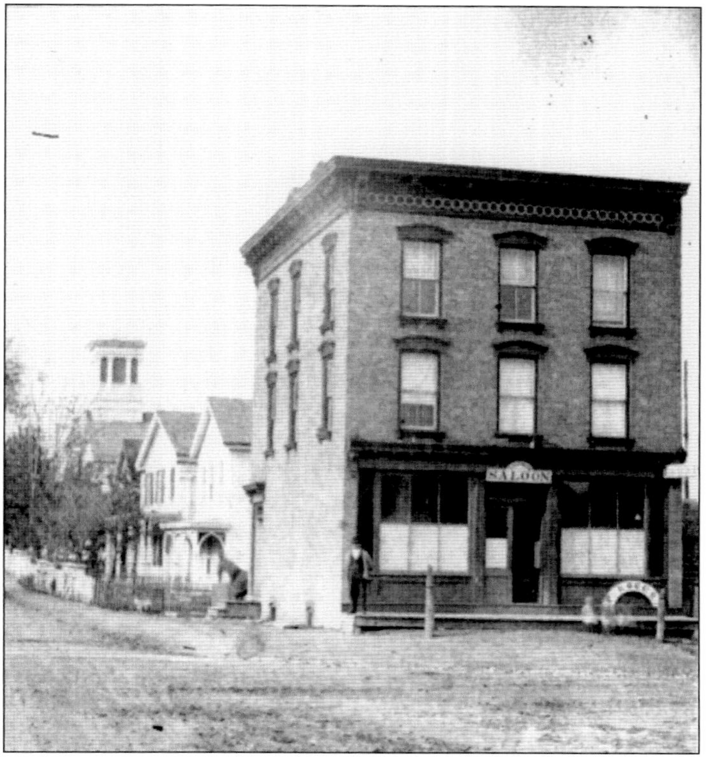

This central square view shows Koger's Saloon with a gentleman and young children in front. When the public school became overcrowded, high school classes were held within the Koger building. In the background, the Methodist church spire rises from its wooden church at 13 Kinderhook Street. (Courtesy of Jon Meredith.)

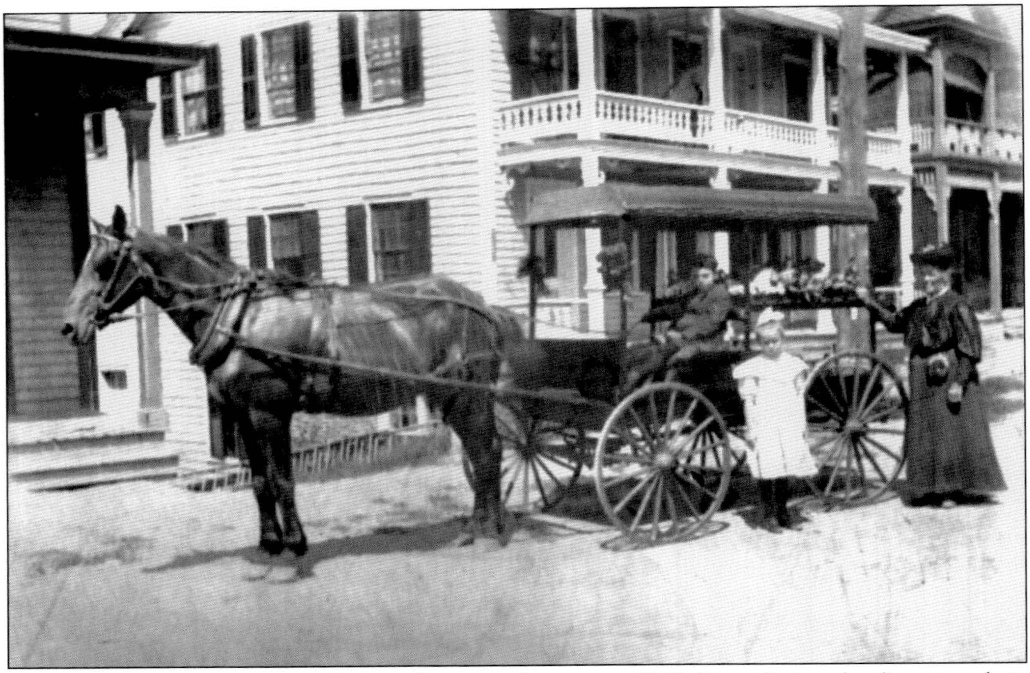

Young Eva Betz was photographed on the central square in 1912. Considering the direction their carriage was headed, they may have been going to Peter Swab's or past his business down Center Street. Kinderhook Street was straight ahead. Trotting down that road they could have turned left onto Woodbridge Avenue, where the grammar and high school buildings stood. (Courtesy of CVHS.)

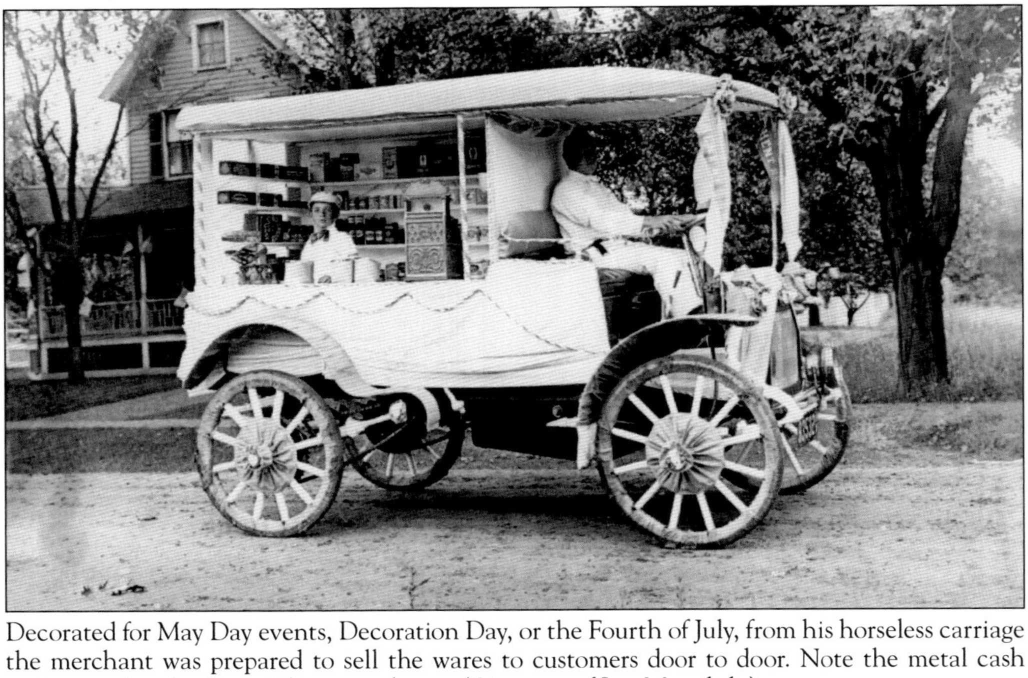

Decorated for May Day events, Decoration Day, or the Fourth of July, from his horseless carriage the merchant was prepared to sell the wares to customers door to door. Note the metal cash register and scales for weighing purchases. (Courtesy of Jon Meredith.)

Four

The Railroads Came

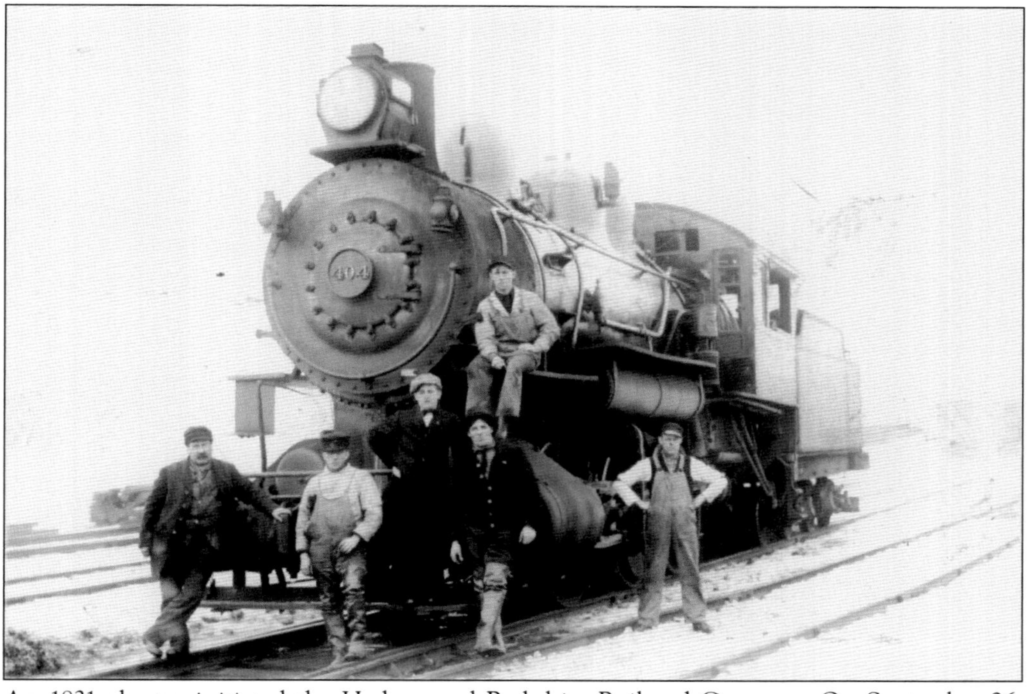

An 1831 charter initiated the Hudson and Berkshire Railroad Company. On September 26, 1838, the West Stockbridge-to-Hudson run was established. There were no specific stops along the route so farmhands were sometimes sent ahead to inform the stationmaster where to have the train stop. This photograph was taken around 1919 near the railroad yard turntable. (Courtesy of CVHS.)

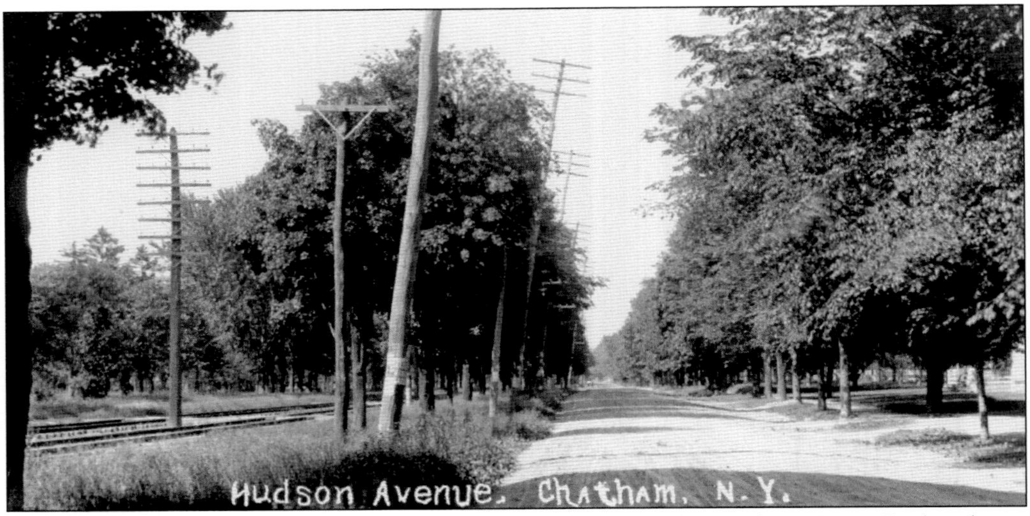

The merger of the New York and Harlem Railroad with the Hudson River Railroad was accomplished by Cornelius Vanderbilt. "Old No. 1" would ease up Hudson Avenue from New York City to the Chatham depot as the first engine of the day. It carried with it a mailbag full of *New York Tribunes* from the Horace Greeley Press. The train crew would deliver the latest fashion news and hum the newest tunes while they unloaded. The train was the direct connecting link with New York City and the rest of the world. (Courtesy of CPL.)

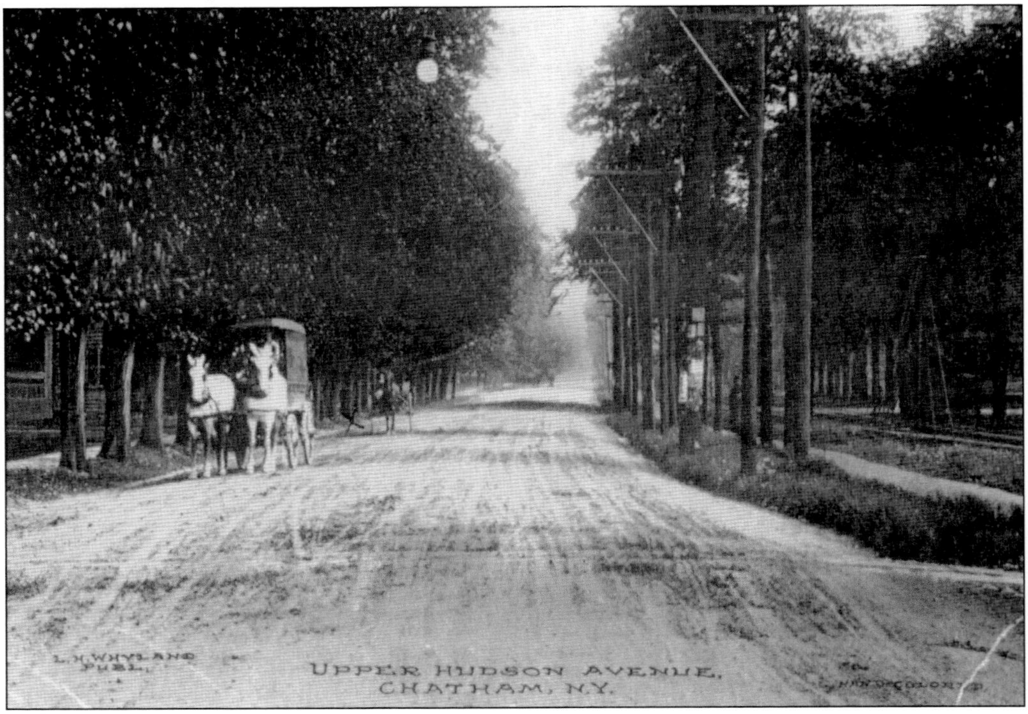

Hudson Avenue's horse-drawn carriages were driven parallel to the Harlem Railway line shown on the right of this photograph. Looking south, beautiful Victorian homes were constructed on either side of these roadbeds, protected from the dust and soot by a continual line of tall, mature trees. (Courtesy of CVHS.)

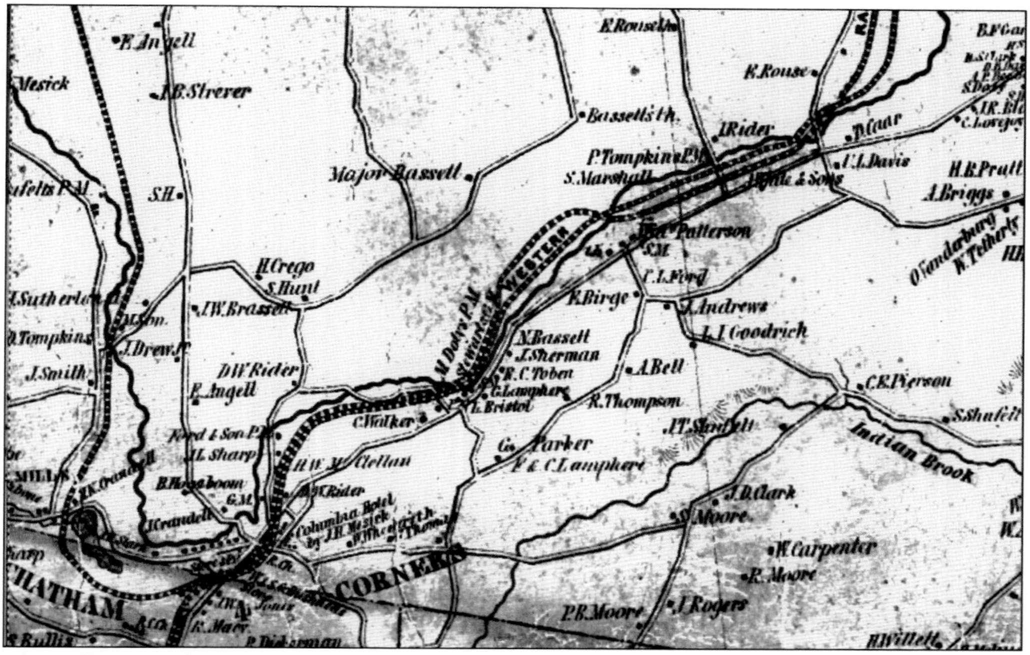

The Albany and West Stockbridge Railroad (Western Railroad) opened to Chatham Four Corners on December 21, 1841. Abraham Lincoln, having spoken in Boston along with Gov. William H. Seward, traveled over the Boston and Worcester Railroad, changing to the Western Railroad. On September 23, 1848, that train stopped at Chatham Four Corners around 4:30 that evening with the future president aboard. (Courtesy of CVHS.)

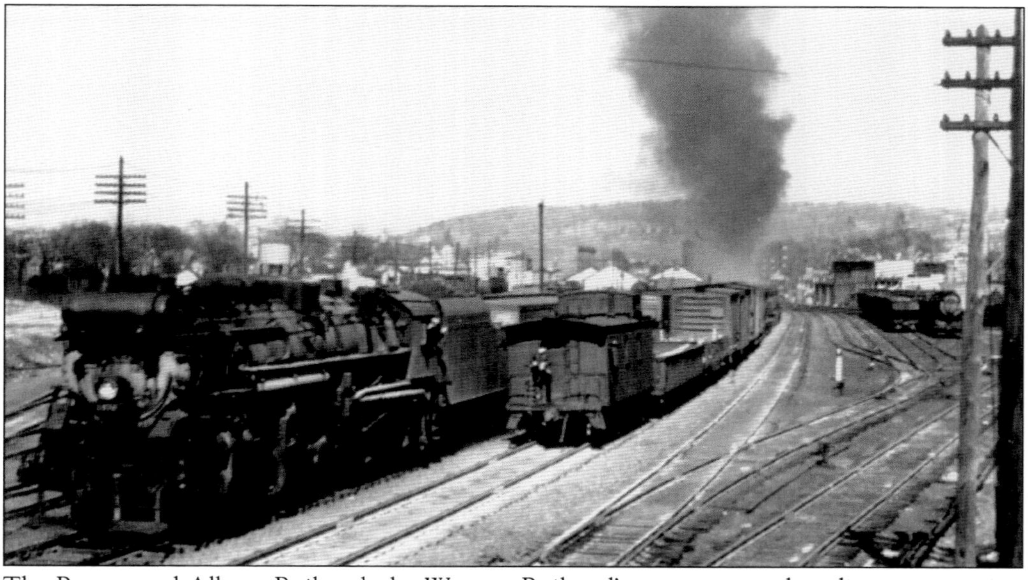

The Boston and Albany Railroad, the Western Railroad's successor, made a direct connection between the Erie Canal and the New York Central Railroad terminal in Albany to the East Coast city of Boston. The Boston and Albany was the northern terminus of the New York Central Harlem Division and the southern terminal of the Rutland Railroad. Chatham's massive train yard, viewed here from tower 66, had two turntables. (Courtesy of CCHS.)

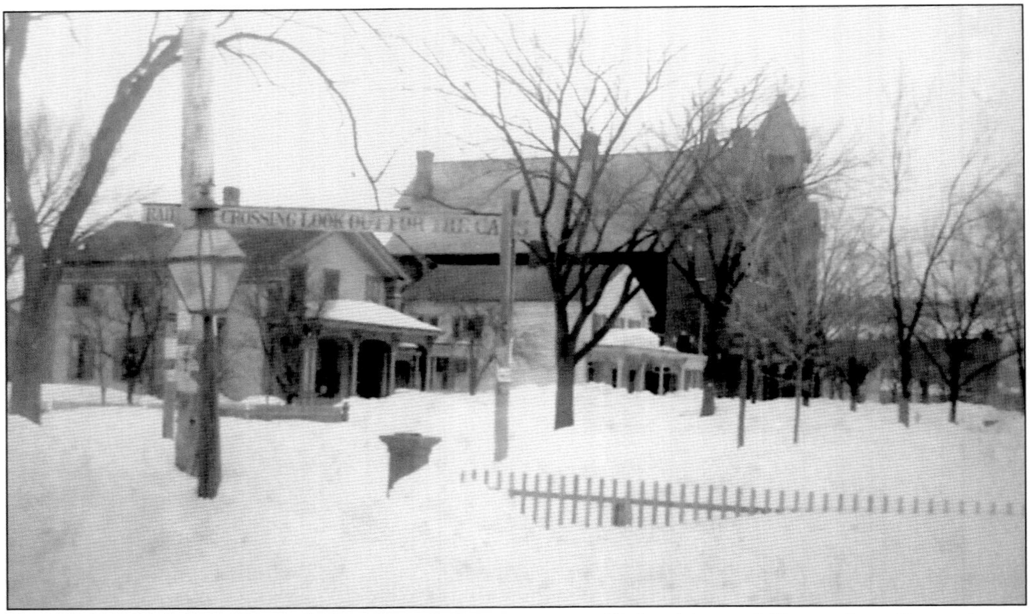

Bonds were sold to the inhabitants of the towns in Columbia and Rensselaer Counties to construct the Chatham and Lebanon Valley Railroad. Elmer LaPointe was a telegrapher in Chatham when its two trains left and returned daily from Bennington, Vermont, pulled by wood-burning engines that towed wooden coaches. The renamed Rutland Railroad reached Chatham Village in 1869, crossing Kinderhook Street, left of this intersection, to its small depot on Park Row. (Courtesy of CPL.)

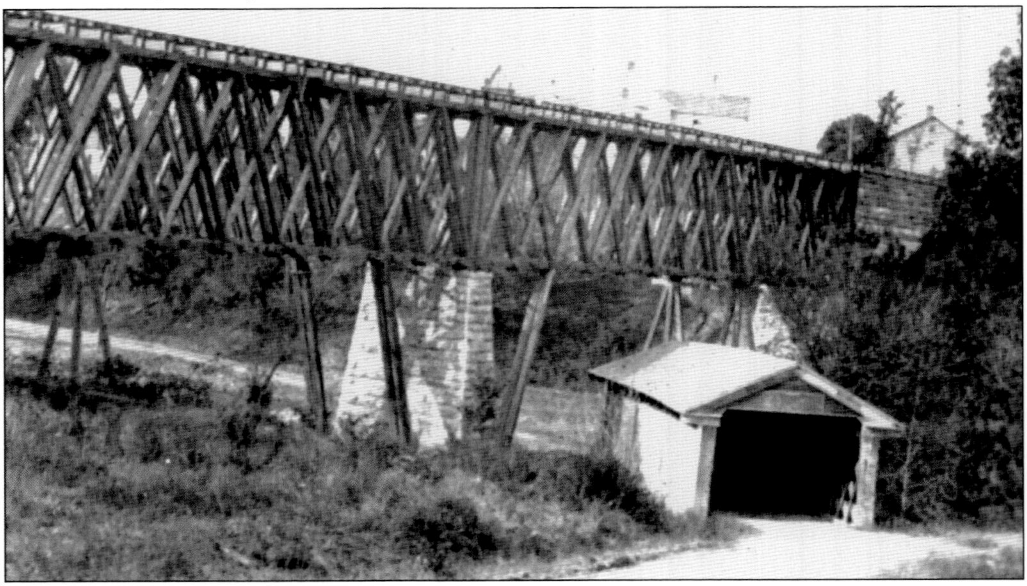

The original trestle was made of wood (see page 31 panoramic photograph of the village) in 1869. Elephants aboard a Rutland train carrying a circus became so upset when the train was crossing the old wooden trestle that they were off-loaded and walked into the village. New York Central had control of the Rutland timetable by 1908 and rebuilt the trestle with steel. (Courtesy of CPL.)

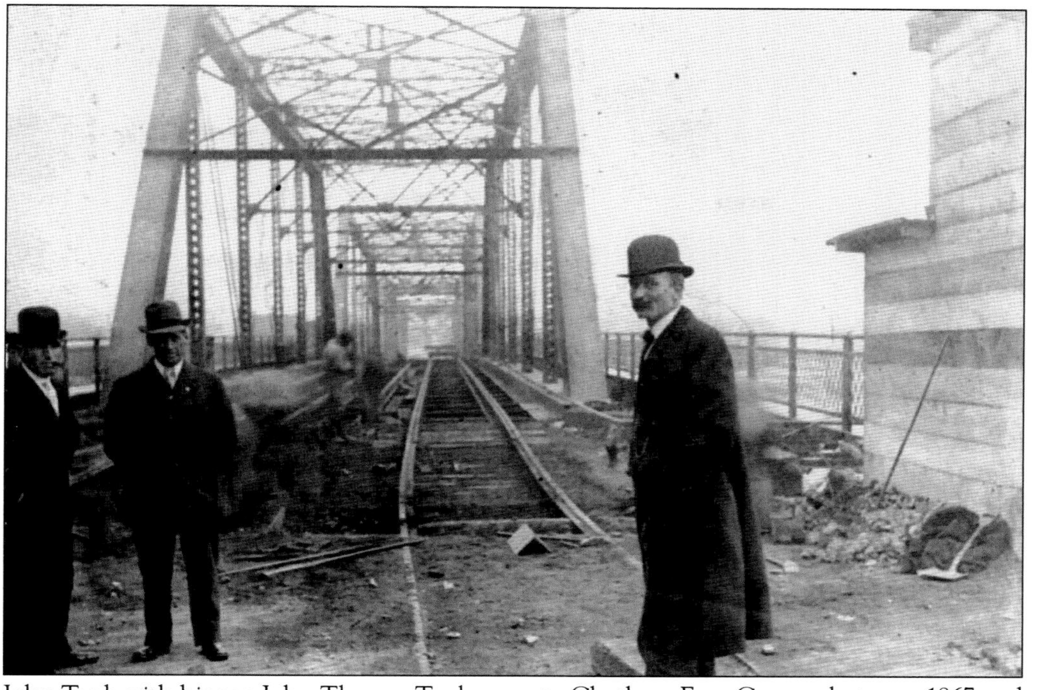

John Tank with his son John Thomas Tank came to Chatham Four Corners between 1867 and 1868. He had contracted to build the stonework for the railroad bridge for Lebanon Springs Railroad, the Harlem Extension. Their engineering feat created 1,453,031 cubic yards of stone masonry that included the culverts. (Courtesy of Jon Meredith.)

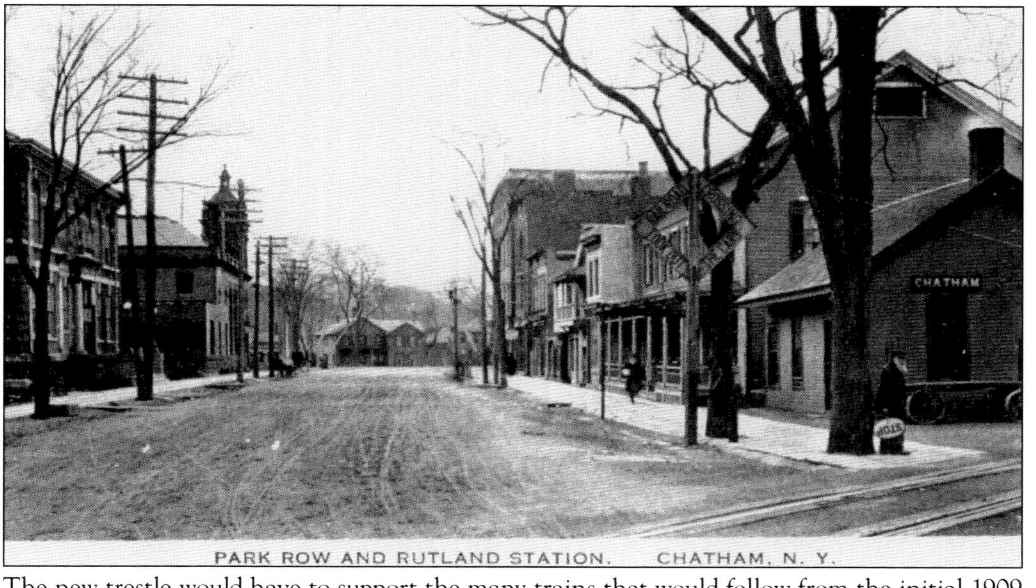

The new trestle would have to support the many trains that would follow from the initial 1909 "milk train" routed through Chatham over the panhandle to New York City. The "rut" or "milk" trains had priority over passenger trains. Train cars were pushed over the Boston and Albany crossover and onto the New York Central wye where the Harlem crew then took it to New York City. (Courtesy of CPL.)

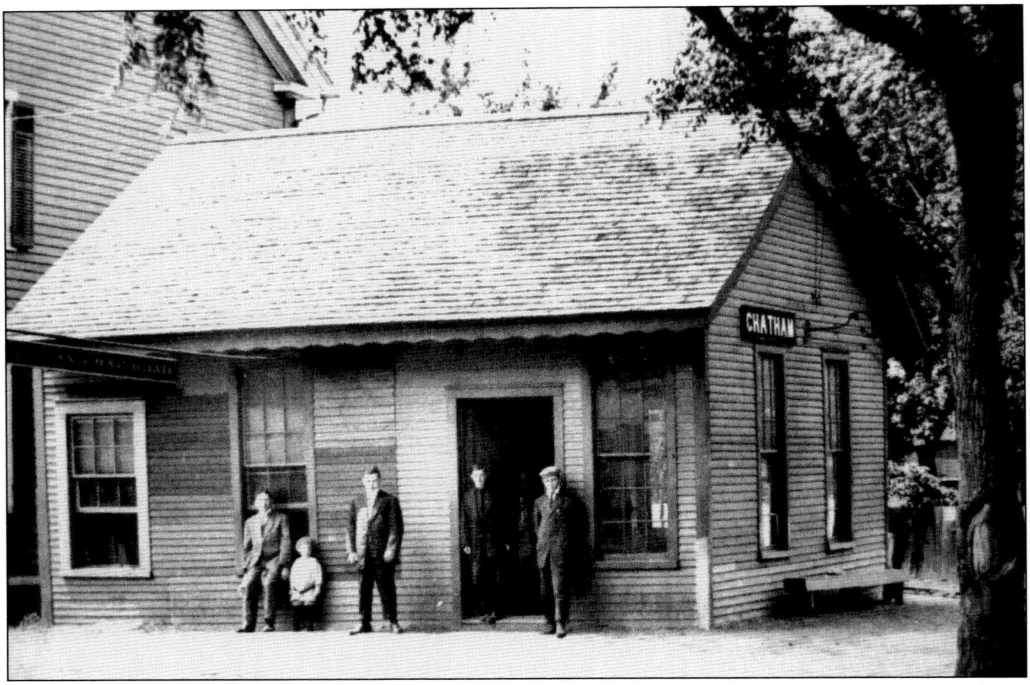

Big passenger train days happened when there were Lebanon Springs Revival meetings and the three- or four-day Columbia County Fair. (Courtesy of Ed Grogan.)

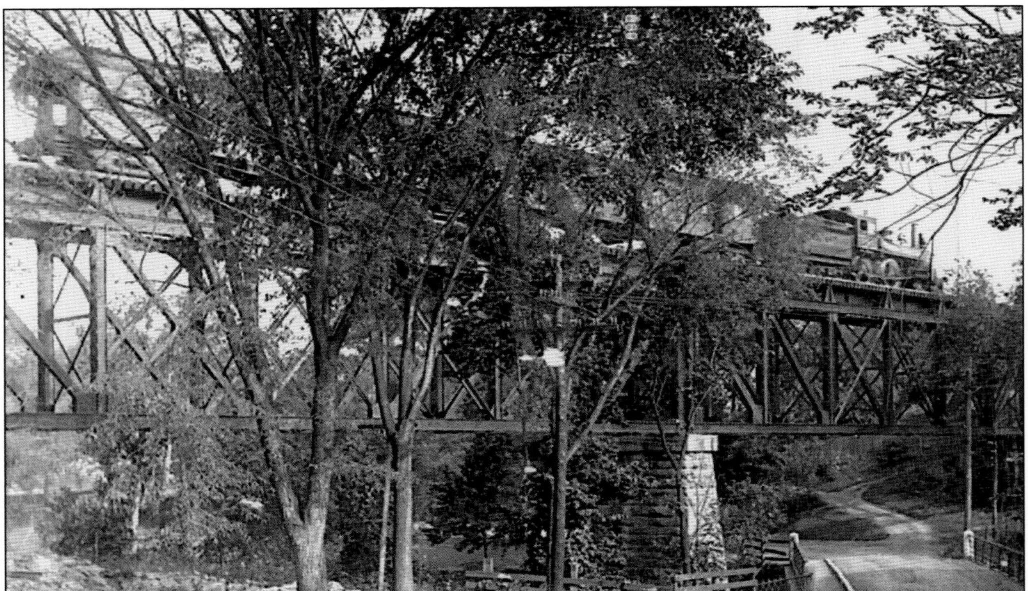

Engineer Ray Graigon's fireman Clyde Olney said Graigon was a "speed artist." Engine No. 82 rocked and reeled, burning soft coal and painting the trackside buildings with its soot. The Rutland Railroad operated the "Stephentown Scute" in 1908. The morning run went from Stephentown, also called Riders, to Chatham where commuters connected to the Albany and Hudson line. In the evening there was a reverse run. (Courtesy of CPL.)

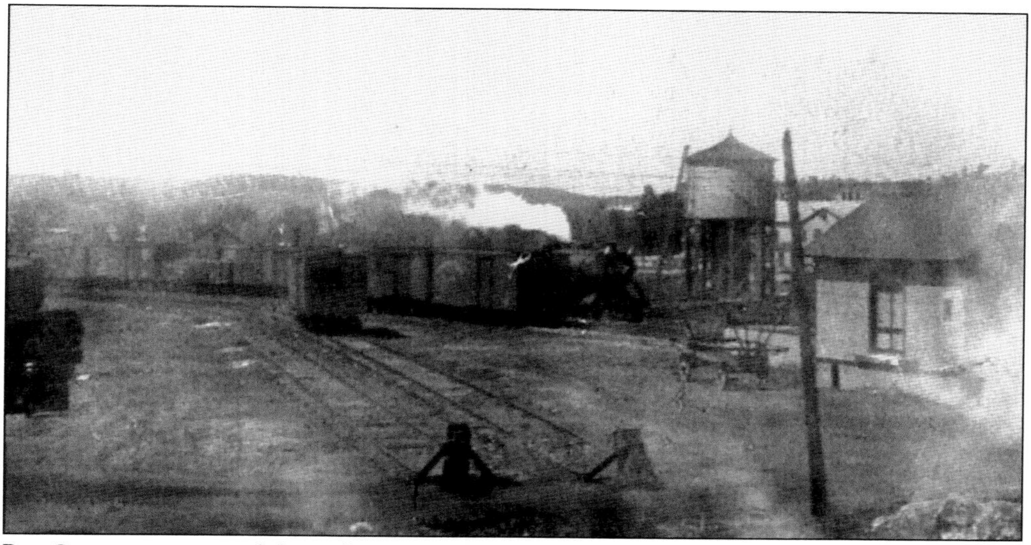

Ray Graigon engineered the milk train, and his brakeman would say "they wore their good suits under their overalls so if they went in the ditch, they'd have something good to be laid out in." By 1918, 10-wheeler engines brought 20 or more milk cars to New York City by way of the village across Fairview Avenue. The Rutland's 46 years was labeled "a glorious streak of rust," according to *The Coming of the New York and Harlem Railroad*, by Louis V. Grogan. (Courtesy of Dwight Sawyer-Miller Collection.)

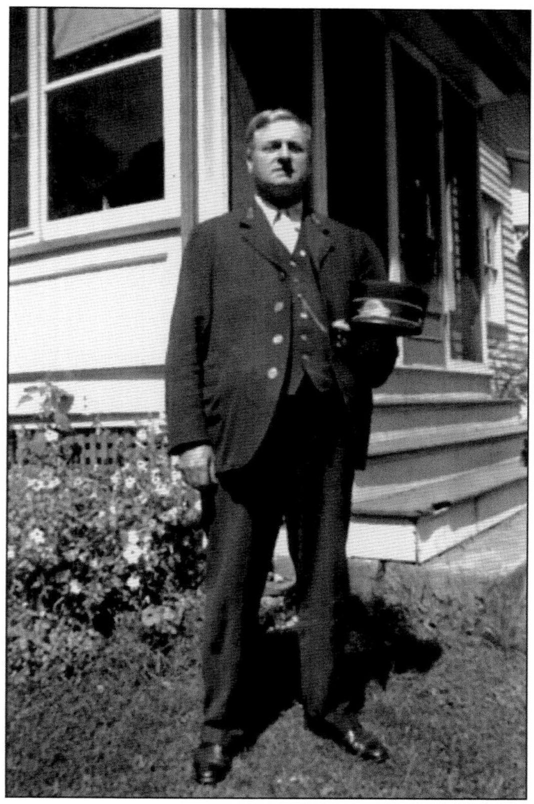

Conductor Grant Blass started with the Boston and Albany before working for the New York Central system. The Harlem Division of the New York Central opened on May 10, 1852, to Chatham. It was a 127-mile run from New York City. It was a fast and curvy eight-to-nine mile ride downhill from Philmont and Chatham. "Those men [conductors] acted as ambassadors of good will for the railroad and for the village of Chatham, and they made a good job of it," claims *The Coming of the New York and Harlem Railroad*. (Author's collection.)

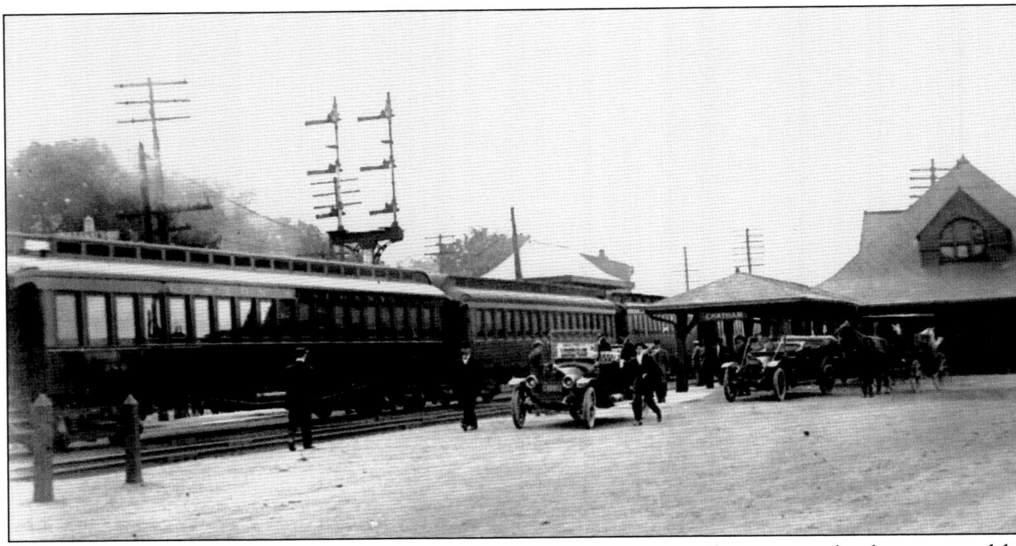

"Chatham Fair Specials" had reduced prices and were met at the station by liverymen like George "Hotstuff" Coffin, who offered a quick ride in his rig "straightaway to the fairgrounds." The Boston and Albany depot later was referred to as the union depot. (Courtesy of CCAS.)

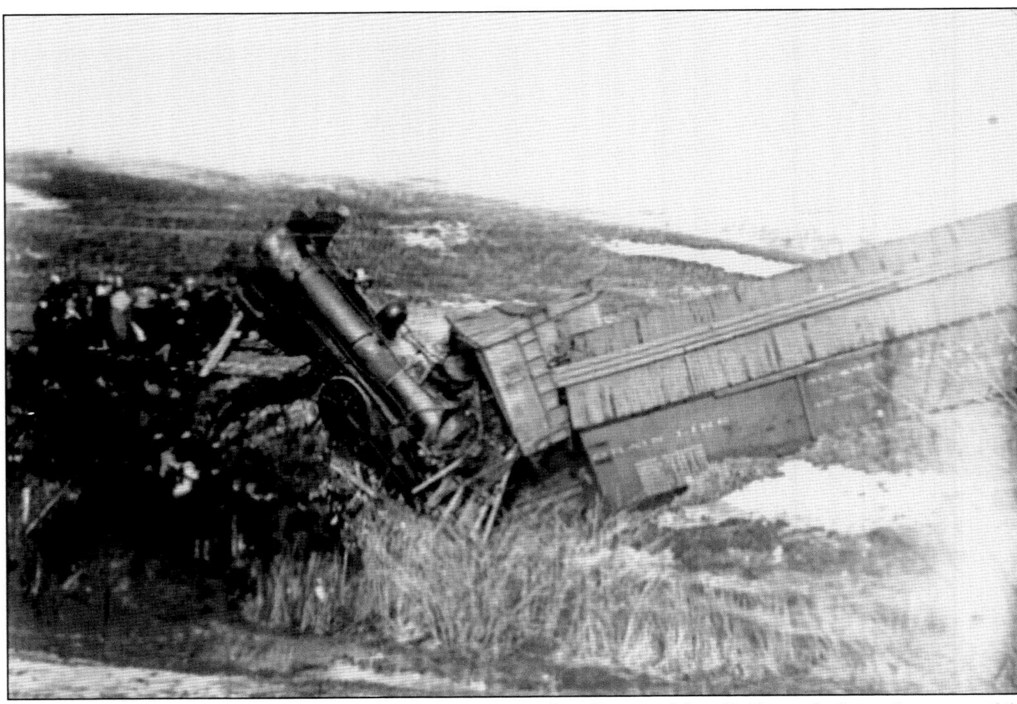

The unlucky engine referred to locally as the "Hoodoo Engine No. 696" was believed responsible for many accidents and lives lost. The repetition of broken axles, blown-out cylinder heads, and snapped drive rods was puzzling. The engine's end came near Philmont when a bridge span gave way during a torrential storm, driving the tender and freight car into the engine, killing the engineer, fireman, and brakeman. (Courtesy of Bill Wood.)

R. H. Bartlett was appointed as a replacement agent at Chatham Four Corners, beginning work on May 1, 1857. As acting general freight agent, he received $200 compensation and a letter of appreciation from Cornelius Vanderbilt, treasurer. (Courtesy of CPL, Dardess Collection.)

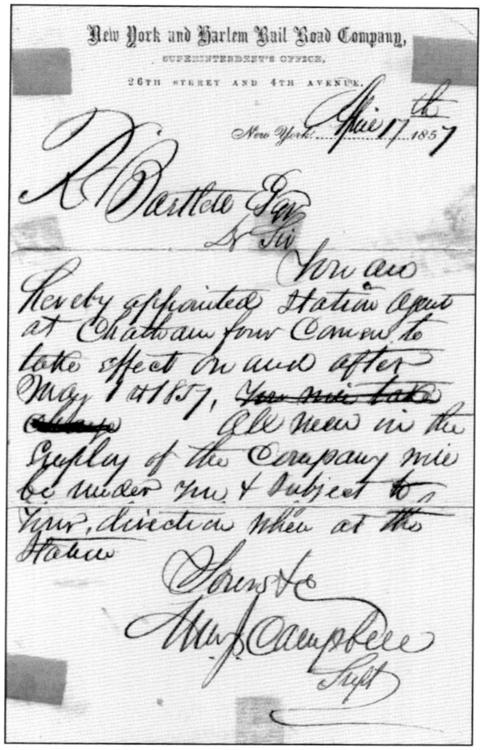

New York and Harlem Rail Road Company,
SUPERINTENDENT'S OFFICE,
26TH STREET AND 4TH AVENUE.

New York April 17th 1857

R. Bartlett Esq.
Dr Sir
You are hereby appointed Station Agent at Chatham four Corners to take effect on and after May 1st 1857, ~~You will take charge~~ All men in the Employ of the Company will be under you & subject to your direction when at the Station

Yours &c
Wm J. Campbell
Supt

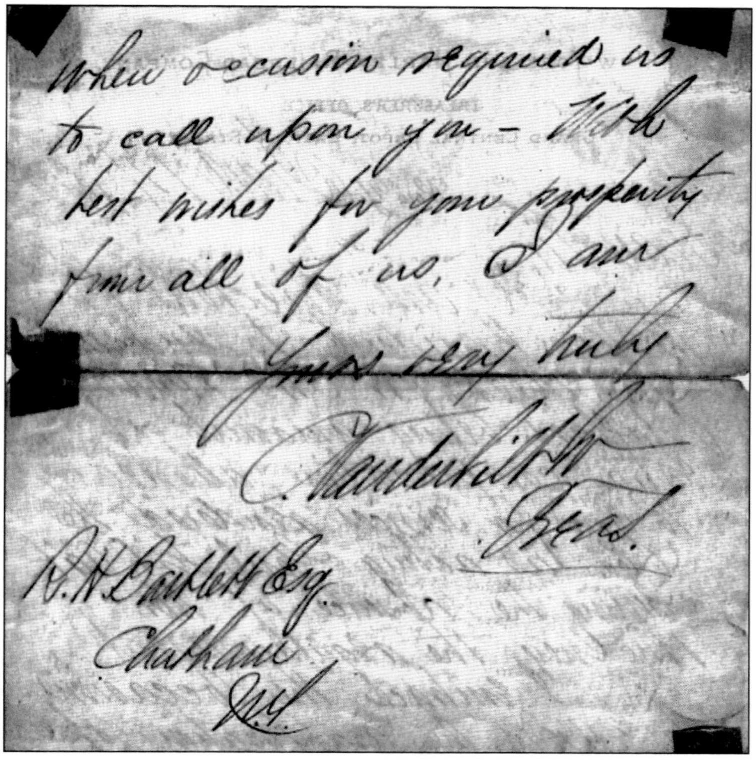

when occasion required us to call upon you — With best wishes for your prosperity from all of us, I am

Yours very truly
C. Vanderbilt
Treas.

R. H. Bartlett Esq.
Chatham
N.Y.

Cornelius Vanderbilt's letter to R. H. Bartlerr reads in part "thank you for the cordial and prompt aid rendered us when occasion required us to call upon you—With best wishes for your prosperity from all of us." (Courtesy of CPL, Dardess Collection.)

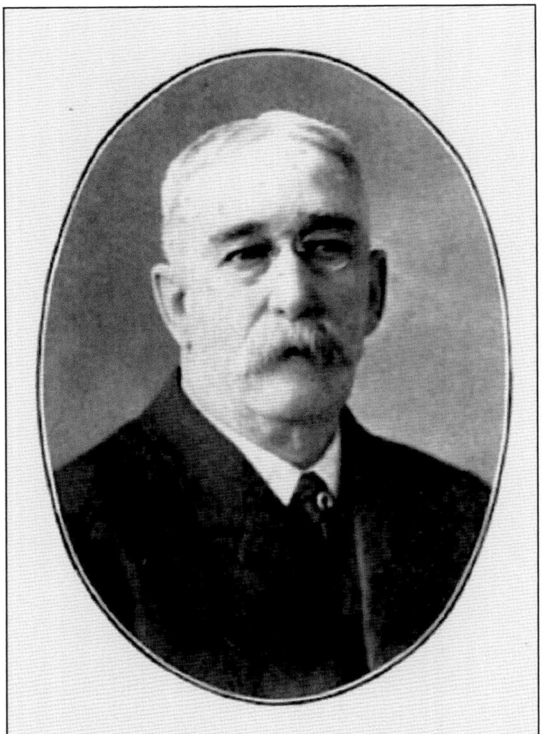

JOHN P. MICKLE

John P. Mickle entered into service with the Harlem Division in 1863, becoming a passenger conductor in 1866. In a 1910 letter to John Mickle, Parker Bruzie wrote: "A stranger went into William H. Vanderbilt's office one day and said: 'Mr. Vanderbilt your company employs a lot of bright, clean-cut young conductors, and…', 'I always liked Johnny Mickle myself.' interrupted Mr. Vanderbilt." On November 1, 1910, Mickle, one of the best-dressed men in uniform on the Harlem, retired. (Courtesy of CPL, Dardess Collection.)

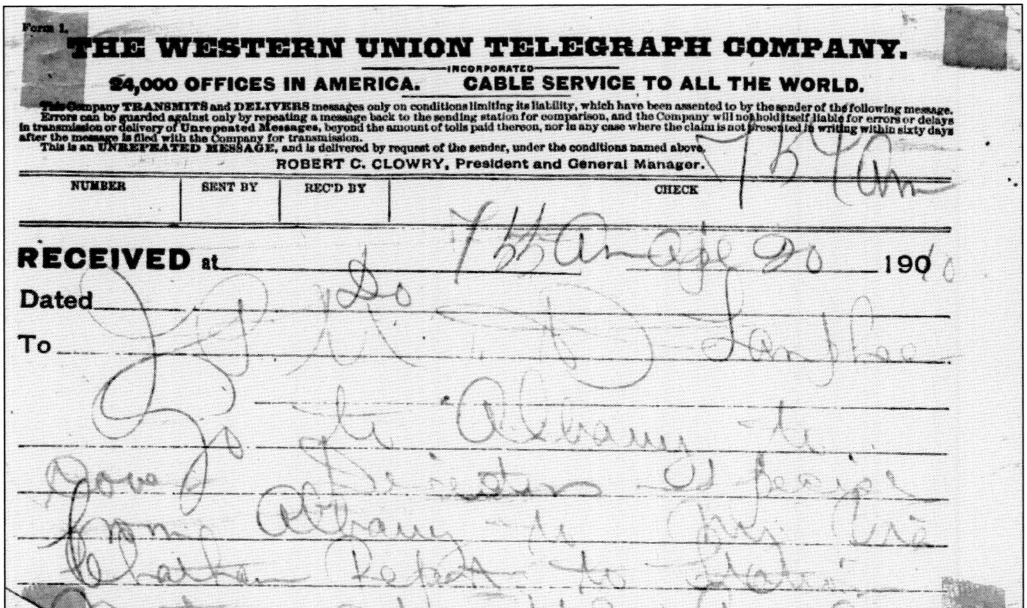

Form 1.

THE WESTERN UNION TELEGRAPH COMPANY.

INCORPORATED

24,000 OFFICES IN AMERICA. CABLE SERVICE TO ALL THE WORLD.

This Company TRANSMITS and DELIVERS messages only on conditions limiting its liability, which have been assented to by the sender of the following message. Errors can be guarded against only by repeating a message back to the sending station for comparison, and the Company will not hold itself liable for errors or delays in transmission or delivery of Unrepeated Messages, beyond the amount of tolls paid thereon, nor in any case where the claim is not presented in writing within sixty days after the message is filed with the Company for transmission.
This is an UNREPEATED MESSAGE, and is delivered by request of the sender, under the conditions named above.

ROBERT C. CLOWRY, President and General Manager.

NUMBER	SENT BY	REC'D BY	CHECK

RECEIVED at 190

Dated

To

The April 20, 1910, Western Union telegraph received by John Mickle reads in part, "To J. P. M. Go to Albany to cover directors' special from Albany to NY via Chatham. Report to stationmaster at 11:30 a.m." (Courtesy of CPL, Dardess Collection.)

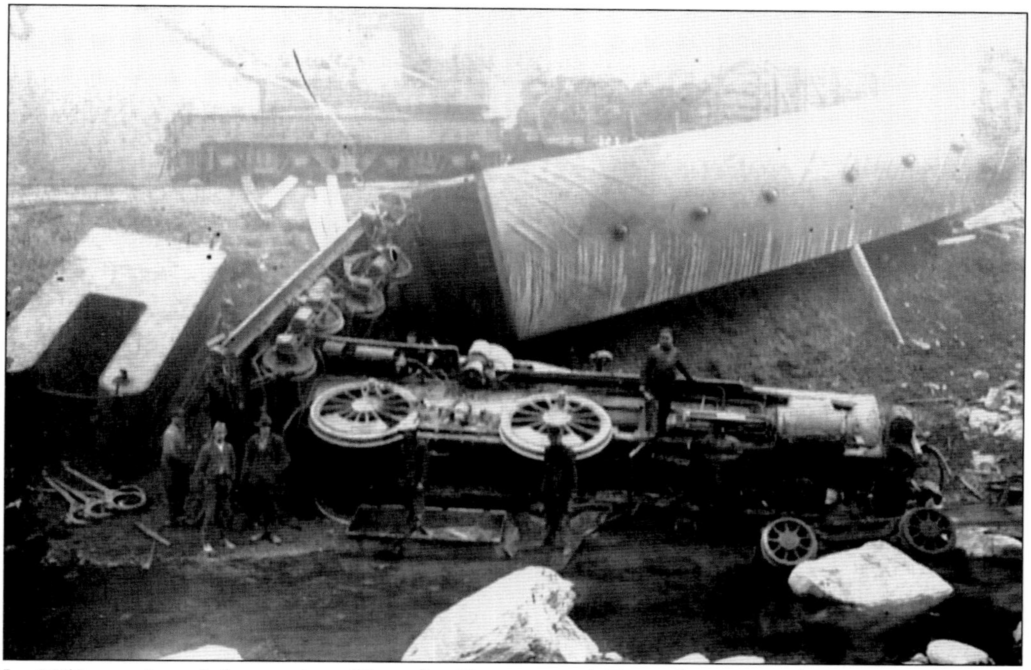

In 1852, service of the engines *Tornado*, *Tempest*, and *Terror* began on the Harlem Division. An entire Chatham crew lost their lives near Martindale in the 1890s. Whenever word got out of another wreck on the Harlem, citizens hurried to the station for details, hoping not to hear how many Chatham men lost their lives. This photograph captures one accident near Railroad Avenue. (Courtesy of Ike Harvey.)

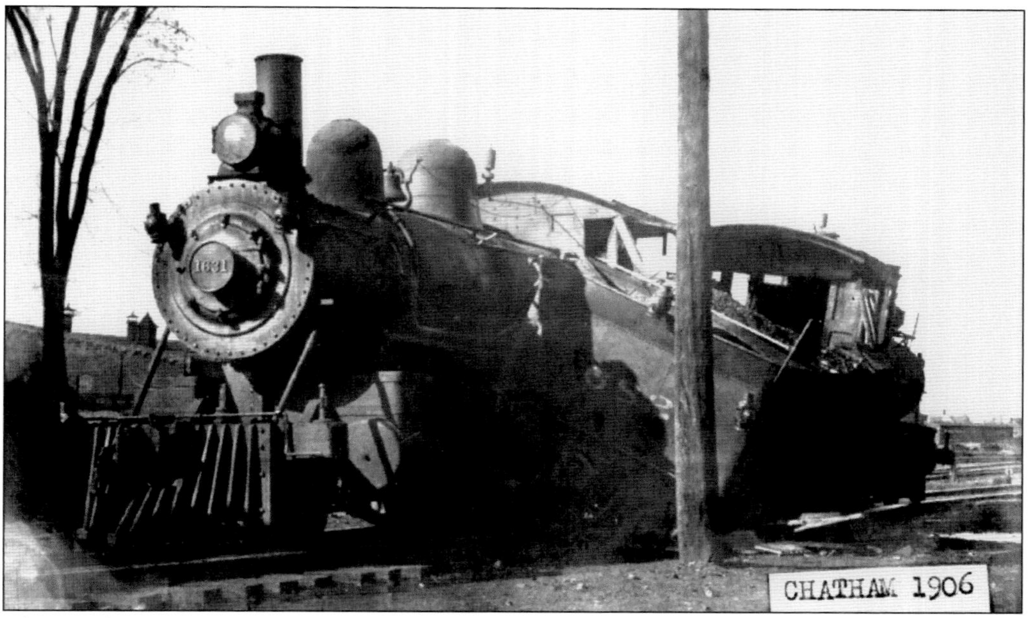

This Harlem train wreck occurred in the village railroad yards. The high level of activity proportionately caused more mishaps. One photograph captured a steam engine that had derailed and fallen off into the turntable. (Courtesy of Jon Meredith.)

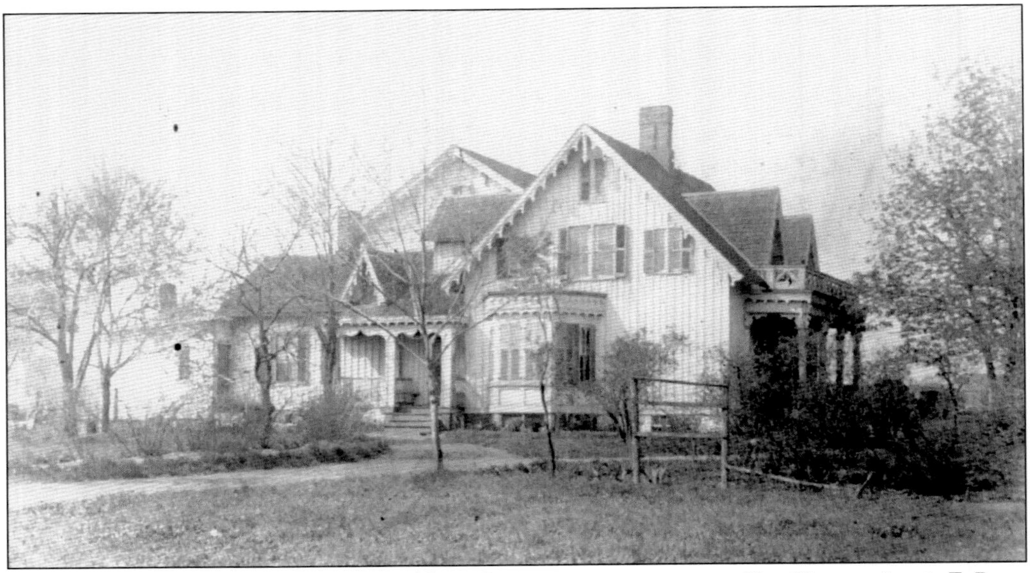

Charles Allen's home was constructed by a Spencertown carpenter. For 12 years Louis F. Payn made the house his home. A long addition was added by J. Smith as a sanatorium, but it was never used. Eventually Charles Francisco rented the Smith house as a hostelry. The addition became a ballroom then hotel rooms. In 1885, Mr. and Mrs. Delan Hoffman became owners of the Hoffman House. (Courtesy of CVHS.)

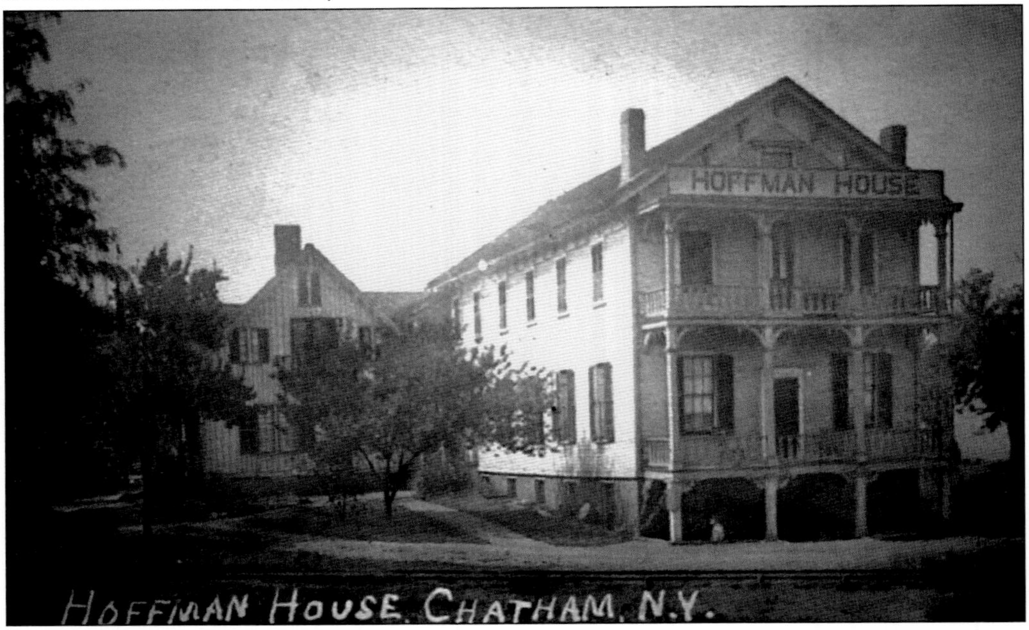

The Hoffman House prospered like no other hostelry. Beginning in 1895, widow Hoffman continued the establishment until 1910 when her daughter Joanne Hoffman Jones became proprietor. Joanne Hoffman Jones was most hospitable to trainmen and their families, earning her the title "mother of all railroad men." During the 1888 snowstorm, she cared for so many that she ran out of food. Farmer Philo Blinn brought her fresh meat. (Courtesy of CCHS, Monthie Collection.)

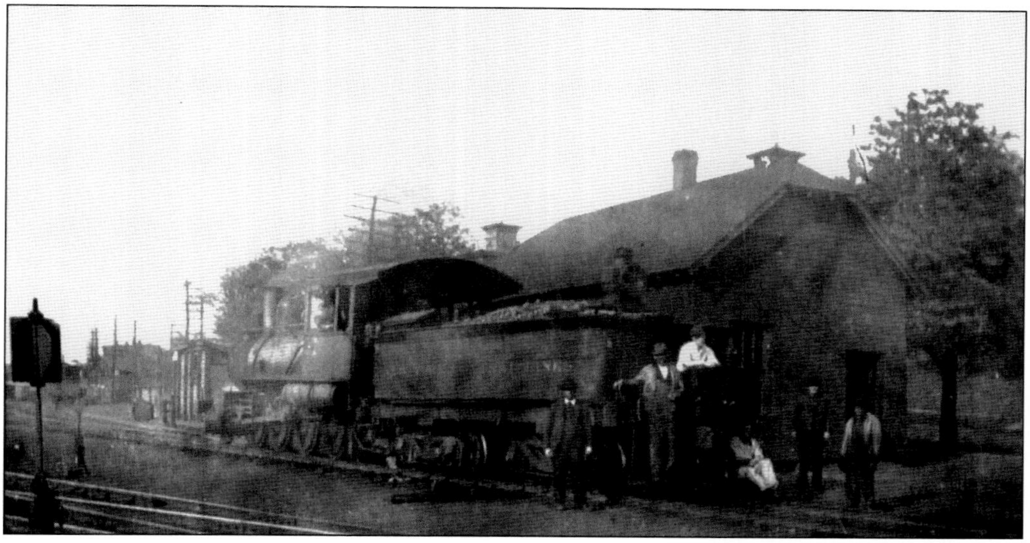

New York Central switching crews used the telephone at the "Green Shanty" located at the southeast end of the rail yard for communication with the towers. In this photograph, Clarence Gardner's grandfather is pictured second from the right. He was the first of three generations of Harlem enginemen, which included his son and grandson Clarence Gardner. There was a close railroad brotherhood. (Courtesy of CVHS, Gardner family collection.)

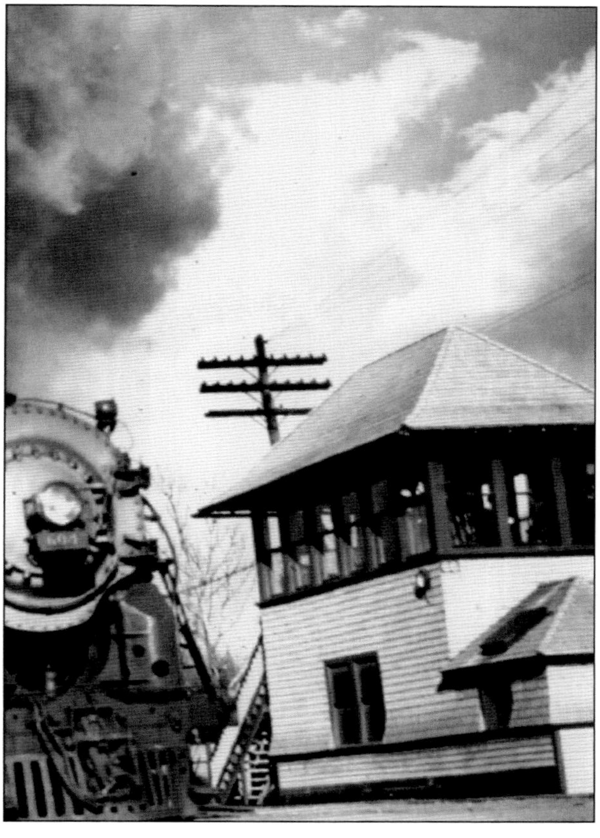

Tower 66 sat on the south side of Woodbridge Avenue at the western end of the Chatham yard. An electric train indicator panel, telegraph "key," dispatcher's telephone, signal equipment (flags, lanterns, torpedoes, and fusees), and operator Keith Steltz would also be found in tower 66. Switch- and signal-operating levers required a strong hand especially in winter. (Courtesy of CVHS.)

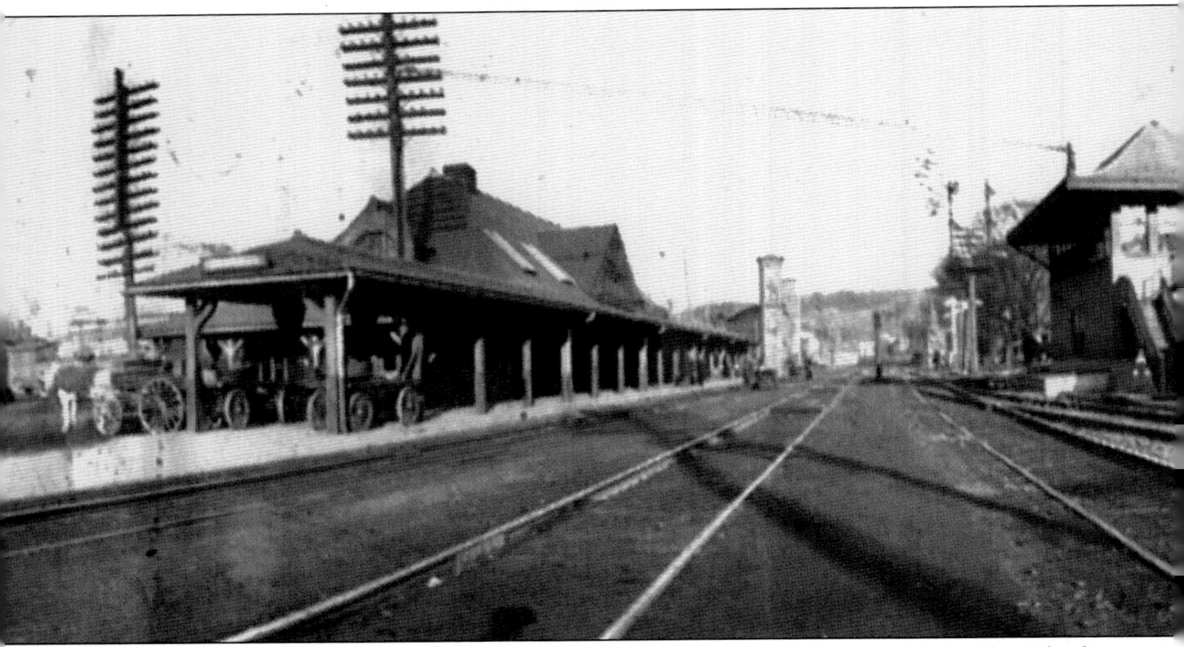

Tower 65 stood at the Main Street crossing next to a powerhouse across from the Chatham Union Station. Signs delineated the track lines of the New York Central from the Boston and Albany. Both towers were involved in the transfer of 450 freight cars per day with and between

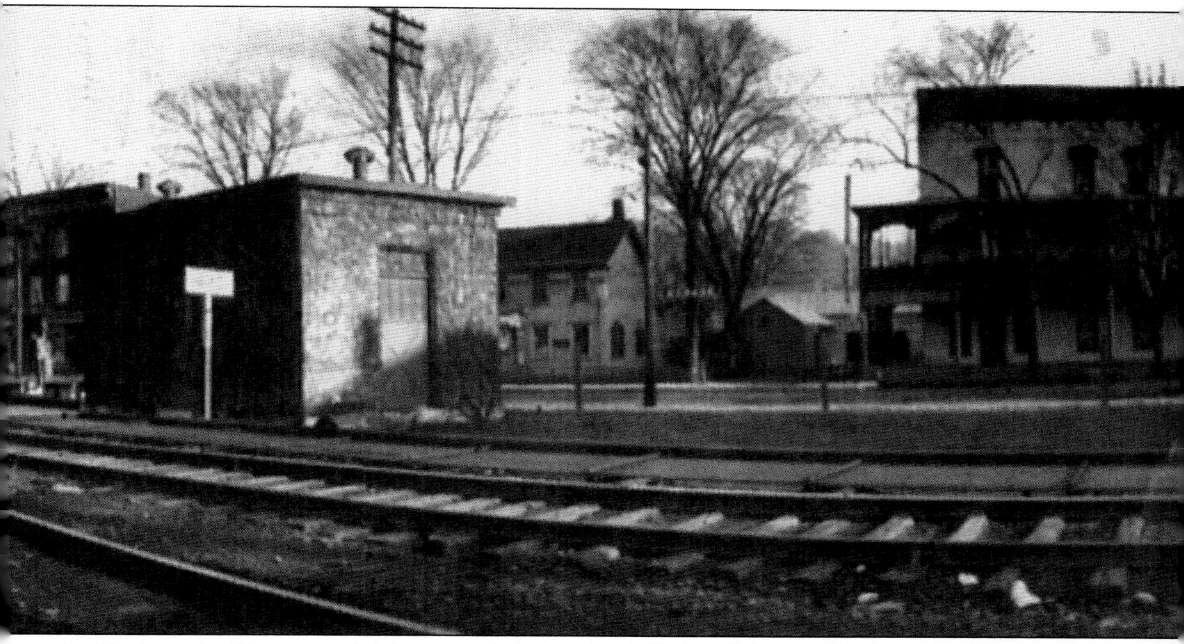

the Harlem, the Boston and Albany, and the Rutland Railroad during the first two decades of the 20th century. The union station, the village clock tower, tower 65, the power station, and the Chatham House are pictured from left to right in this photograph. (Courtesy of CPL.)

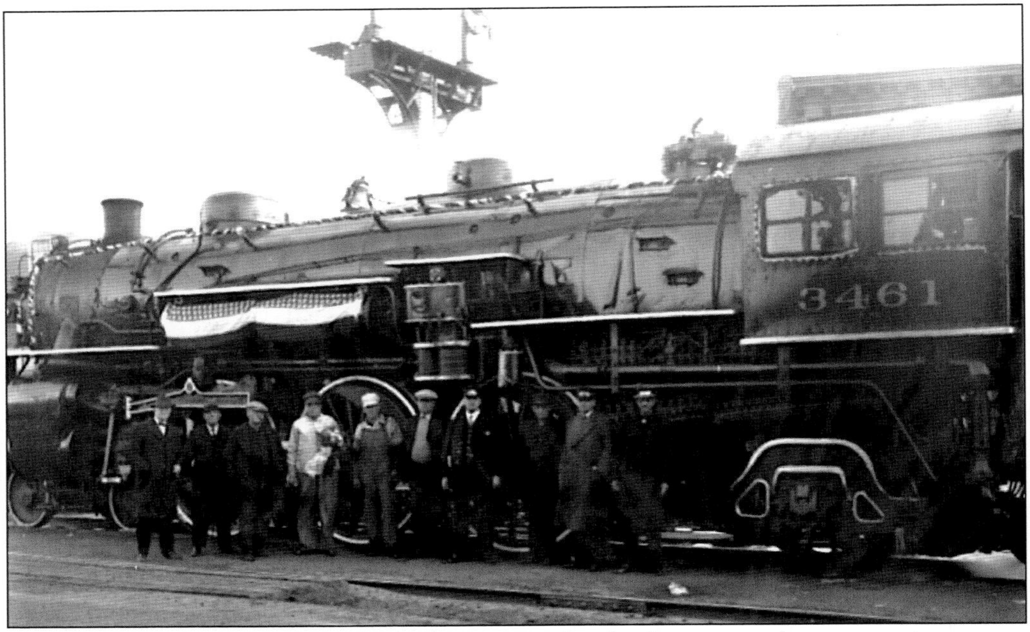

Nearly 200 men worked out of Chatham on railroad jobs: section bosses, car inspectors, postal clerks, hostlers, railroaders, flagmen, watchmen, conductors, section hands, roundhouse employees, yardmaster Edwin Southard, and freight office bookkeeper Jacob B. Waltermire. After an engineer or conductor's last run within a cleaned and highly decorated engine run through the fireworks, the retiree posed with his crew for a memorable photograph. (Courtesy of Ralph Blass family.)

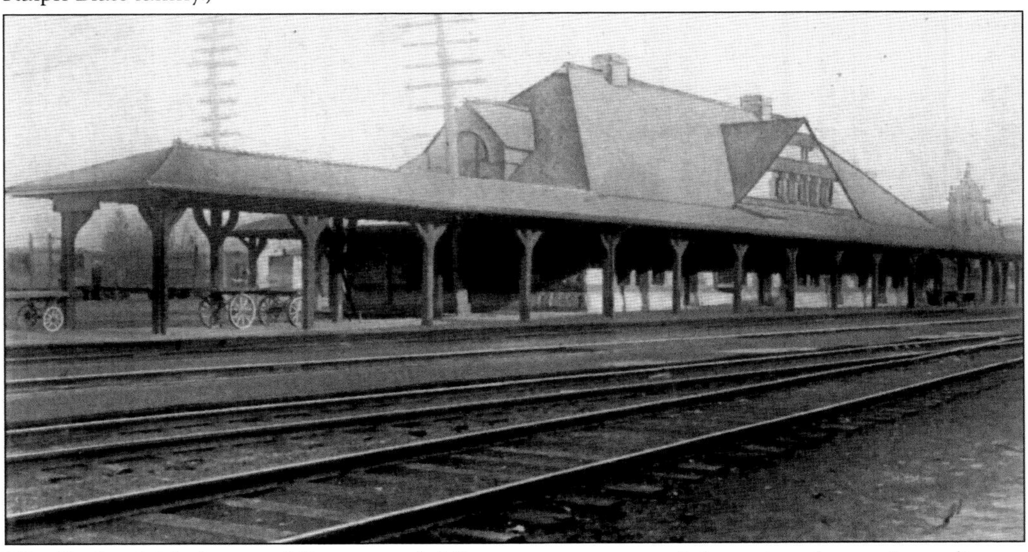

The Rutland, Harlem, and Boston and Albany passengers used the union depot. According to *The Coming of the New York Central and Harlem Railroad*, architect H. H. Richardson's philosophy was carried out to "strive for clearly expressing the building's purpose—that a station is not a house but a shelter. Not a place to live in but to wait under." It incorporated dual pitched hipped roof, bracketed post porch that wrapped completely around, and ribbon windows that allowed light indoors. (Courtesy of CPL.)

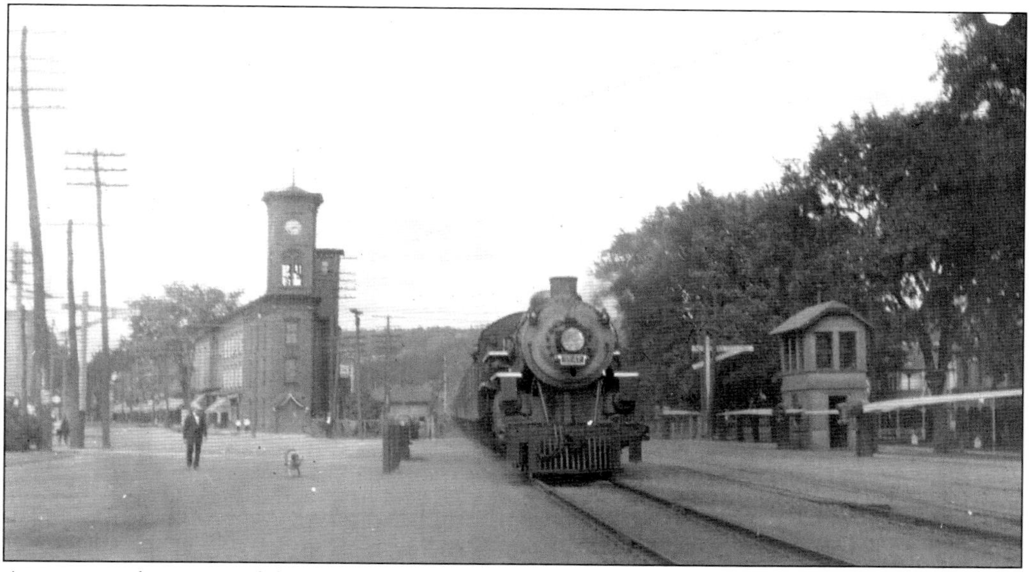

A trainman leans out of the engine at the Main Street crossing. Nothing separates the man and his dog from the tracks. Is the engineer watching them or looking ahead to the depot that is just yards away on the same side? When gates were ordered for this crossing, they were the longest ever constructed. (Courtesy of CCHS, Monthie Collection.)

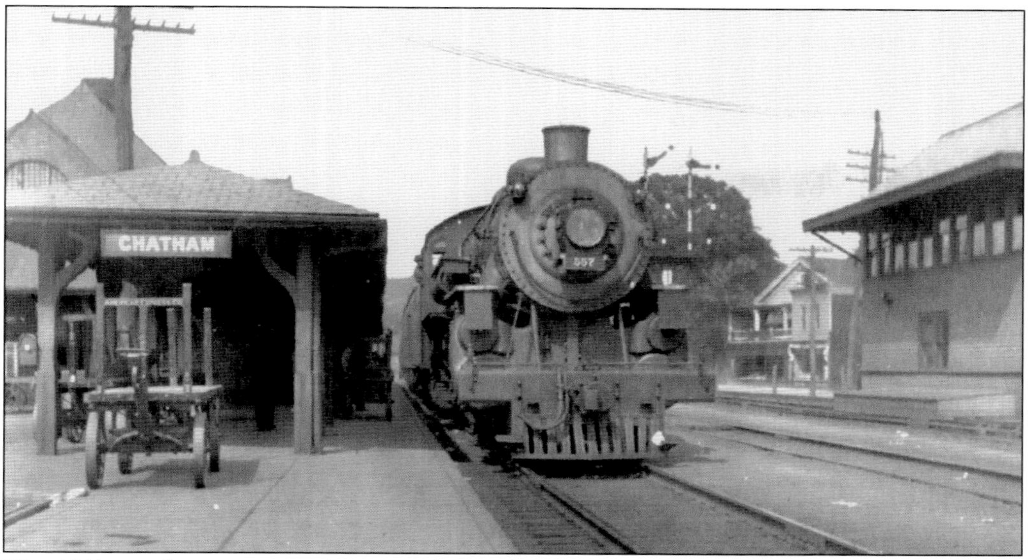

The 1841 wooden station sat between the tracks where the trains for Albany came in on one side and those heading to New York picked up and discharged passengers on the other side. The new 1887 Chatham Union Station built of stone and masonry sat alongside both railways with more than 80 trains per day originating, terminating, making a station stop, or passing through its village. (Courtesy of CCHS, Monthie Collection.)

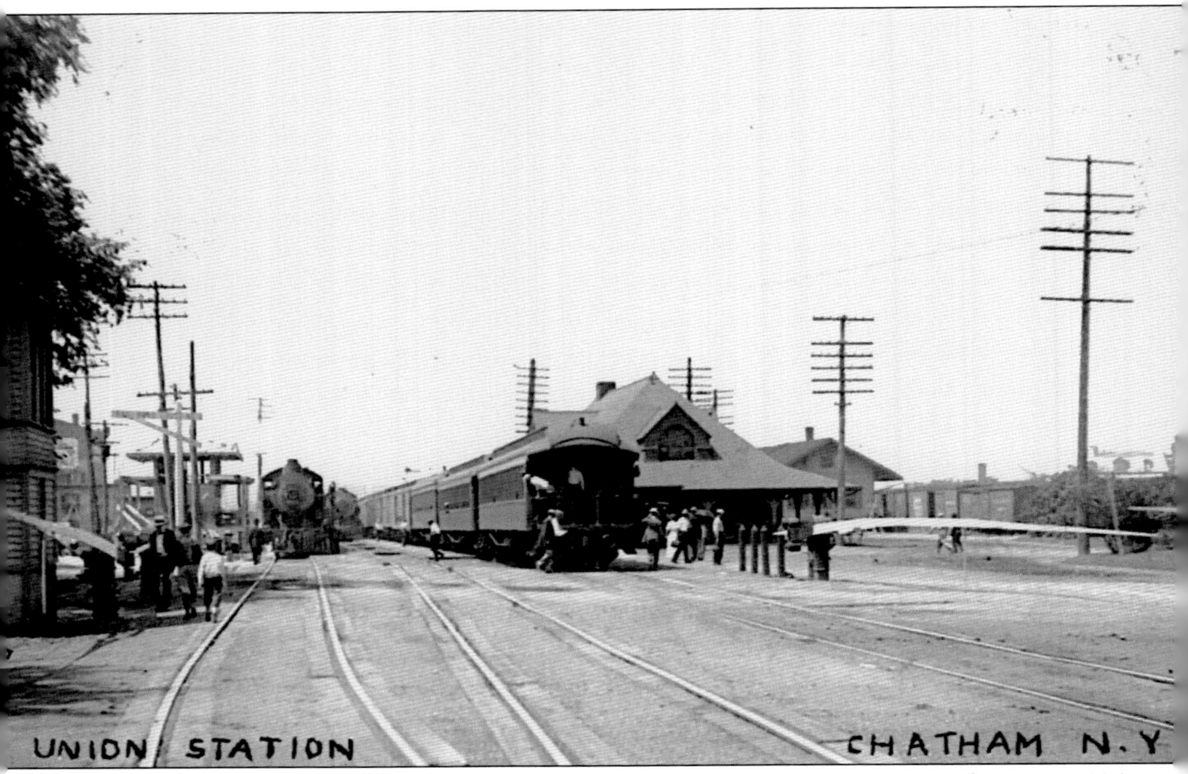

Twenty-eight passenger trains arrived and departed from Chatham every 24 hours in 1906. According to the *Chatham Republican*, "You can enter a Pullman at Chatham every day at 6 o'clock and arrive in New York in time for the theatre that evening. You can board a Rutland flier in the morning and eat dinner on Lake Champlain. You can take a B&A train most any hour of the day and within a few minutes find yourself in the heart of the Berkshires, or going further, land in the White Mountains, or perchance the coast of Maine." (Courtesy of Jon Meredith.)

Five

Water and Fire

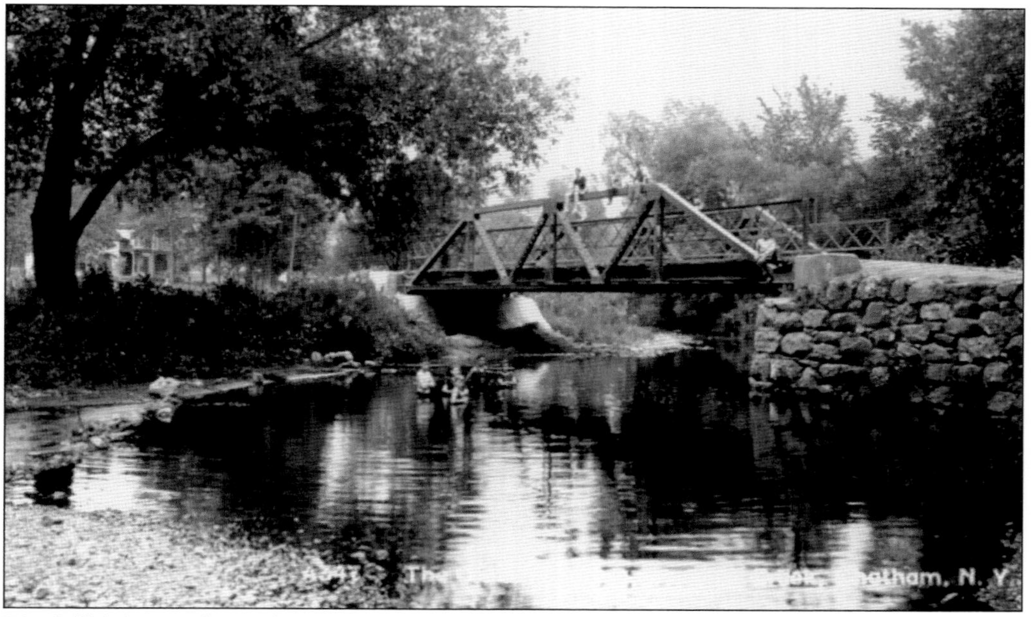

The *kill(e)* (water channel or riverbed) was appealing to the earliest Groat's Corners settlers. For generations the swimming holes provided warm weather fun even if the bottom was mostly *stein* (stone or rock). The 18th-century Dutch settlers had given the village creek the practical name of Stein Kill (found spelled Steine [plural], Steeny, or even Stony) and found a power source contained in the falls and rapids. (Courtesy of CPL.)

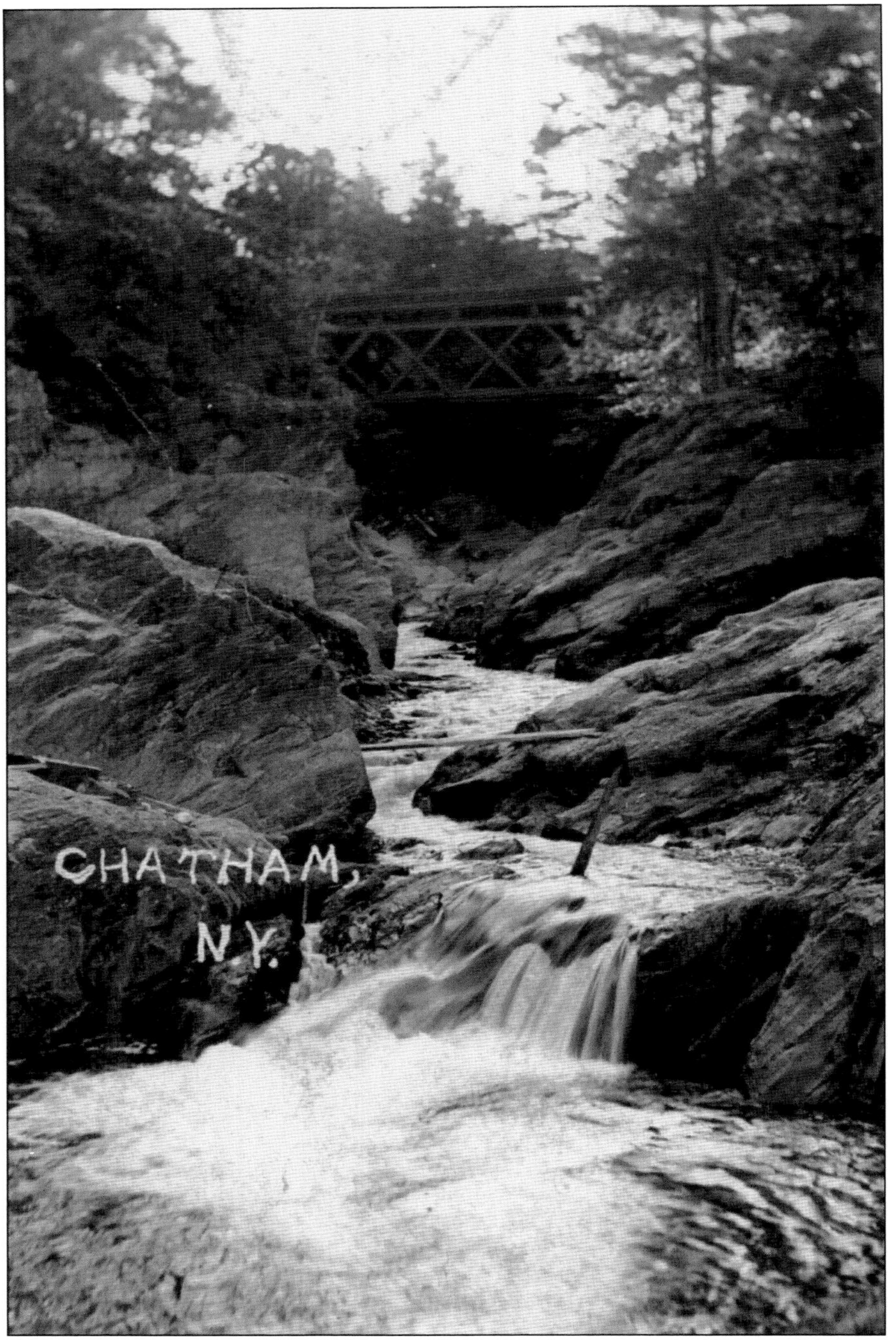

Around 1828 a hand-operated gristmill first harnessed the power of Stein Kill. North of this gristmill was J. H. Garner's paper mill, vacated by 1900. The Columbia Mill experimented with making paper from wood unsuccessfully. Within the northern limits of the village was another gristmill owned by Joseph R. Coleman that later became a distillery. The Tompkins and Eagle Mills, farther downstream, made straw wrapping paper. The Mesick Paper Company on Mill Street made A1 grade tissue paper. (Courtesy of CPL, E. B. Collection.)

The Payn Paper Mill was situated on the former Stewart gristmill site, producing seven tons of strawboard daily. The Honorable Louis F. Payn, proprietor, was in New York City when he learned that the plant had suffered a fire. He speedily rebuilt it in 1907 to save the many jobs the plant provided. Columbia Box Board Mills, Inc., purchased the property in 1916. (Courtesy of Dwight Sawyer, Miller Collection.)

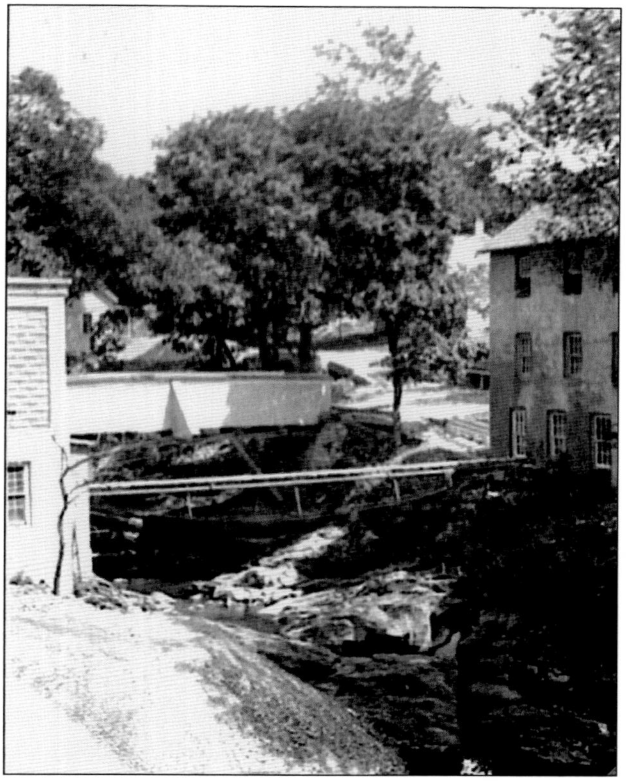

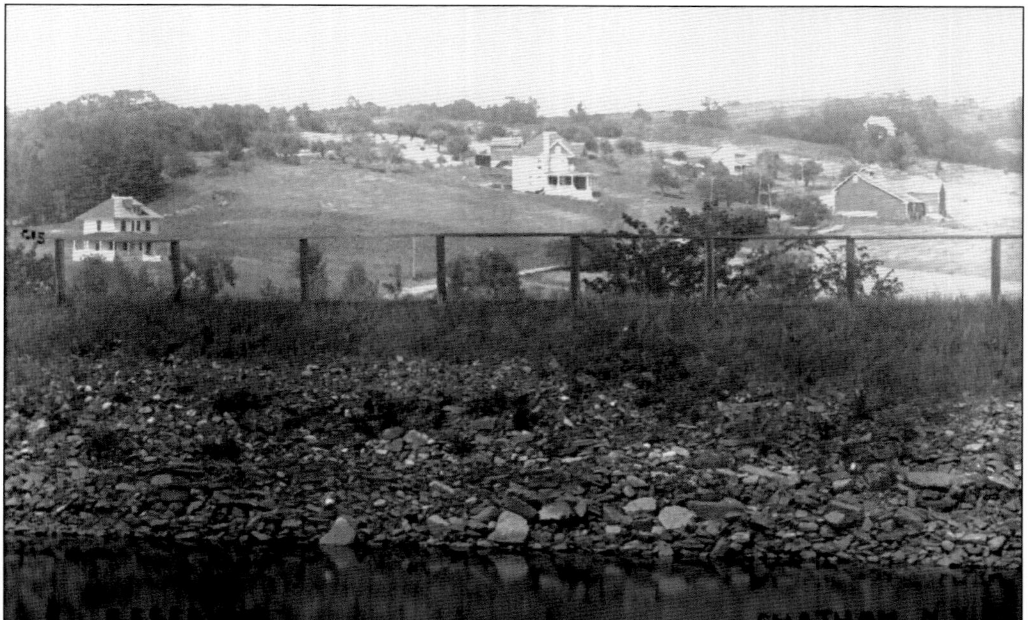

John Mickle was president of the waterworks when the village purchased it in 1912. The windmills stopped and noise subsided when a reservoir was dug at the location of the old academy school. (Courtesy of CPL.)

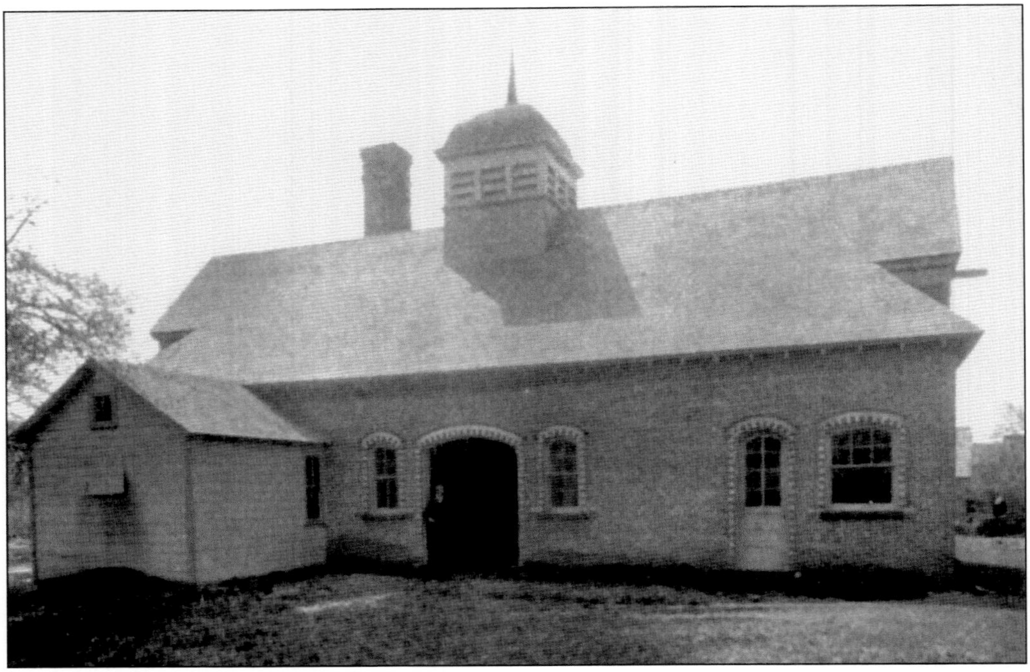

The Chatham Water Works applied for a charter and organized in April 1886 with H. W. McClellan, president; George E. Drumm, vice president; Philo B. Blinn, treasurer; and Philo B. Blinn Jr., secretary. The 21 wells powered by steam and windmills were extremely noisy. The brick pumping station, bordering Payn Avenue, was built on Philo Blinn's farmland. (Courtesy of CVHS.)

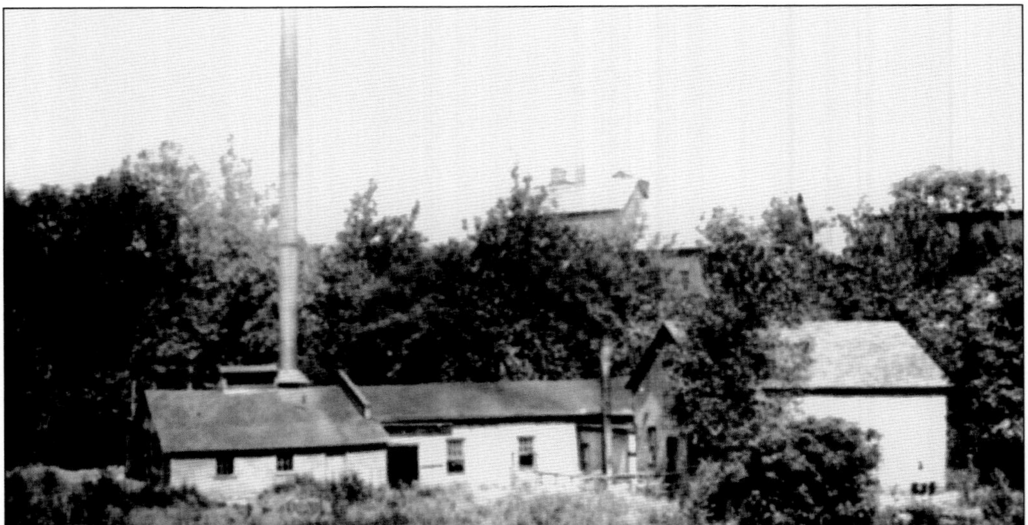

The Chatham Electric Light Company organized on October 29, 1889, and built a brick electric light station next to the Stein Kill near the Center Street bridge. At the first public display of electric street lighting, on February 6, 1890, witnesses gasped with excitement. General Electric Company bought the power plant in 1893, moving it to Mill Street. Note the iron foundry in the photograph background. (Courtesy of CPL, Lee Collection.)

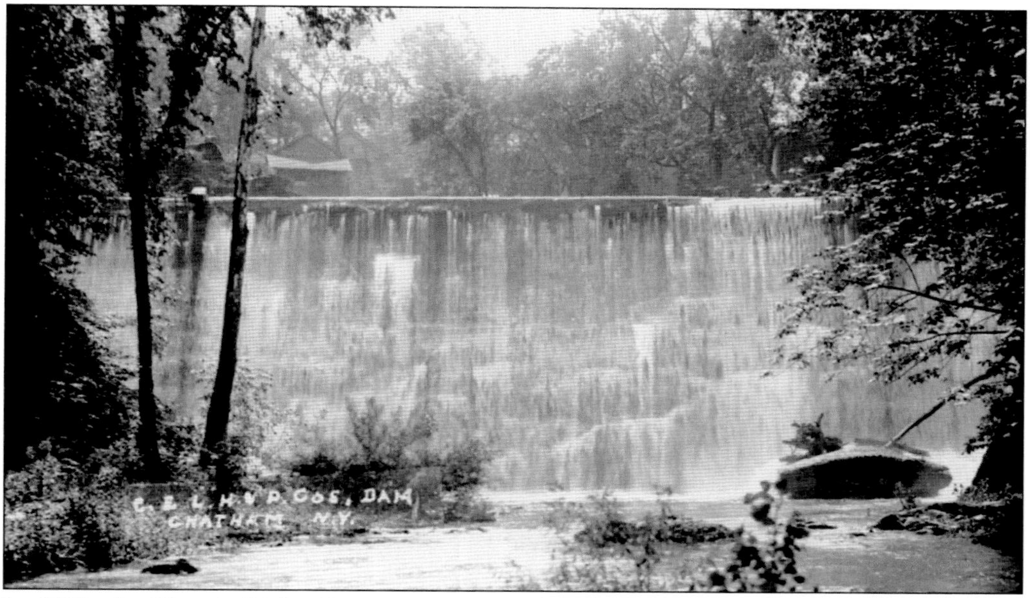

In 1898, the Electric Light Company contracted with the waterworks to furnish power for pumping 10 years. The president and treasurer at that time was J. M. Klingelsmith. Sanford W. Smith was secretary. The falls operated the power circuit for the Chatham Electric Light, Heat, and Power Company. The Chatham Center waterpower plant operated the electric light circuit. (Courtesy of CPL, Lee Collection.)

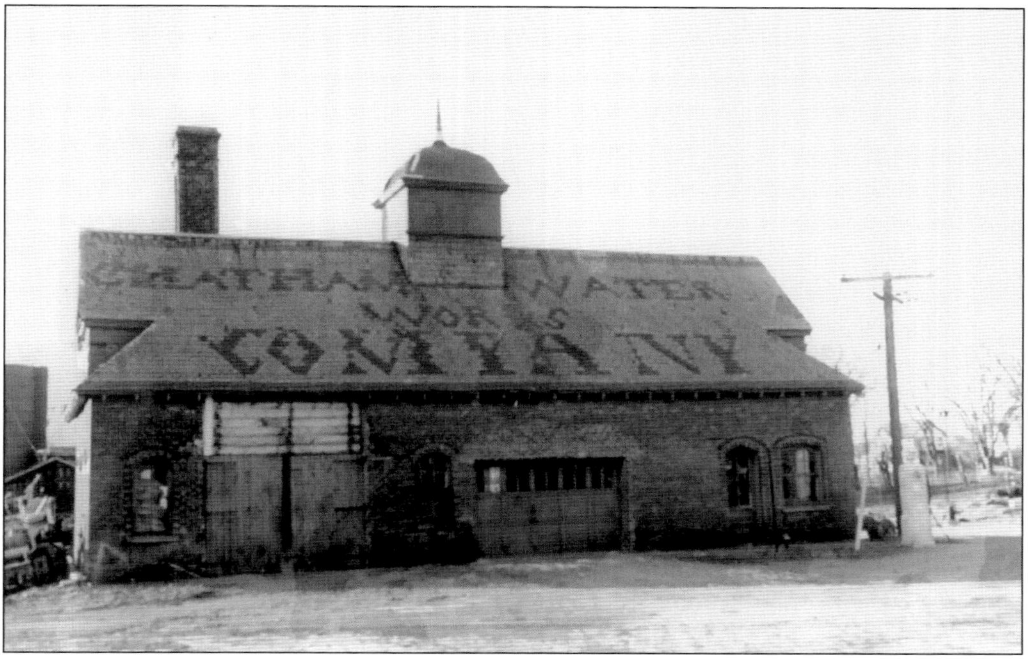

On June 26, 1858, the Ocean Engine and Hose Company No. 1 of Chatham Four Corners was formed. Wells and cisterns provided water for their hand-drawn carts. When the village waterworks was constructed, four more hand-drawn carts were purchased for placement at strategic places around the village. (Courtesy of CPL.)

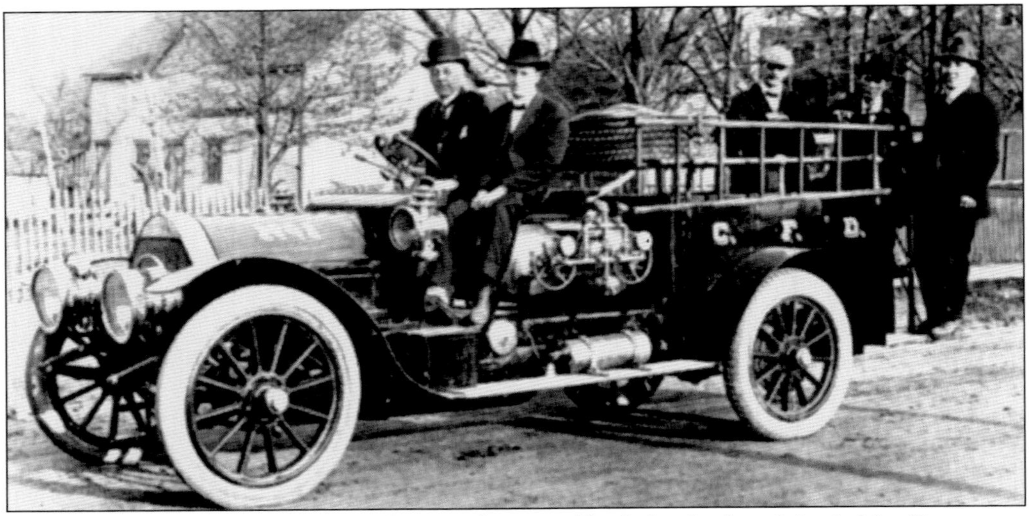

Sanford W. Smith, born in 1869 in the same house in Kinderhook where Martin Van Buren was, volunteered for the Ocean Fire Company No. 1 starting in 1894, when dark gray, double-breasted frock coats were uniform. He donated his Pierce Arrow automobile to the fire department to be used as a fire vehicle. Representing the firemen at the dedication of their new home at the Tracy Memorial, he said, "there is no more important institution in the village than that composed of these brave, sturdy men of the fire department." (Courtesy of CPL.)

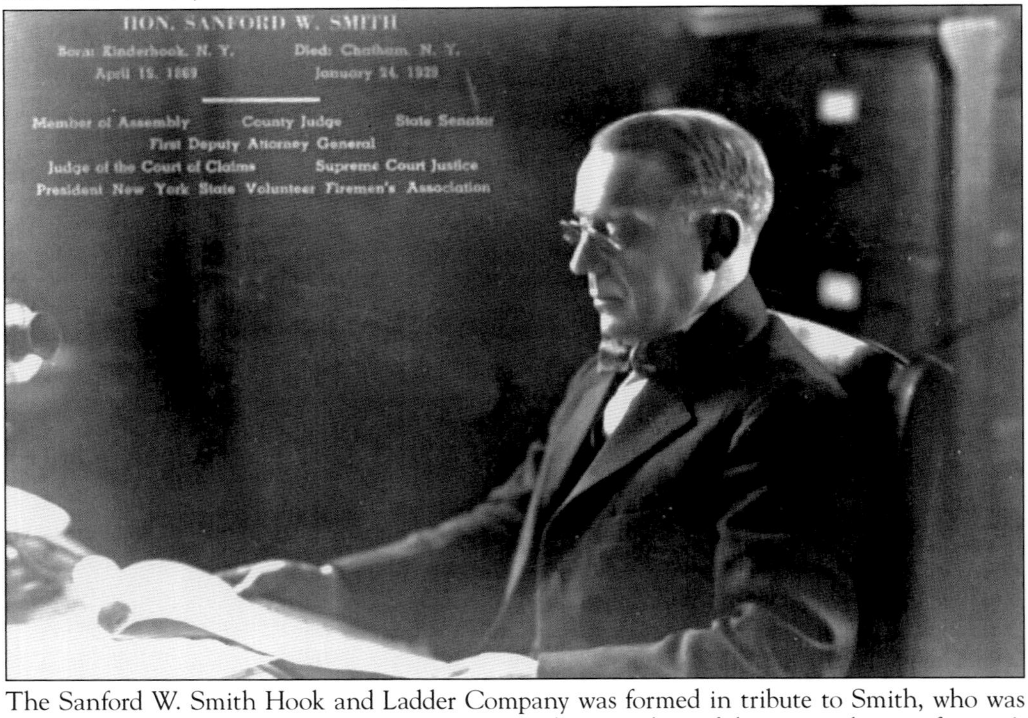

The Sanford W. Smith Hook and Ladder Company was formed in tribute to Smith, who was an active fireman until his death in 1929. He served as president of the state volunteer firemen's association for two years, sponsored a bill in the New York State Assembly to tax foreign fire insurance companies for the benefit of the state firemen's home, and was a member of the board of trustees at the home. (Courtesy of Chatham Fire Department.)

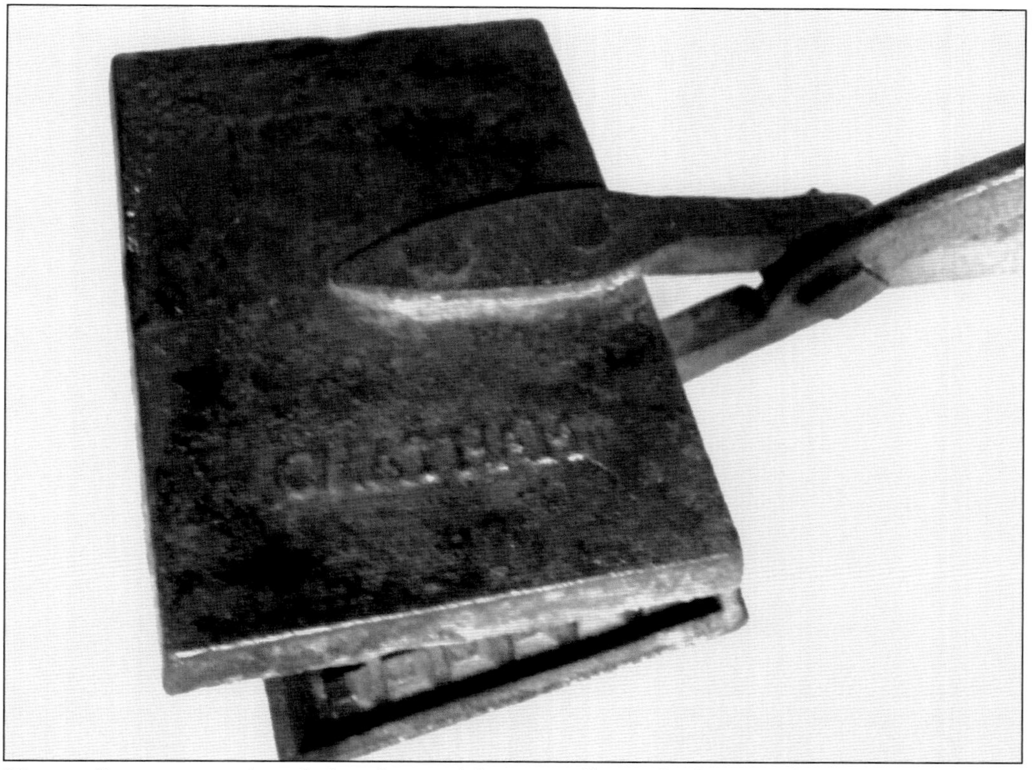

This waffle iron was identified with raised letters spelling Chatham. Perhaps it was produced under management of engineers Michael Glynn or Matthew Powers. Always alert for fires, the blast furnace whistle at one time was the fire alarm. If the wind was right the whistle could be heard as far away as East Chatham. (Author's collection.)

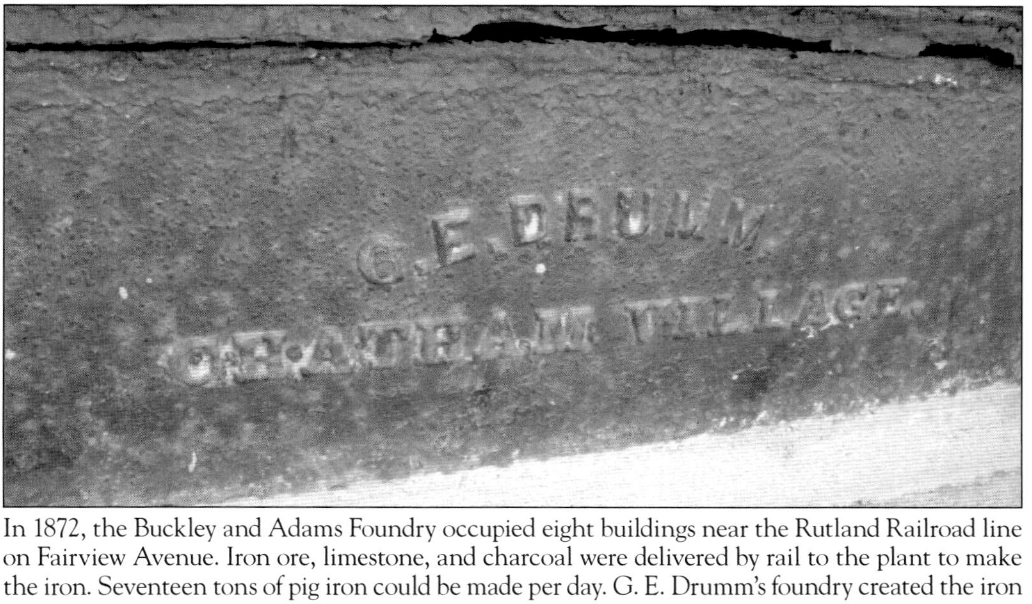

In 1872, the Buckley and Adams Foundry occupied eight buildings near the Rutland Railroad line on Fairview Avenue. Iron ore, limestone, and charcoal were delivered by rail to the plant to make the iron. Seventeen tons of pig iron could be made per day. G. E. Drumm's foundry created the iron step faceplates on five of the new brick business buildings on Main Street. (Courtesy of CVHS.)

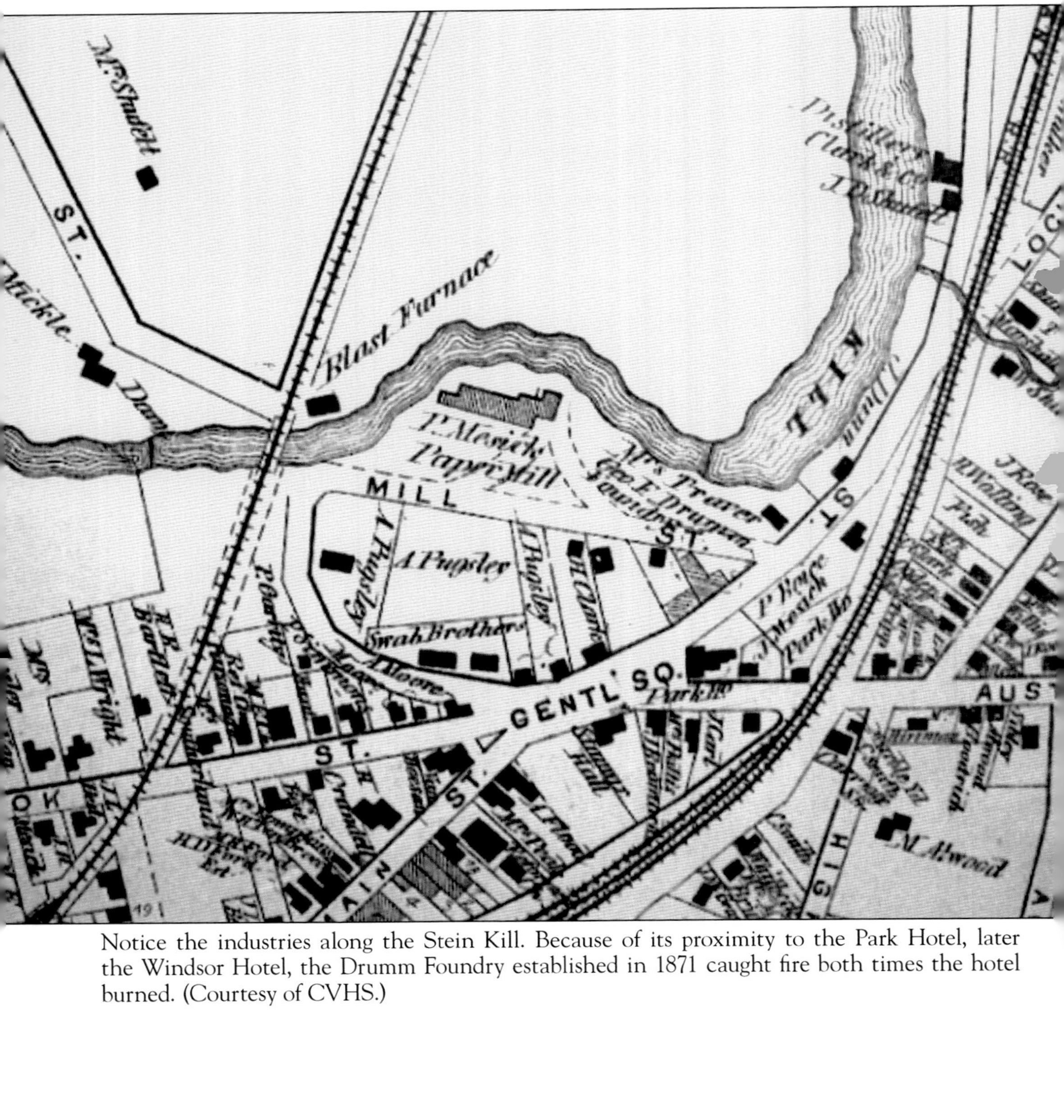

Notice the industries along the Stein Kill. Because of its proximity to the Park Hotel, later the Windsor Hotel, the Drumm Foundry established in 1871 caught fire both times the hotel burned. (Courtesy of CVHS.)

Six

THE CHATHAM FAIR

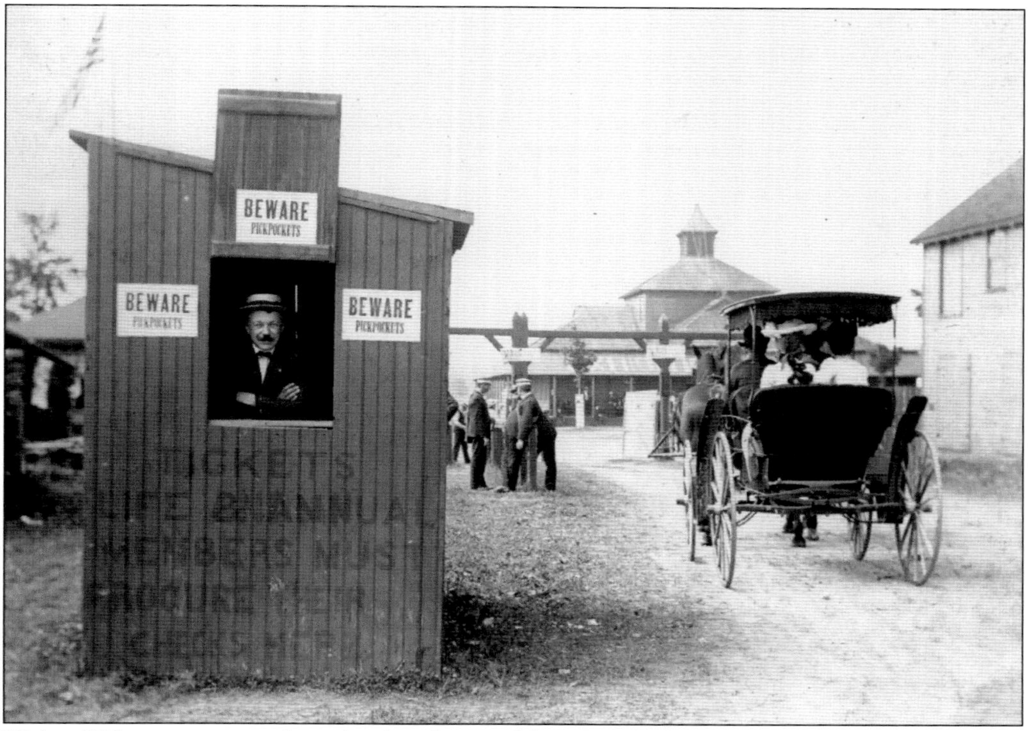

Walter Wilcox, manning the ticket booth, posed for John Eberle to take his photograph in 1903. The Columbia County Agricultural Society was formed to "improve the condition of agriculture, horticulture, manufacturees, and domestic economy." On August 13, 1841, at a meeting at the Hudson Court House, the plan was to accomplish this goal in five years. (Courtesy of CCAS.)

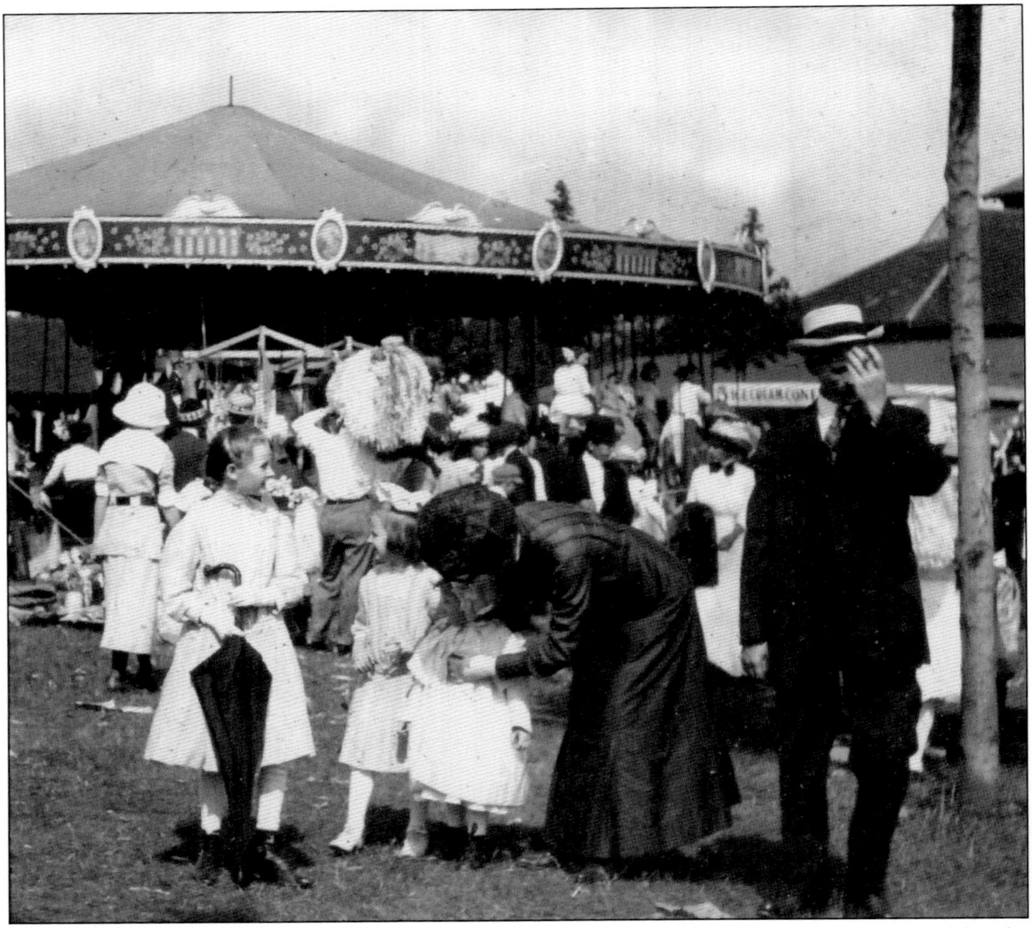

Originally the fair was held in Hudson but with the added convenience of passenger and freight train service, the event was removed to Chatham Four Corners in 1855. The next year 15 acres bordering Church Street was purchased for $2,400 from Mr. Bullis. These young ladies are enjoying the day at the fairgrounds. (Courtesy of CCAS.)

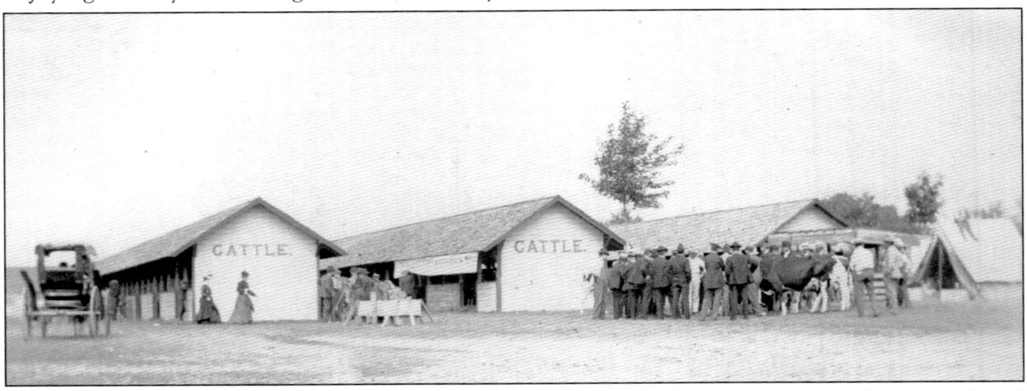

Cattle were judged before the newly erected cow sheds. In a county where the agricultural industry dominated the economy alongside the railroad industry, it was important to keep a healthy stock of dairy cows. (Courtesy of CCAS.)

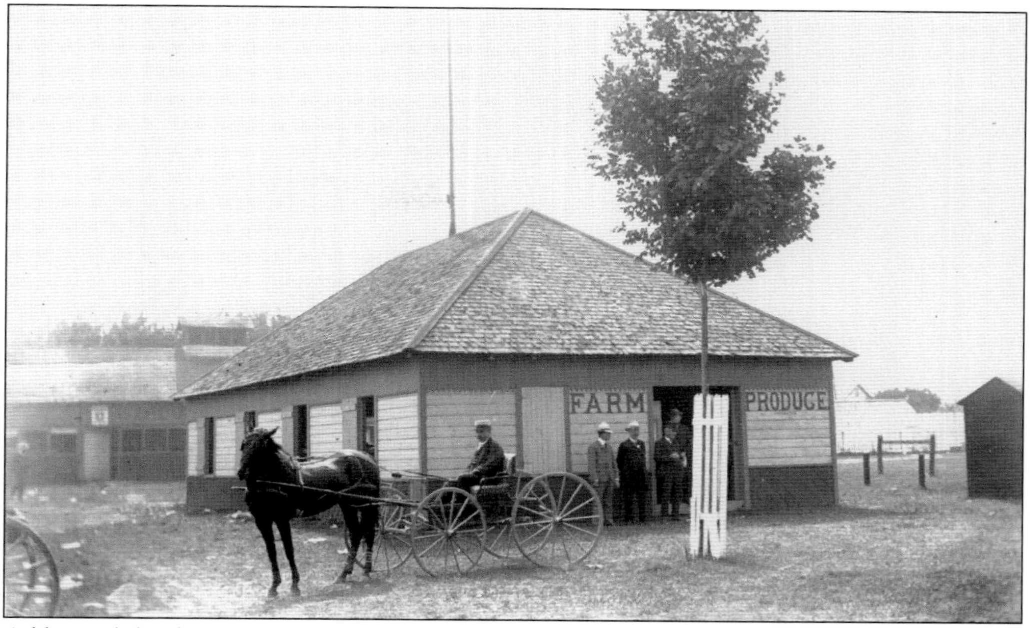

Additional land was purchased in 1865, 1868, and again in 1898. The fairgrounds now encompassed 27 acres with room for permanent buildings. A produce barn displayed the products of Columbia County farms, giving those in the agricultural market a chance to view and learn from the competition. Advancements in agricultural methods were also discussed. In 1882, the poultry house and horse barns were built. (Courtesy of CCAS.)

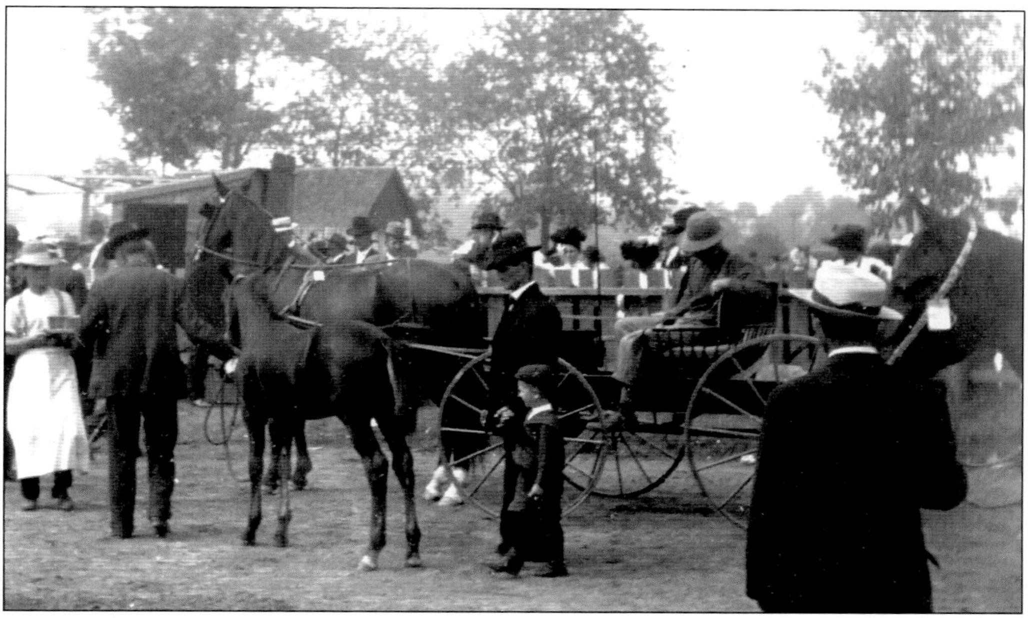

In 1876, the theme was transportation with "100 horses on exhibition." Horse trainers who had easy access to the racetrack on the grounds would utilize stables year-round. Proud owners parade their horses for all to see in this photograph. (Courtesy of CCAS.)

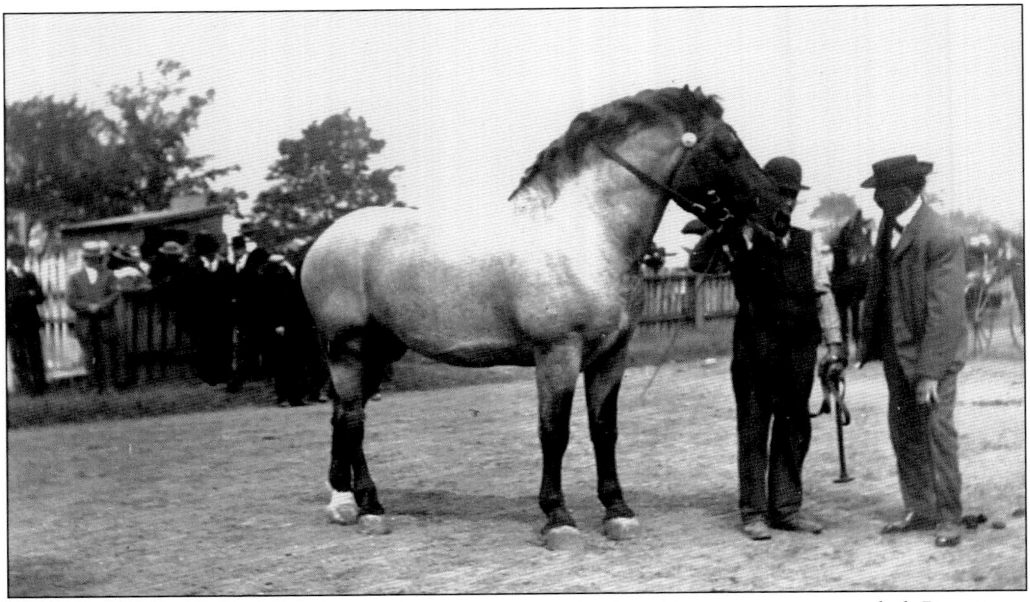

The muscular horse was the farmer's horsepower. At the fair this power was rewarded. Premiums were paid for the three levels of prizewinners. Under the supervision of John P. Mickle, president; Abram Vosburgh, vice president; H. J. Baringer, treasurer; and William A. Dardess, secretary, $4,586 in premiums were paid out in the early 1900s. (Courtesy of CCAS.)

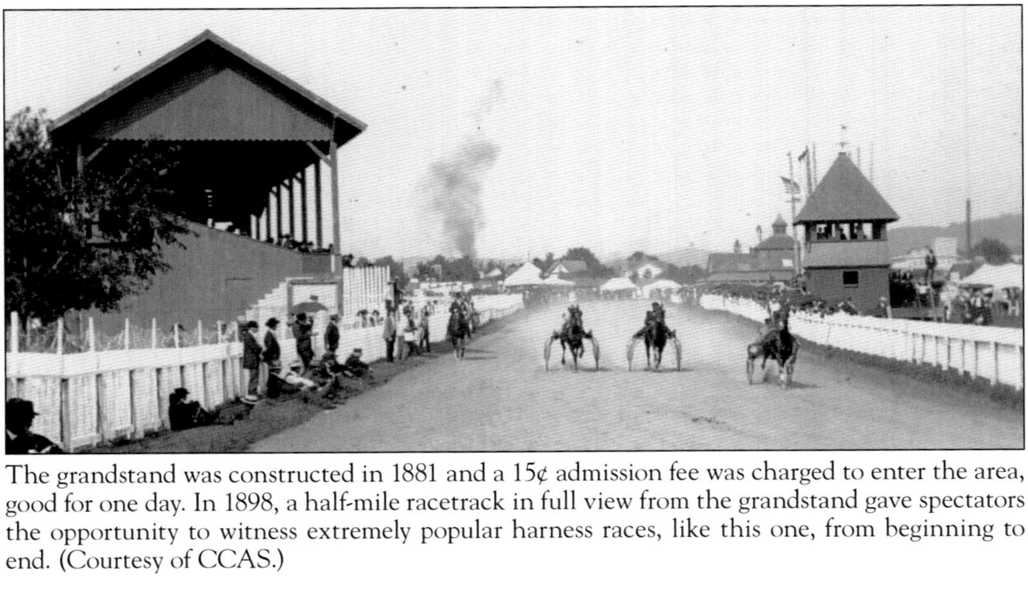

The grandstand was constructed in 1881 and a 15¢ admission fee was charged to enter the area, good for one day. In 1898, a half-mile racetrack in full view from the grandstand gave spectators the opportunity to witness extremely popular harness races, like this one, from beginning to end. (Courtesy of CCAS.)

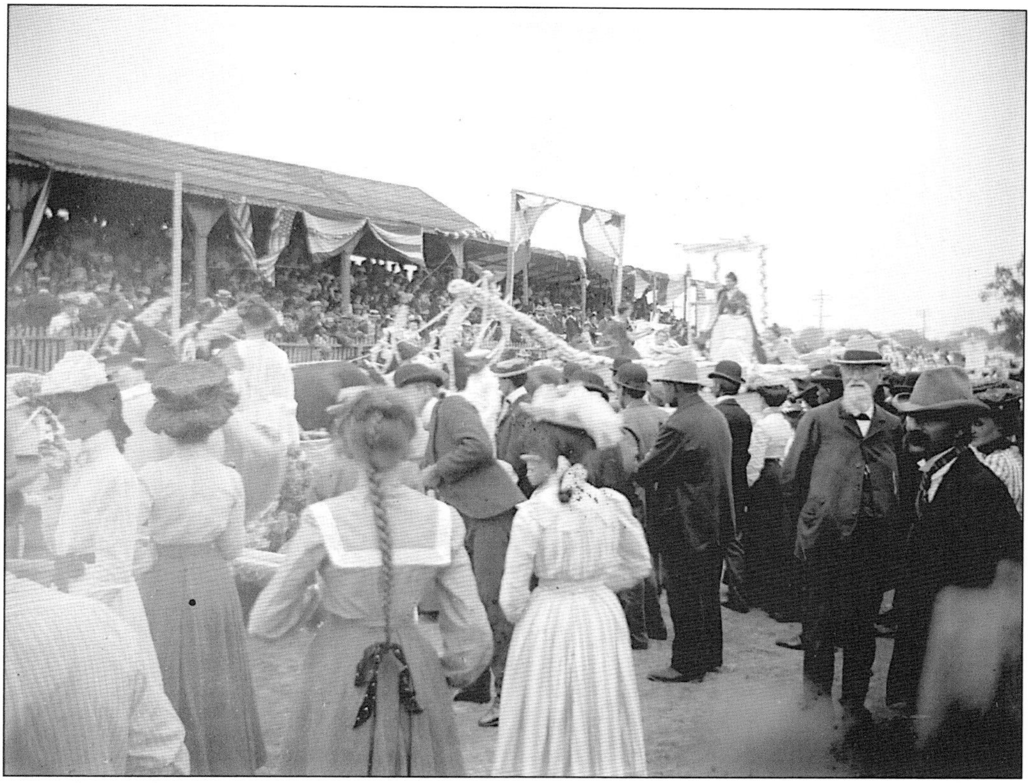

According to the October 12, 1909, edition of the *Chatham Courier*, "The Chatham Floral Company have started in their carnation shipments and an average of 1000 are being cut daily which will increase as the season advances." The annual floral parades began in 1897 and were a highly anticipated event. Home blossoms or those from George Shufelt's Chatham Floral Company, later owned by Mortimer Tank, would cover all kinds of conveyances. (Courtesy of CCAS.)

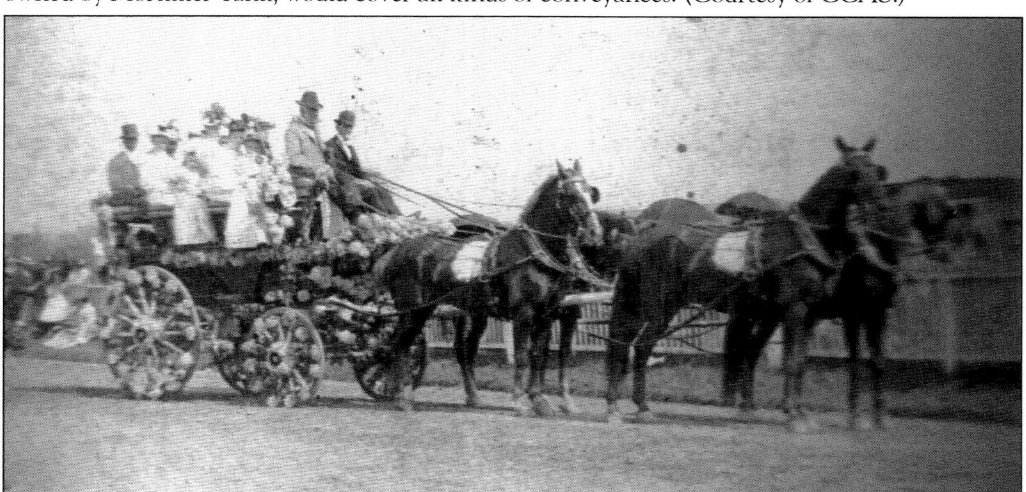

Floats with varied themes carried mayors, politicians, and many local individuals who enjoyed participating in the public display. The Honorable Louis F. Payn is driving a wagon decorated for the theme "Tally Ho." (Courtesy of CCAS.)

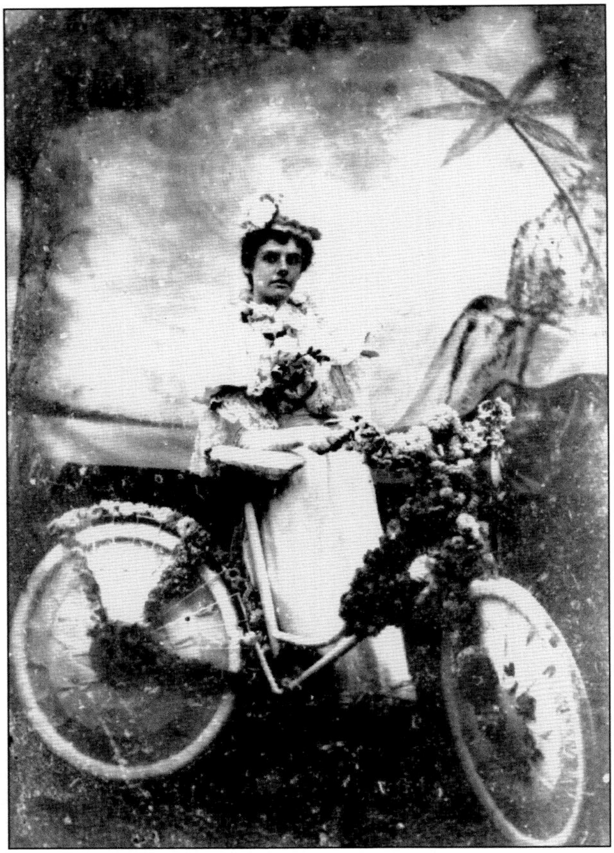

Floral parade bicycle winners on September 17, 1902, were Grover Wilcox and Horace McGinnis of Ghent, gentlemen bicycle riders, and Mrs. J. Boyle and Helen Boyle of Albany and Ethel McGinnis of Ghent, lady bicycle riders. (Courtesy of CPL.)

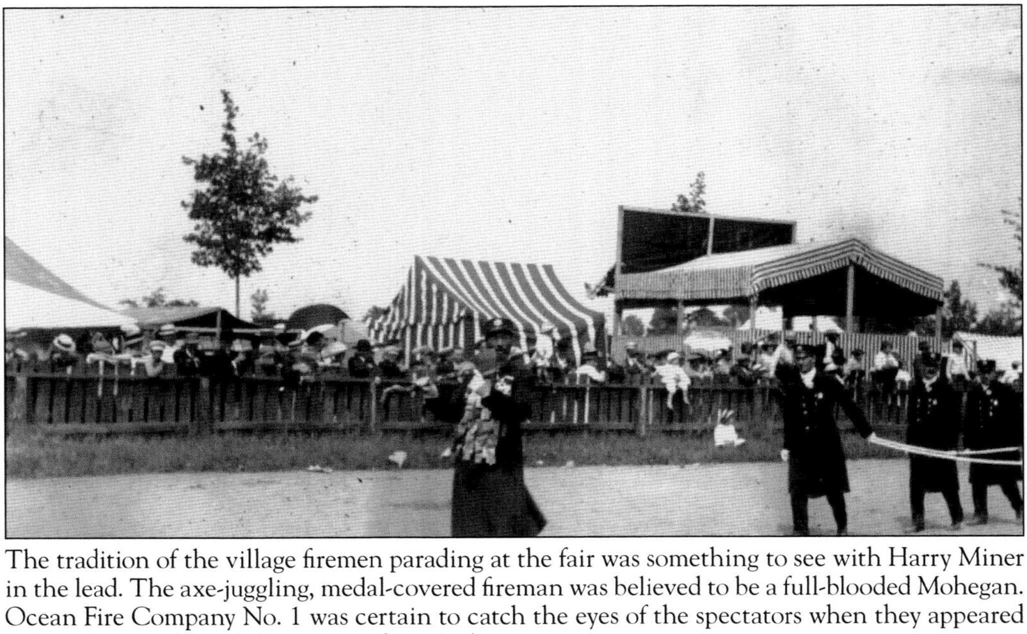

The tradition of the village firemen parading at the fair was something to see with Harry Miner in the lead. The axe-juggling, medal-covered fireman was believed to be a full-blooded Mohegan. Ocean Fire Company No. 1 was certain to catch the eyes of the spectators when they appeared before the grandstand. (Courtesy of CCAS.)

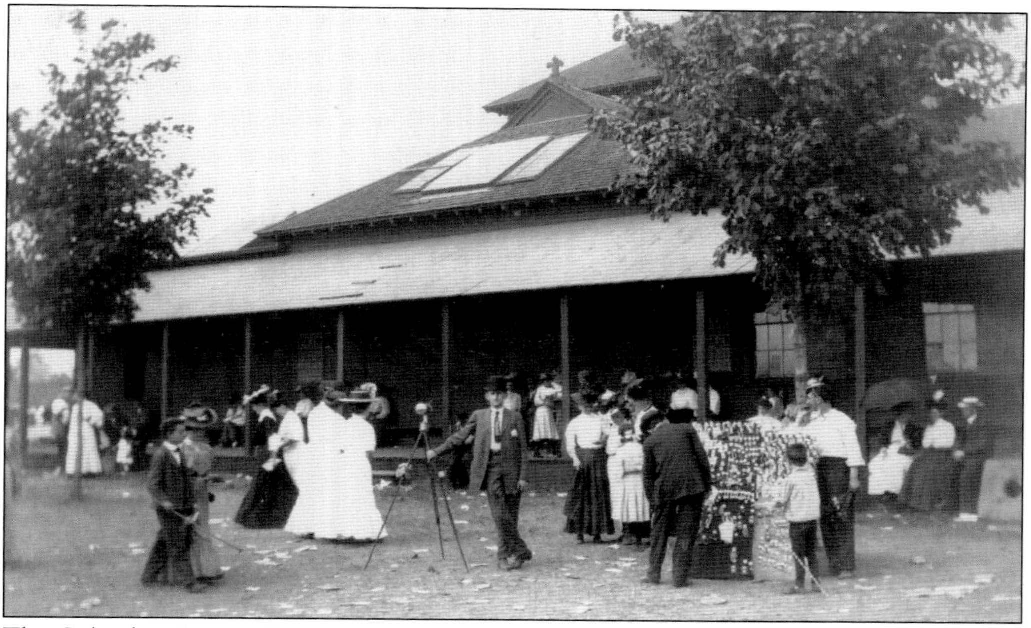

The Columbia County Fair ran October 2–5 in 1906. George McClellan was president, and William A. Dardess was secretary then. Photographer John Eberle between 1908 and 1914 captured Chatham Fair images for posterity and all the delectable fair moments that seem ageless except for the fairgoers' attire. (Courtesy of CCAS.)

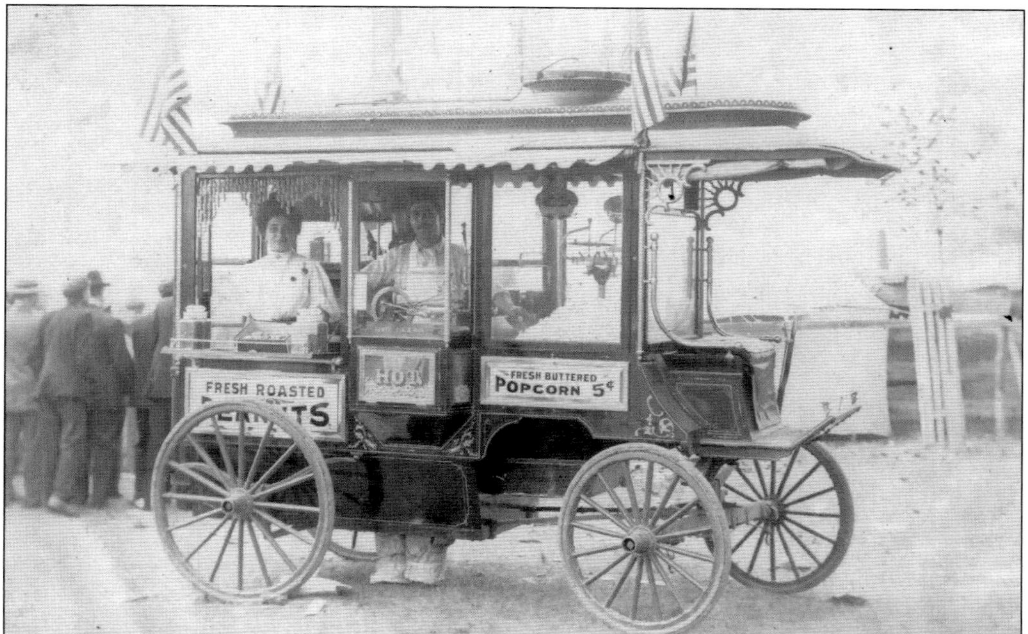

Homemade food was provided by church groups and served under tents. Robert Coon's frankfurters were advertised as "Coney Island Hots." The purest of real cream was used to make dainty old-fashioned ice-cream wafers sold by Howard Wild. Popcorn and peanut wagons in 1908 appeared much the same as they do now. (Courtesy of CCAS.)

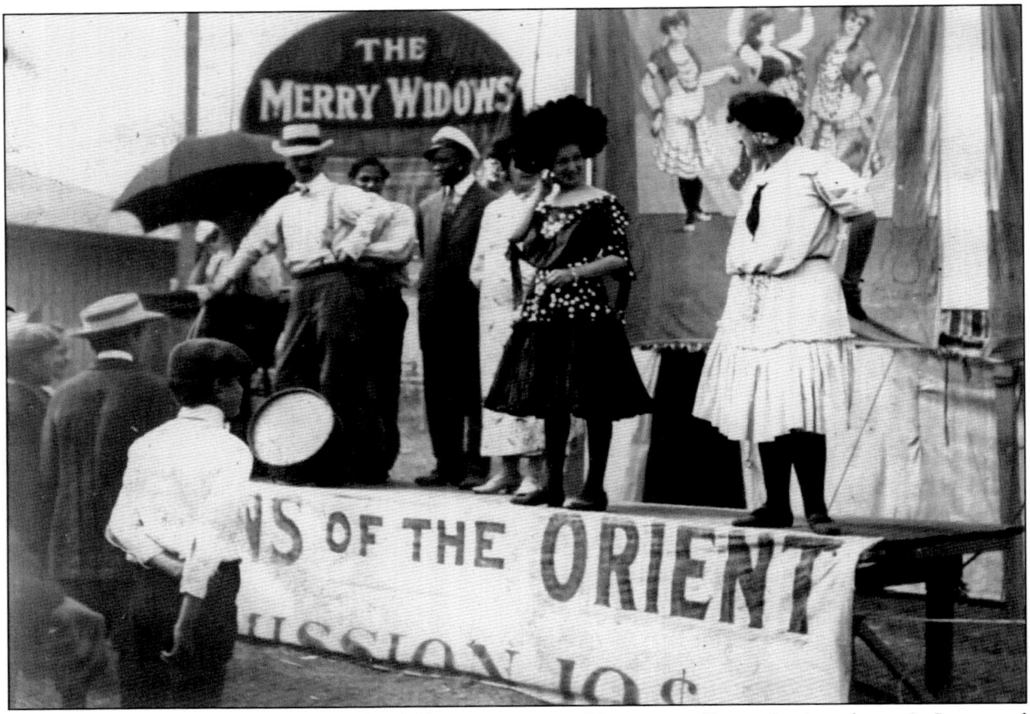

The *Chatham Republican* listed the following events: European Comedy Acrobats, LaJour and LaJour Chinese Comiques, Madame Lockhart's Balloon Ascension and Thrilling Parachute Jump, and a baby show in the exhibition hall. Babies were on display from 1:00 p.m. to 3:00 p.m. In the future, Columbia County School Queen pageants would replace the baby contest. These merry widows gather a crowd outside their sideshow tent. (Courtesy of CCAS.)

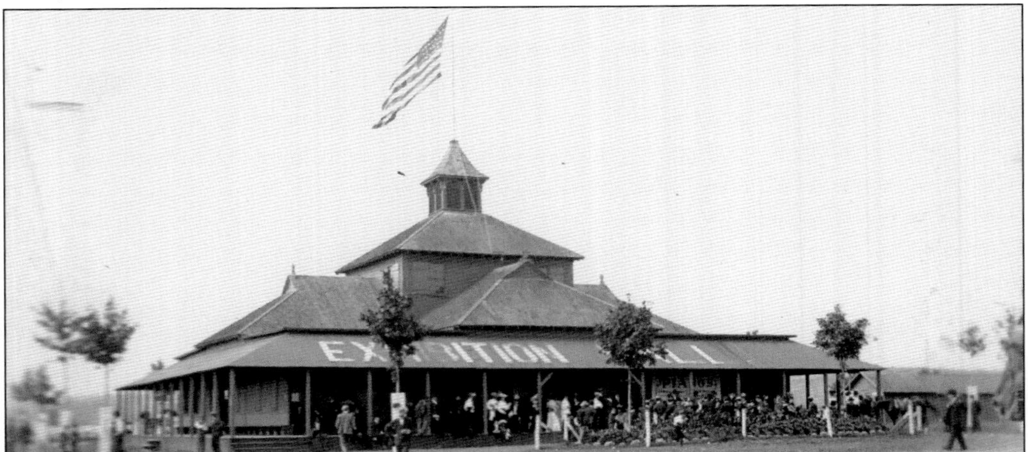

According to the August 30, 1902, *Chatham Courier Extra Edition*, "The Chatham Fair is not a money-making institution, some of the purposes which it serves are: to provide recreation and enjoyment for the thousands who attend and to be of educational value by showing to the farmer, . . . in brief to broaden and elevate the mind of the onlooker, to bring him to a realizing sense of what is being accomplished outside the circle of this daily observation." (Courtesy of CPL.)

Seven

Industry

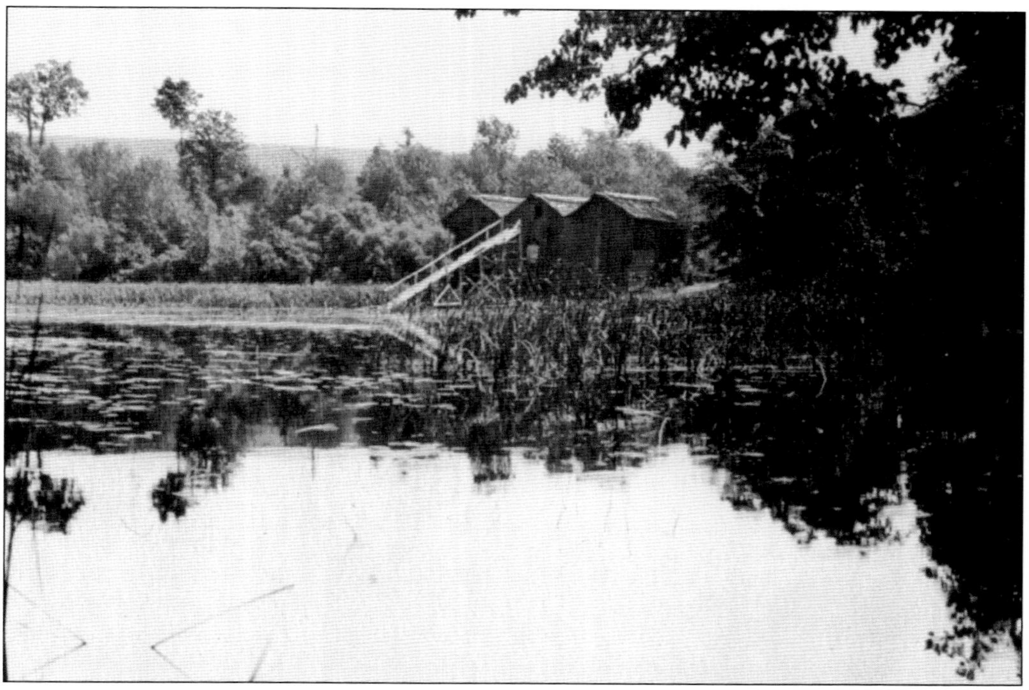

Ice harvesting from several ponds, including Chatham Lake (the old pond), was a necessary seasonal task prior to electric refrigeration. The Borden Milk station ice crop harvest was crucial. Once it took 35 teams to haul an ice crop to the milk plant. It took 3,000 tons to supply the quantity of ice needed at the station. Ice farmers earned 2.5¢ per eight- or nine-inch cake. (Courtesy of Dwight Sawyer, Miller Collection.)

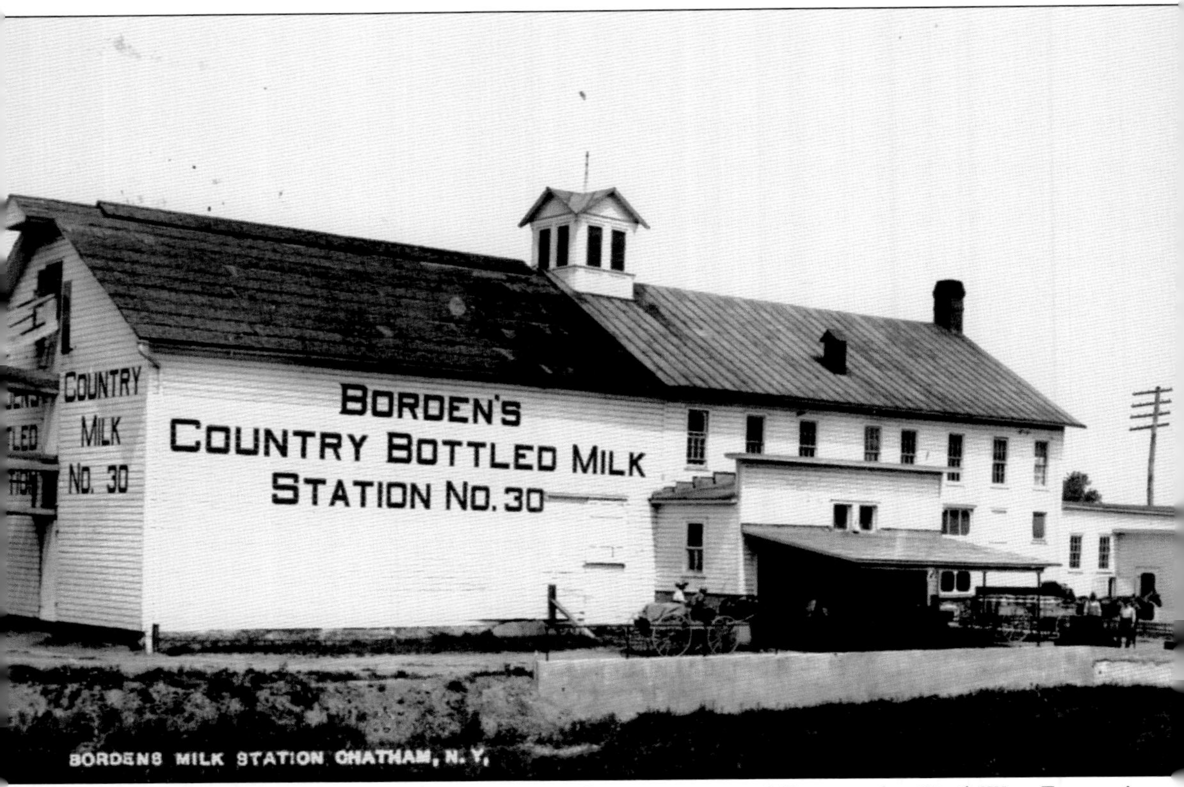

The Borden Grade B bottling plant started as a creamery following the Civil War. Farmers' horse-drawn wagons arriving at receiving docks sometimes carried multiple deliveries from neighboring farms, each can bearing a serial number. "Contract day" re-signed many old patrons who could earn between $7,000 and $9,000 a week in 1910 depending on the amount of butterfat the raw milk contained. The station opened in the former butter and cheese factory of Wright and Evans. The creamery burned in 1913 but was rebuilt and updated. (Courtesy of Chatham Press.)

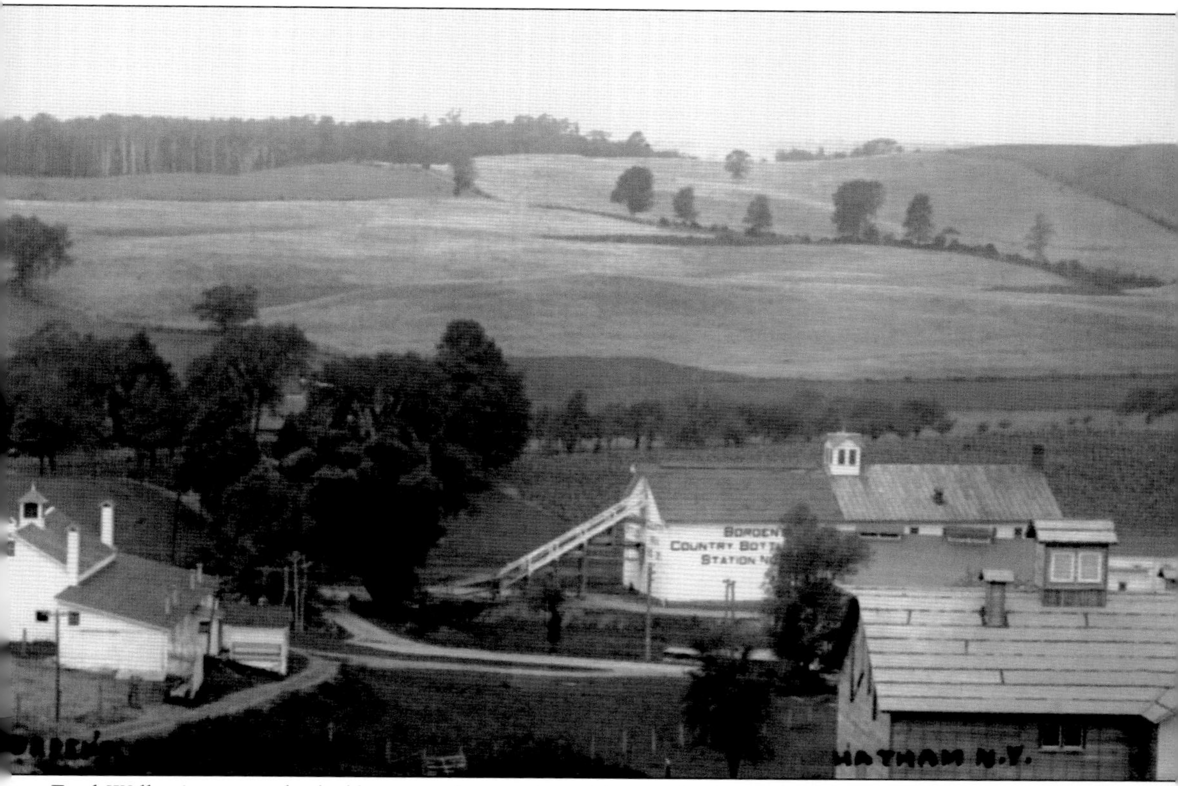

Fred Wilbor's one-and-a-half-ton truck met the 3:00 a.m. Rutland milk train in the rail yards. He would make three round-trips on this roadway to retrieve all the milk for the plant by 5:00 a.m. Raw milk was rejected if it had a high bacteria count, smelled of wild onions, or was too overheated. Accepted milk was pasteurized, chilled, then bottled, crated with ice chips, and stacked in milk cars on the Harlem siding. In 1929, these employees (see page 90) performed the inspections and processing stages: William Alamillo, Perry Knoblock, George Winn, Theodore Sherman, Ralph Roraback, Clarence Dallas, Allan Van Tassel, Arthur Roraback, George Westover, Charles Weeler, Gus Hedrick, Charles Decker, William Cornelius, Elbert Pulver, Vedela Feathers, Ezra Kern, Stewart Wooley, George Sipperly, Donald Wooley, Archie Callender, Irving Arnold, Fenton Allen, Anthony Brahm, and superintendent Charles Hansen. (Courtesy of Chatham Press.)

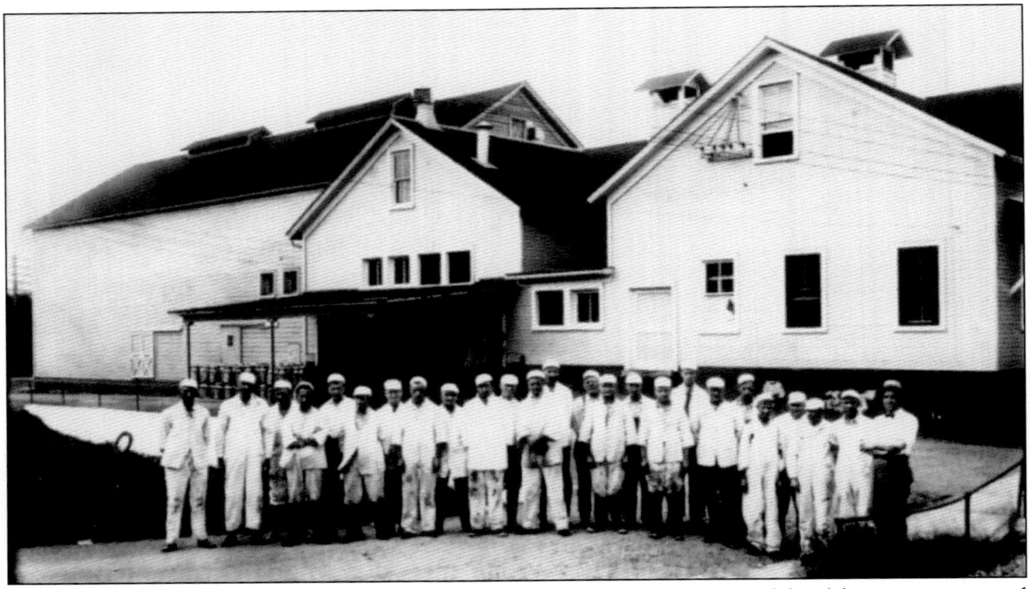

On the eastern side of the turnpike, 200 of the most productive and healthy cows received constant care at the Borden Farm and Milk Center. Twenty local men made sure the cows were fed on a regular schedule, and the barn was kept spotless and sterilized. The animals' health was constantly monitored with throat cultures, and preventative measures were taken with injections. Local veterinarians were on call. New York State inspectors qualified the product as Grade A milk. (Courtesy of Chatham Press.)

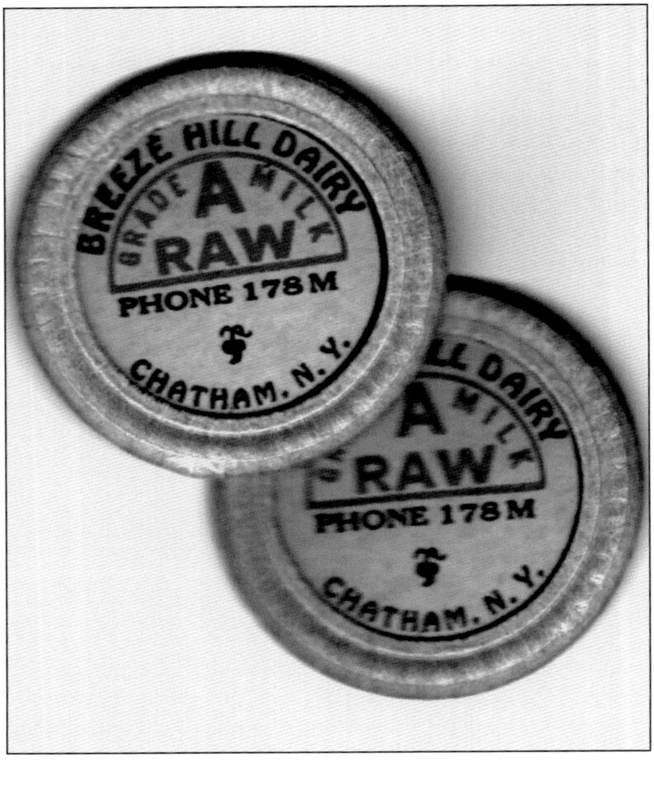

Breeze Hill Dairy bottled Grade A milk at its processing plant on the Valatie road. John "Babe" Kraft owned the plant and employed Louis Hartcorn, Henry Mead, and "Brook" Howe as Breeze Hill milkmen. Empty bottles were picked up, and fresh milk was placed inside a metal insulated box at the household door, an improvement from George Angell's 1887 milk route when milk was hand-dipped from a pail. (Courtesy of CVHS.)

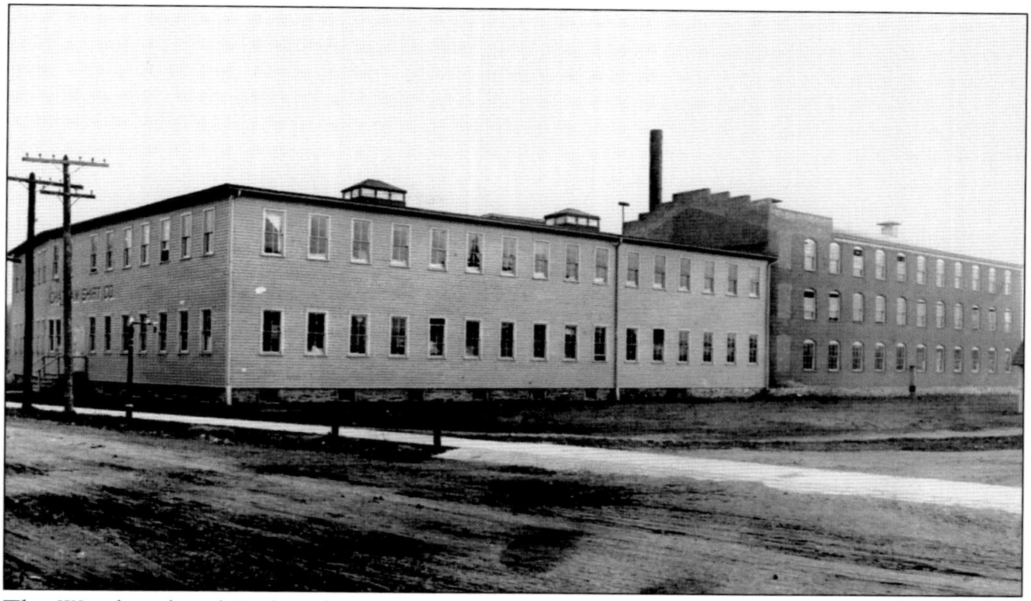

The Woodward and Bailey Shirt Factory, founded by Jerome Hayes, began on School Street in the former school building. The business transferred to the former thermometer factory on Church Street in 1894. In 1902, the Chatham Shirt Factory was expanded to include a second wood-framed building. Later, the three-story brick laundry building was constructed. (Courtesy of Bob Gross.)

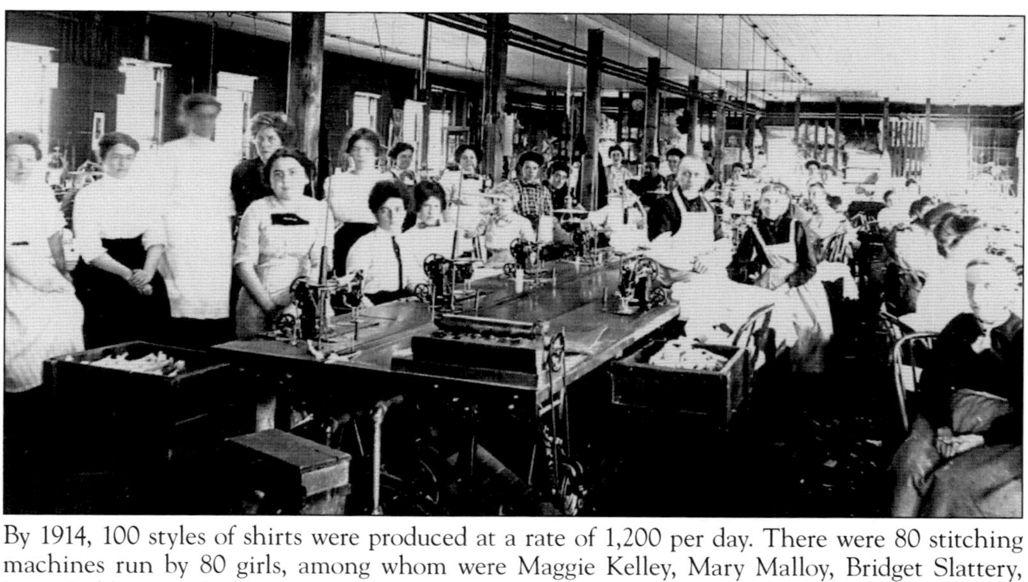

By 1914, 100 styles of shirts were produced at a rate of 1,200 per day. There were 80 stitching machines run by 80 girls, among whom were Maggie Kelley, Mary Malloy, Bridget Slattery, Lizzie Baldwin, and Maggie Keefe. Twelve girls were replaced when the modern buttonholer was introduced. (Courtesy of Bob Gross.)

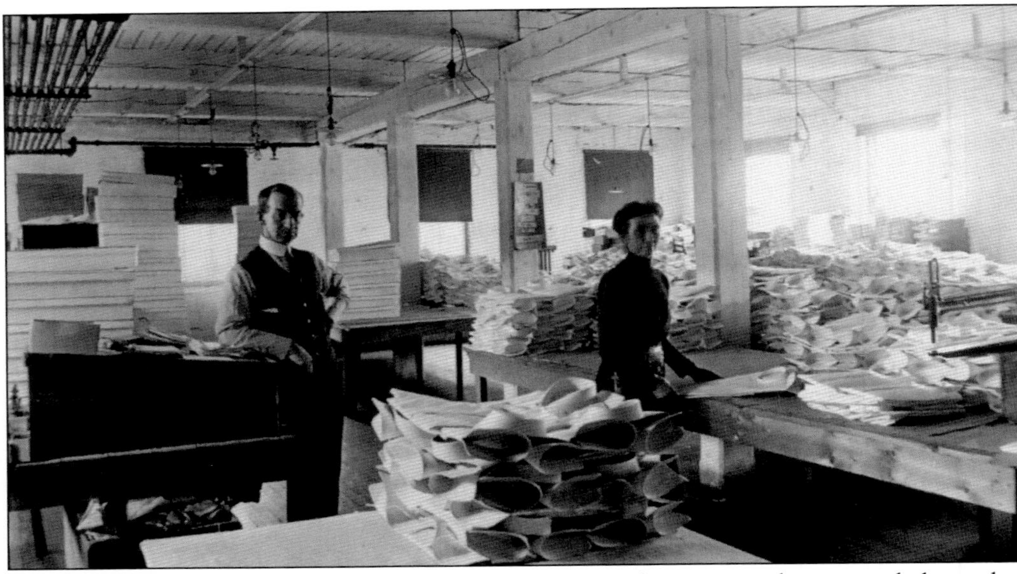

The Chatham Shirt Factory was a profitable business with many employees until the end of World War I. A large order for military union suits was canceled, and despite the adaption of the work suit by local businesses, the factory was forced into bankruptcy in 1922. It sold for a fraction of its actual worth. (Courtesy of Bob Gross.)

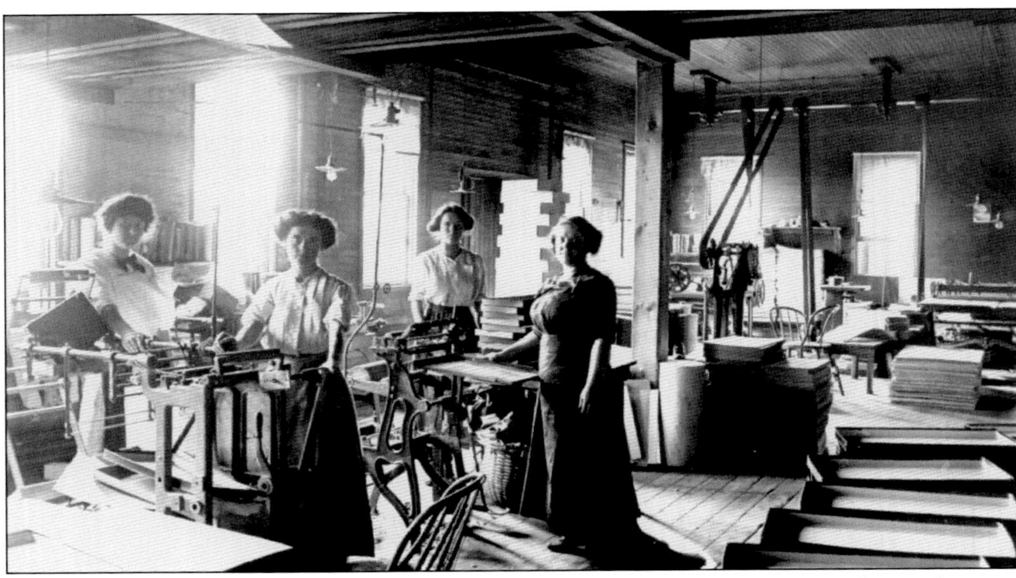

The on-site laundry employed 45 men. Men cut the fabric. The company manufactured its own boxes, and shipments went to New York City and Chicago. Shirtwaist factory workers, from left to right, Hazel Miller, Carey Carty, Flo Bullis, and Grace Bullis Gross were photographed at their workstations. (Courtesy of Bob Gross.)

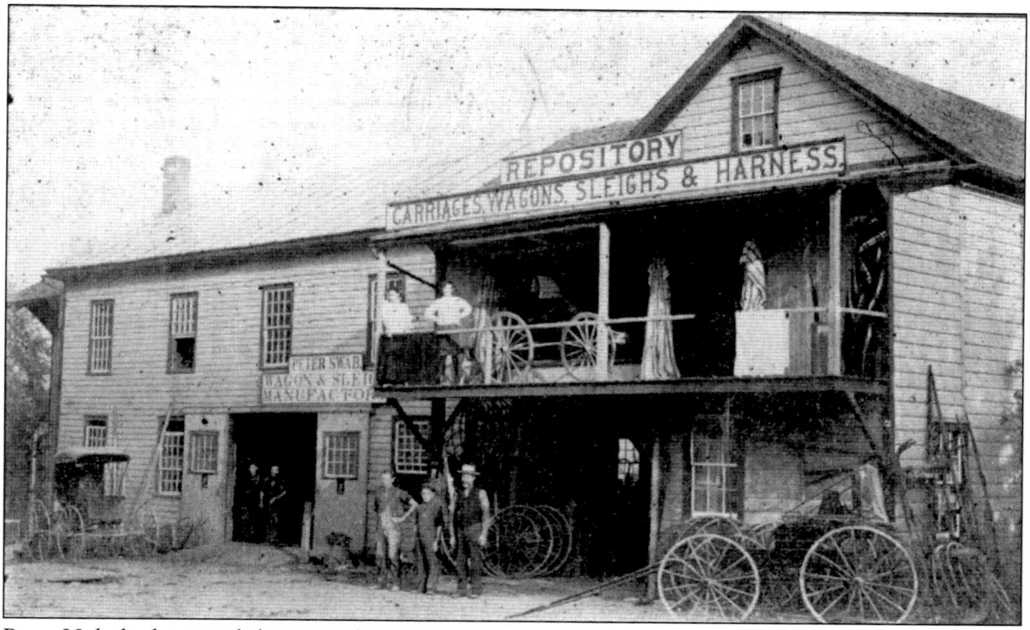

Peter Hobel advertised the manufacture of carriages and wagons in his Main Street shop in 1869. Peter Swab's warerooms were located on the central square near Center Street. He specialized in making fine wagons of every description. The warerooms were, according to the *Chatham Republican*, "filled with the handsomest vehicles placed on wheels." Even when machine-made wagons became available, people came for miles around for his product. (Courtesy of CPL.)

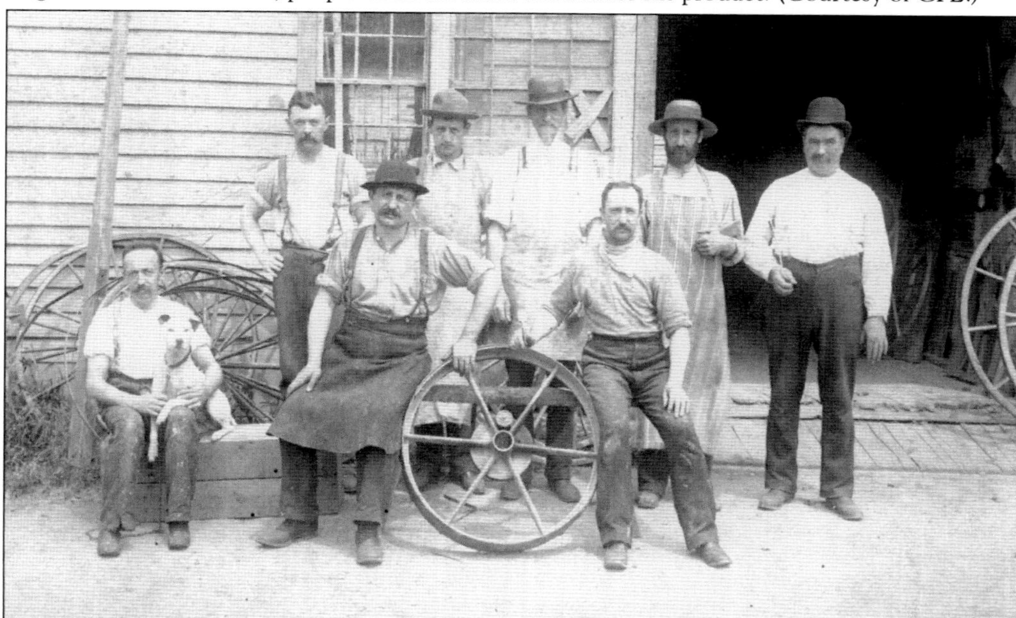

Peter Swab is "surrounded by a corps of competent workmen in every department," wrote the *Republican*. His work crew had a difficult time keeping abreast of all the orders. Peter Swab reportedly gave his personal attention to every aspect of the business and was described as industrious, faithful, honest, and upright, a credit to Chatham. (Courtesy of CPL.)

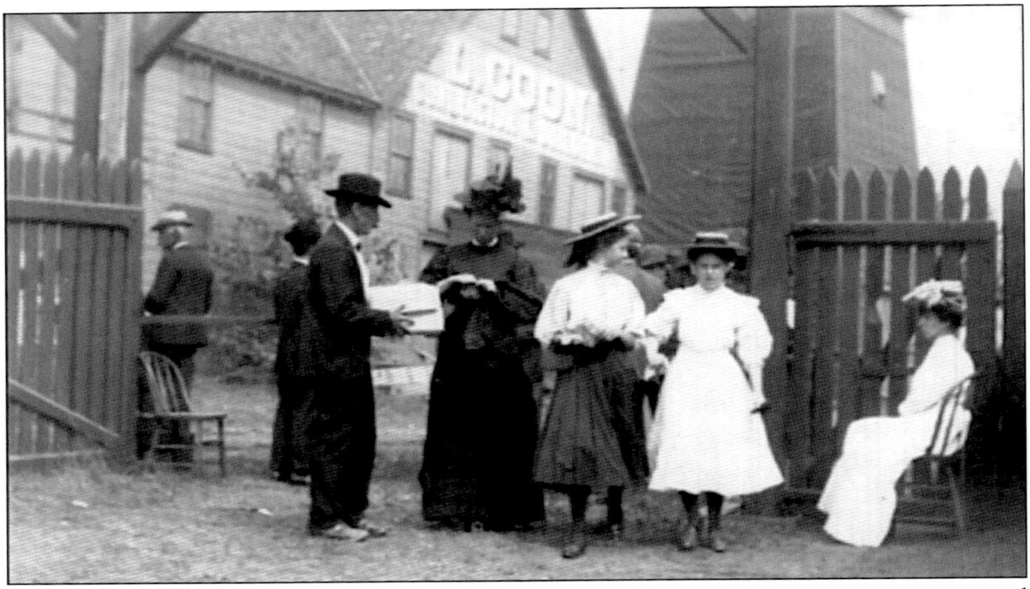

Lewis Coon's building business on Church Street started in 1875. His company constructed most of the houses on Washington Avenue, which he cut through to provide that residential area. He also erected many leading commercial blocks as well as dwellings. From his large place of business on Church Street, he contracted to build homes of every style with made-to-order detailing. The company filled a great need for housing in the rapidly growing village. (Courtesy of CCAS.)

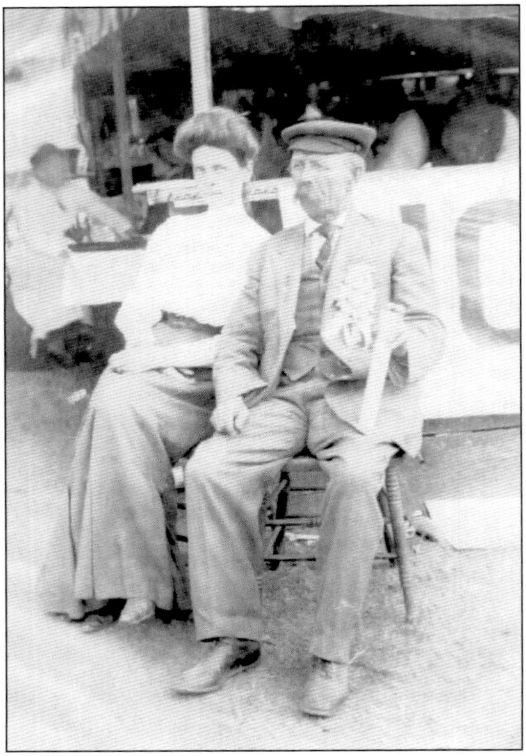

T. S. Buckley, a self-made man, had the most unique plant in this part of the state. His sawmill reportedly turned out lumber and railroad ties faster than much bigger plants. Thousands of bushels of apples were turned into cider. In 1904, Thomas Buckley shipped 30 carloads of cider from the plant's Harlem siding. There was a large volume of activity at "Buckley's Mills" or Buckleyville. (Courtesy of CCAS.)

Eight

SCHOOLING

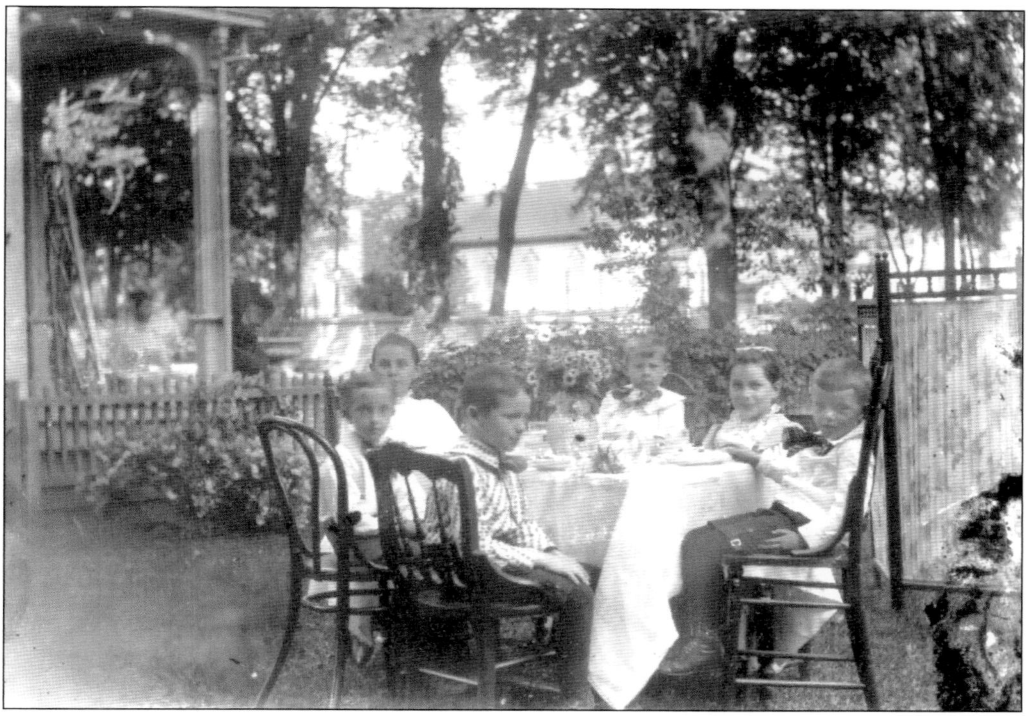

A number of private schools included the 1853 institution Alvah Roe's Burnstead Private School for girls on Center Street. Mrs. Joseph Clark held classes on the second floor of a barn on Kinderhook Street. Ethel Blinn had a kindergarten class. Perhaps one of these tea party guests at the Wheeler home on Kinderhook Street attended one of these schools in 1895. (Courtesy of CVHS, M. Fredericks Collection.)

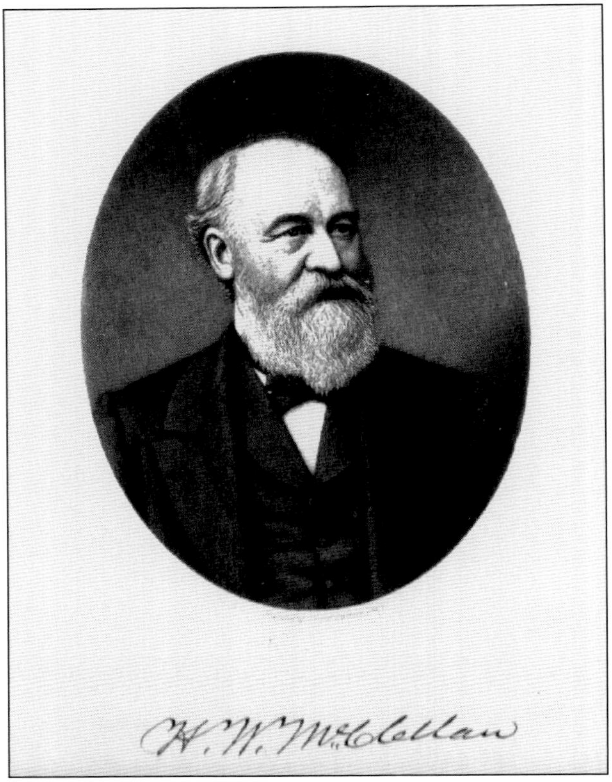

Education was a priority for the area as early as September 12, 1795, when seven school commissioners "Resolved: That the clerk write twelve advertisements reciting part of the act for the encouragement of schools," according to *The History of Columbia County*, written by Capt. Franklin Ellis. Amos Boright and Hugh W. McClellan would each serve as town superintendent of schools, charged with maintaining quality of instruction in small schools in the community. (Courtesy of CPL.)

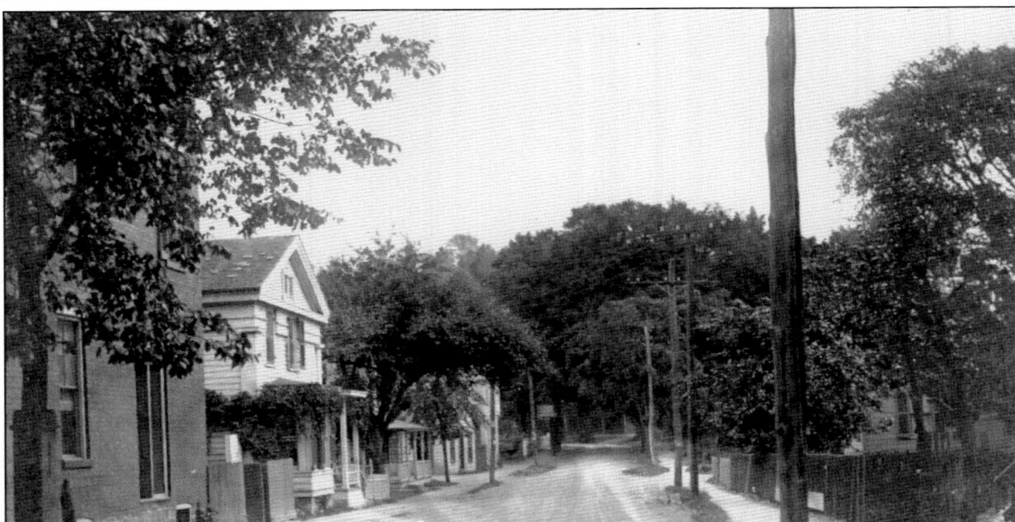

First an old brown Kinderhook Street schoolhouse stood close to the Rutland railroad trestle. Between 1818 and 1833, a *Chatham Courier* interview with a former student reported, "old Miss King made liberal use of the switch and ferule." In 1850, the small-framed schoolhouse was sold and a newer one was built at the same location. Students outgrew that school, and a two-story Chatham and Ghent District No. 22 school was occupied in 1859 on School Street. (Courtesy of CPL.)

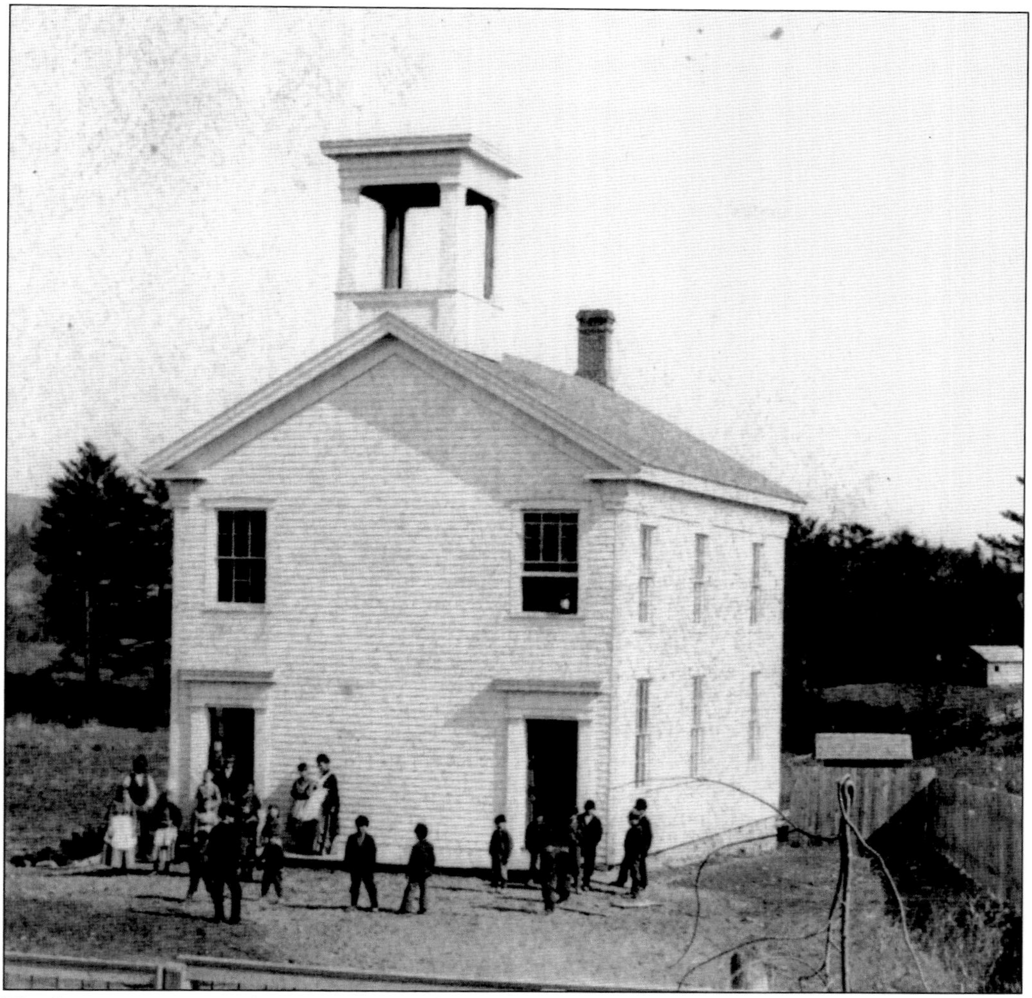

The largest private academy in 1871 was located to the east of the village on a hillside. Gertrude Lake Wheeler and Louis F. Payn were students there. John Cadman, J. D. Shufelt, and D. S. Lovejoy ran the academy in 1873. Thomas Buckley moved it intact to Thomas Street. Recorded in the Shatham centennial souvenir program, "The bell on top of the school clanged all the way down the hill on its trip to the new site." (Courtesy of CPL.)

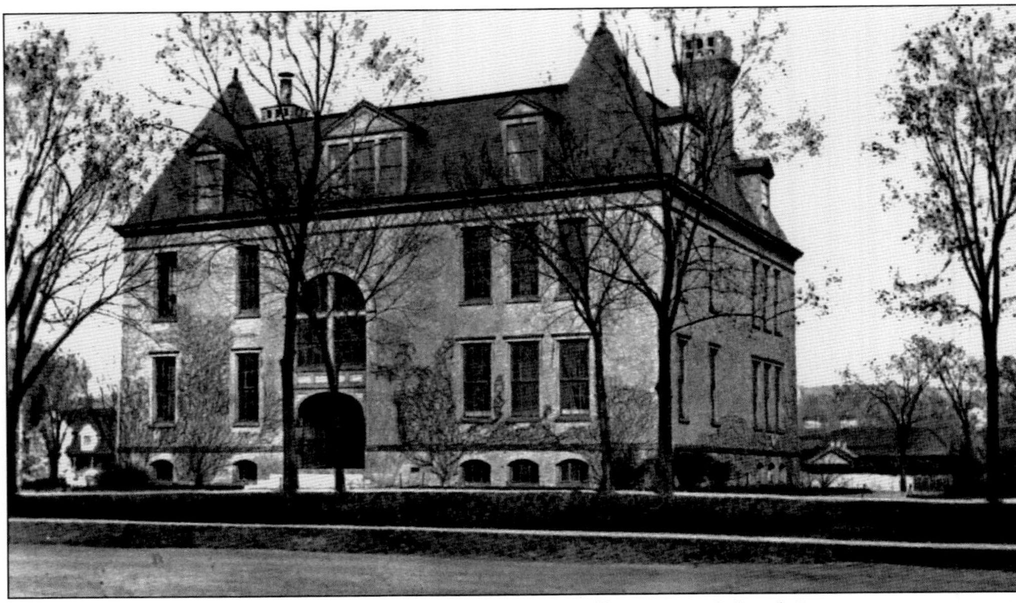

One hundred or so voters arrived at the district schoolhouse on School Street one evening in 1881. They stumbled to the second floor to find a single lantern on the principal's desk. The point was made that a new school was needed. Between two and a quarter to two and a half acres were purchased for $2,500 on Woodbridge Avenue. The first union school building, a three-story brick grammar school, opened in 1883. (Courtesy of CPL.)

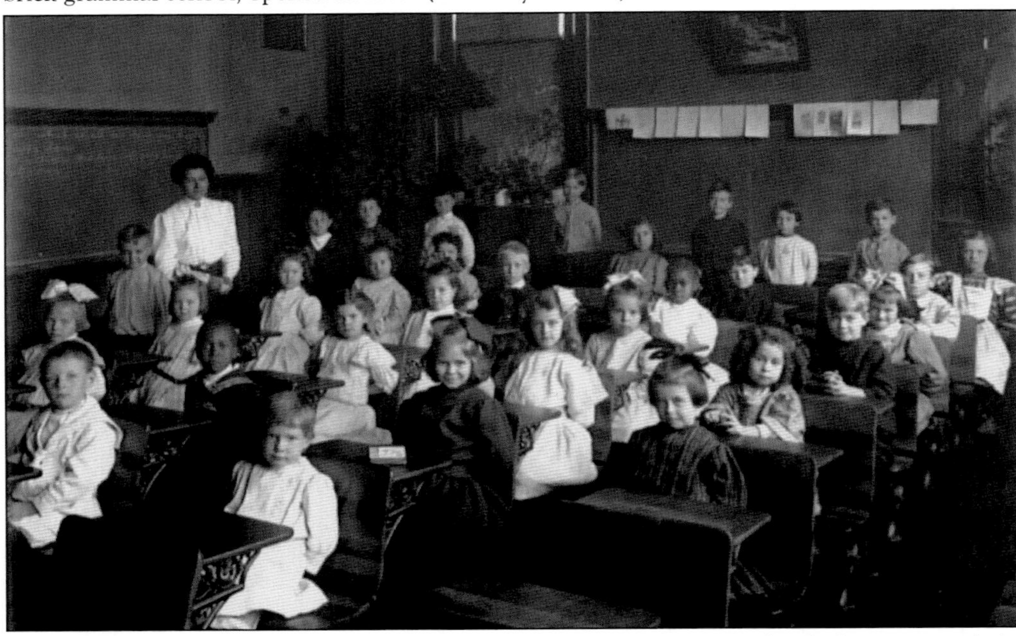

When Union School District No. 1 was proposed in 1880, many individuals questioned the introduction of an academic program. The first trustees were P. H. Garrity, J. D. Shufelt, F. I. Park, Dr. W. C. Bayley, Dr. J. T. Wheeler, and William C. Dayley. Both Park and Wheeler would continue to serve the district for over a quarter of a century. Mary Smith's class poses in their grammar school classroom in 1900. (Courtesy of CPL.)

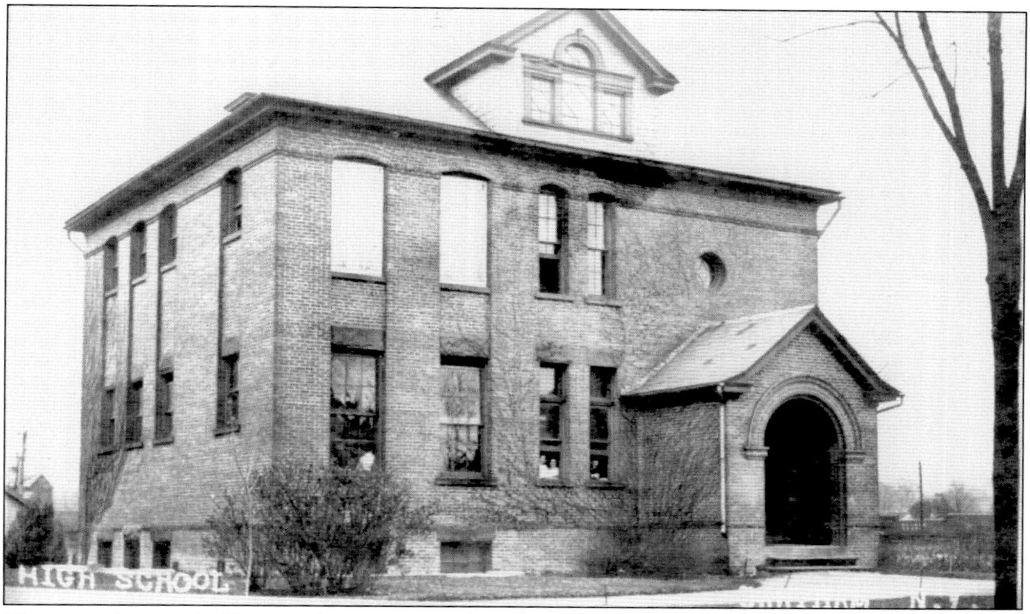

The attendance of village students increased, and in addition students from neighboring districts were attracted to Chatham's school. The new high school would be constructed next to the grammar school in 1894. (Courtesy of CPL.)

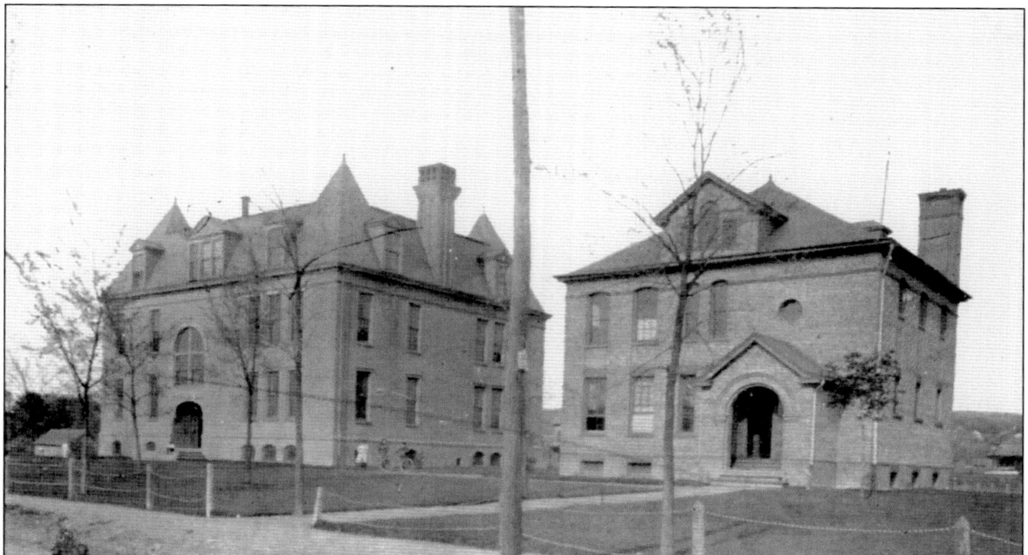

The Union Free School District No. 1 was admitted to the Regents in 1886. William P. Boright, Kirby J. Jones, Lottie M. Vincent, Ethel Percy, Sanford W. Smith, and Dr. Willard Starks were graduates the following year. Dr. John C. Dardess was the single graduating student in 1888. School development was rapid and significant in 1889 under the supervision of principal Frank H. Wood. (Courtesy of Jon Meredith.)

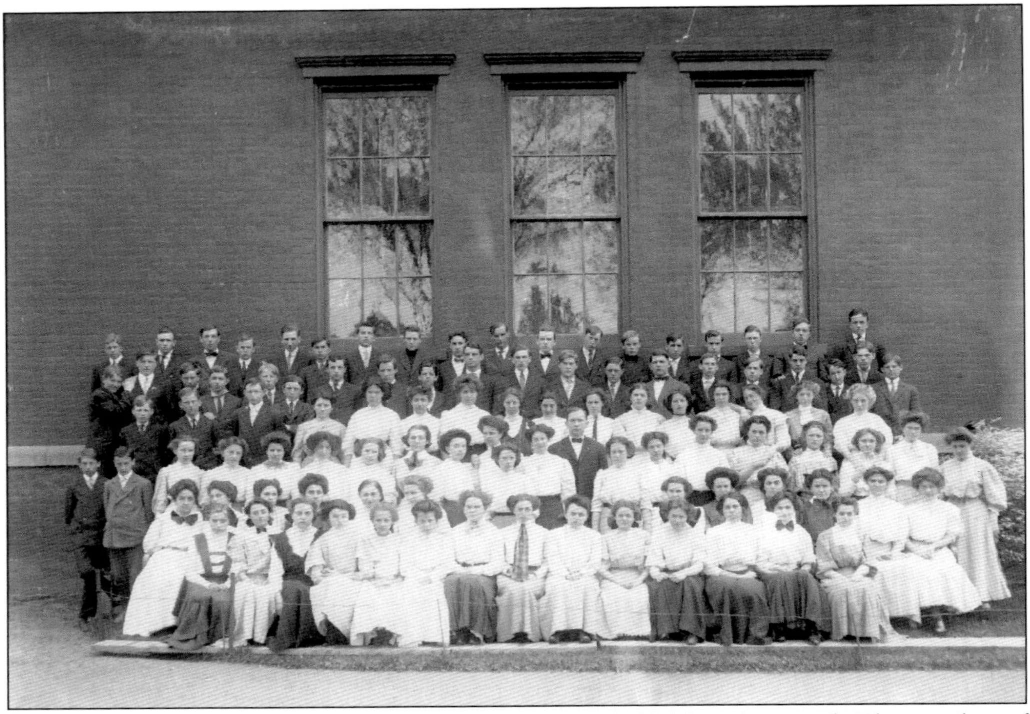

In the beginning of the 20th century, the need for child labor decreased. The number of nonresidential high school pupils increased. Sometimes these students lived in boardinghouses as an alternative to riding the train daily. The commercial course of study, one of four offered graduates, began in 1902. This photograph was taken of Chatham High School students in 1910. (Courtesy of CVHS.)

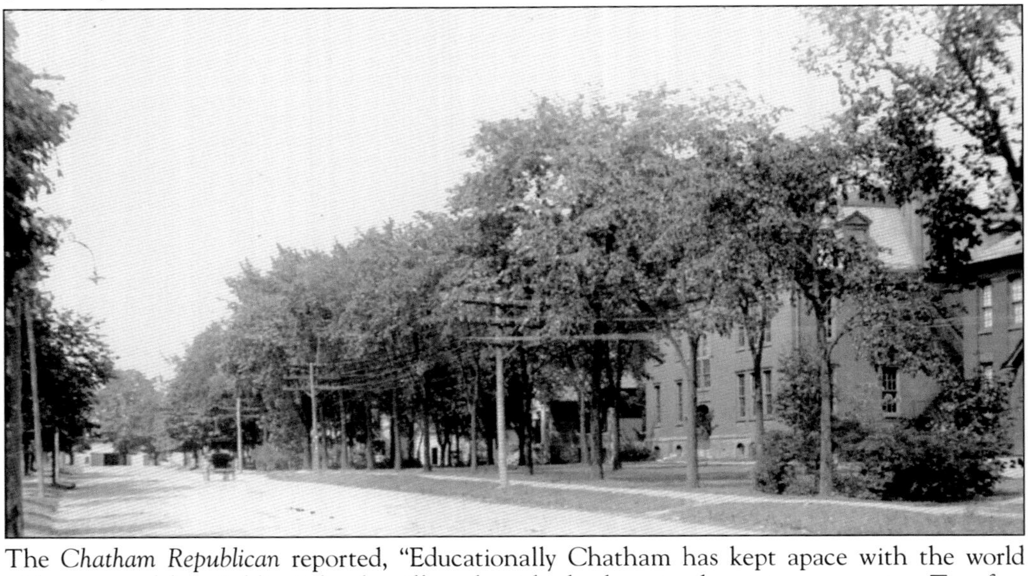

The *Chatham Republican* reported, "Educationally Chatham has kept apace with the world of letters, and her Public Schools will rank with the best in the state or country. Two fine commodious brick buildings harbor one of the most successful and thorough educational systems extant. Chatham graduates are filling scores of responsible positions." (Courtesy of CPL.)

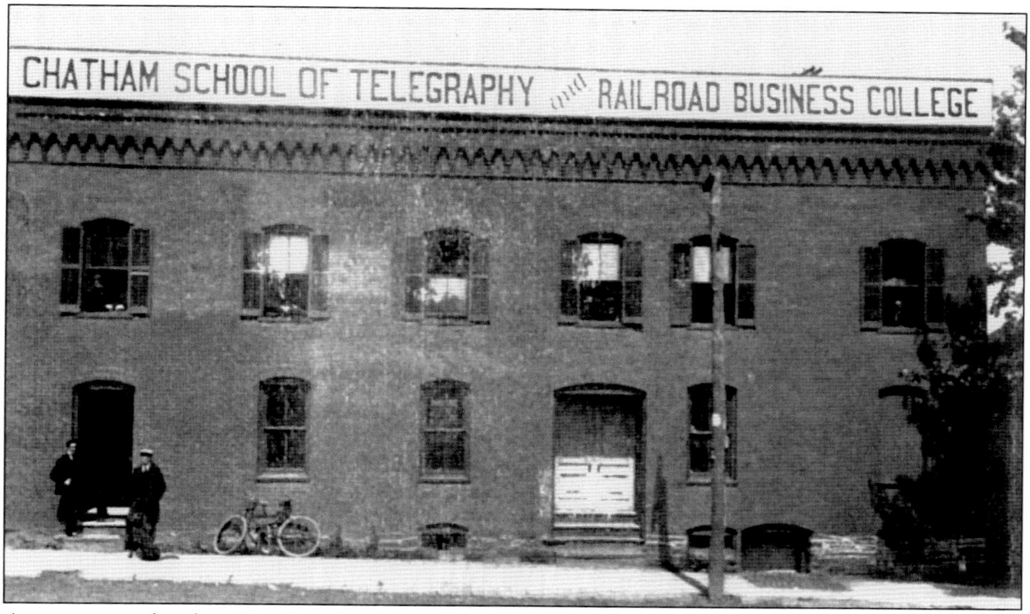

A separate school on Lower Main Street (Hudson Avenue) prepared young men for specific commercial success in the business world. Whiteman's Telegraph School and Railroad Business College would propel a number of prospective students into executive positions on some of the nation's great railroads. D. H. Hoffman was president of the school. Frank Whiteman was the proprietor. (Courtesy of CPL.)

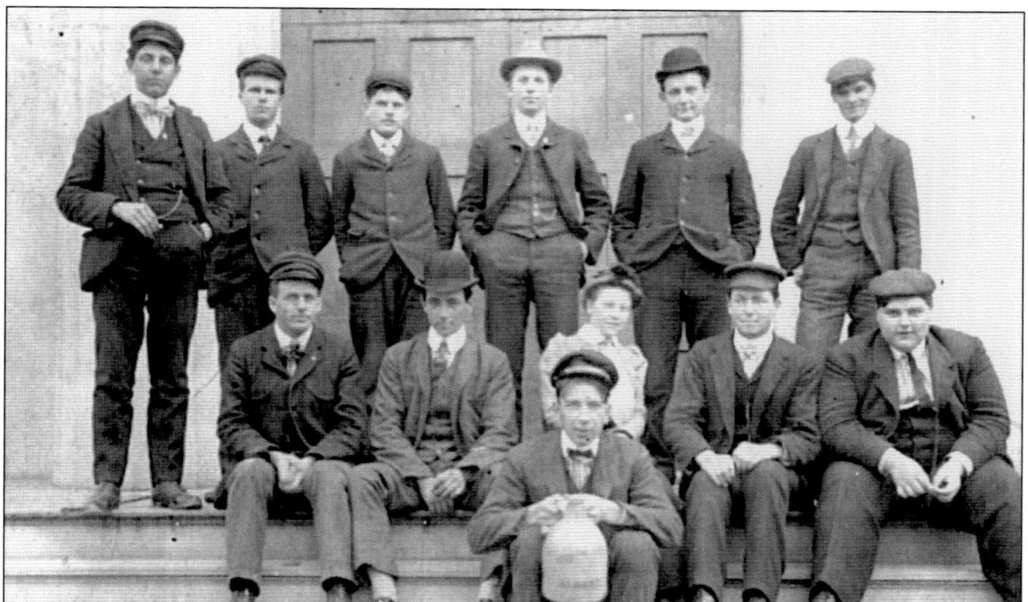

Telegraph students usually paid $3 a week room and board in Chatham homes. This photograph captures the graduating classes of 1902 and 1903. The names of the students were as follows: Stanley Matthews, Ben Evans, John Kelley, Ernest Limes, E. P. Height (professor), Roft Laraway, Ed Swan, Kirbey Brown, Mary Connor, W. P. Young, Frank Judd, and George Fox. (Courtesy of CVHS.)

CHATHAM

UNION FREE SCHOOL

LIBRARY

CATALOGUE.

CHATHAM, N. Y.

1888.

CHATHAM PUBLISHING COMPANY PRINT,

John Wheeler, M.D., had conceived the idea for a Chatham public library when Andrew Carnegie began offering grants in 1886. Ella A. Wagar, librarian, came to the Union Free School District in 1881, the year Dr. Wheeler was first appointed trustee. The classic books listed in the library catalog in 1888 had limited circulation. (Courtesy of CPL.)

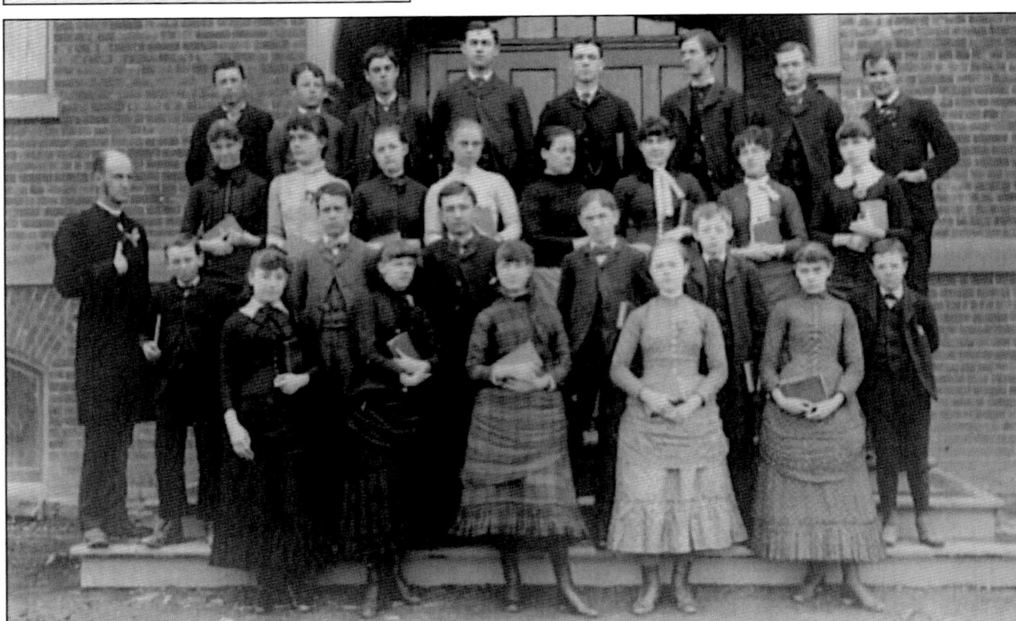

Together Wheeler and Wagar promoted library growth and development in association with the school. Chatham had a literary society that was established in 1879. When the grammar school was built the society donated 70 books to the library. (Courtesy of CPL.)

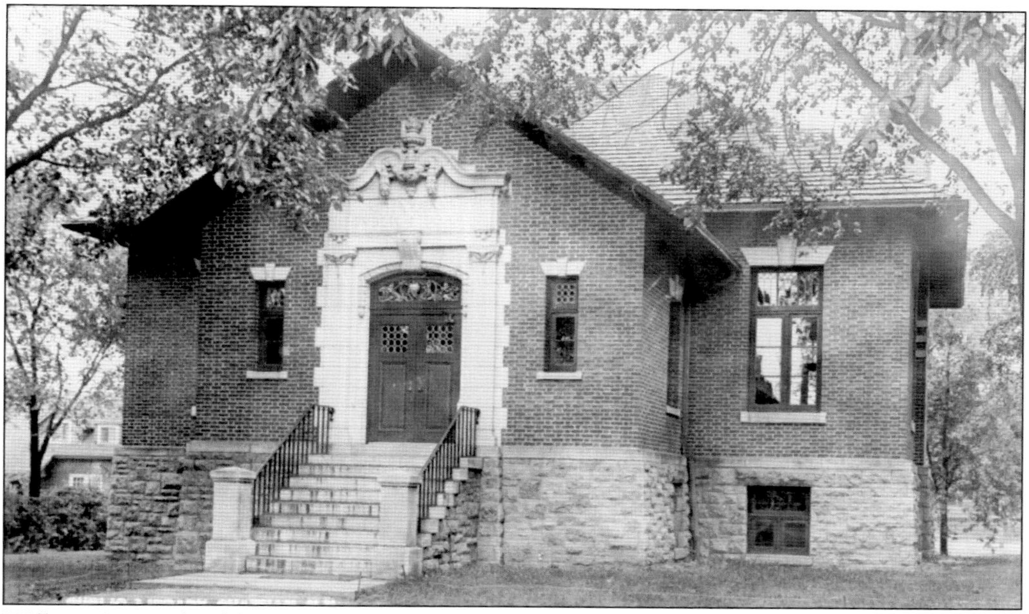

William B. Howland bought and published the *Chatham Courier* from 1875 to 1883. Dr. John Wheeler's request for him to intercede with Andrew Carnegie in order to get a library grant was quickly carried out even though he then lived in New York City. In 1901, Howland wrote Andrew Carnegie and included a memo from Dr. Wheeler. The grant application was accepted on April 8, 1902. (Courtesy of Jon Meredith.)

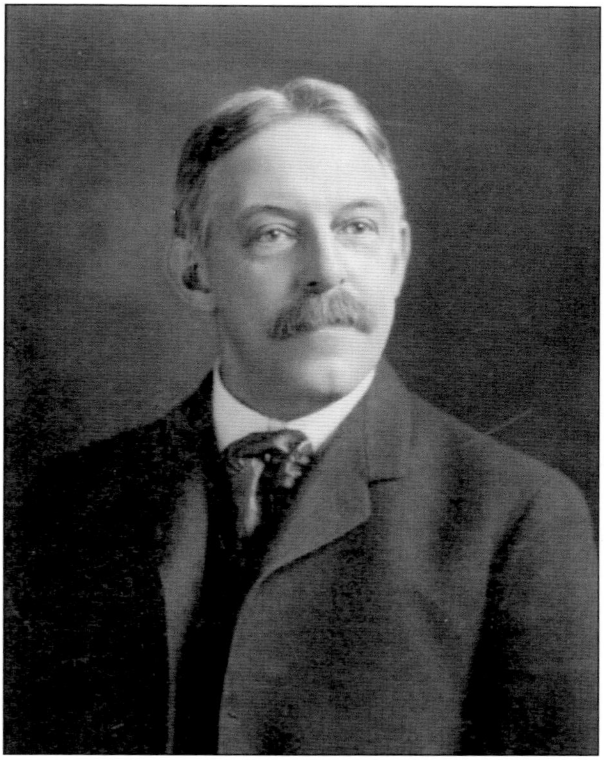

Three years after the library was completed, John T. Wheeler, M.D., suddenly passed away. On December 9, 1908, ten pallbearers from the Masonic lodge escorted by members from the board of education followed his coffin from his Kinderhook Street home into the library where it rested in front of the fireplace. (Courtesy of CPL.)

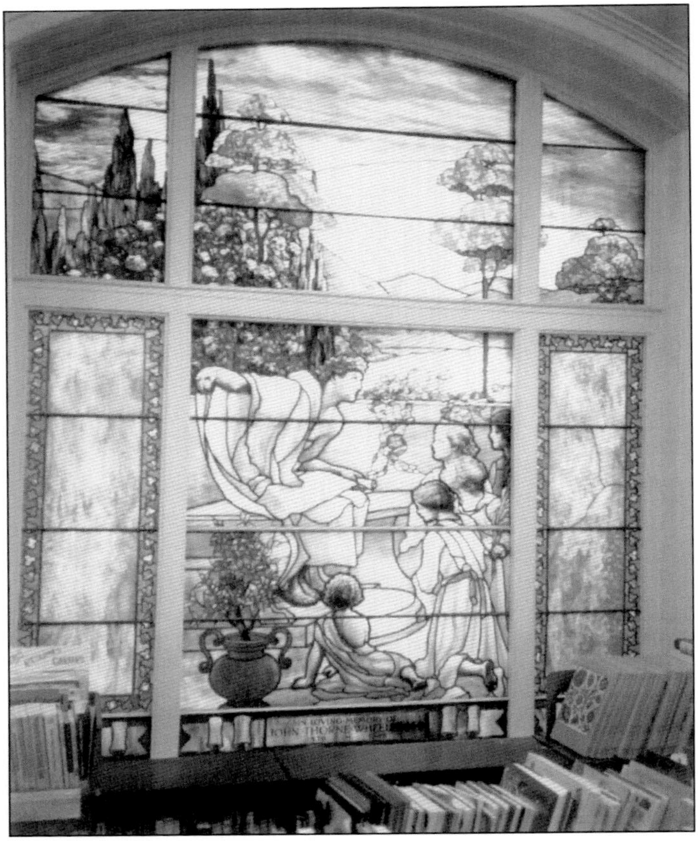

Some 475 students came from the school, and each respectfully placed a small bunch of violets on his coffin during the hour-and-a-half tribute. The stained-glass Tiffany window entitled "Instruction" was dedicated in 1912 as a loving memorial from his wife, Gertrude. (Courtesy of CPL.)

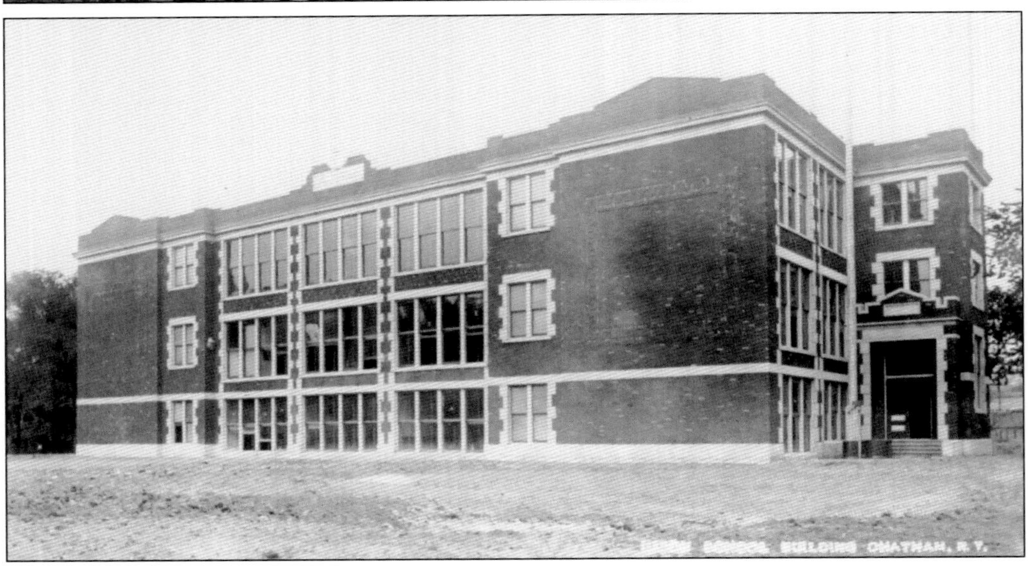

The Honorable Louis F. Payn, Dr. T. C. Washburn, Dr. W. R. Starks, C. E. Covey, the Honorable J. B. Sinclair, W. C. Woodward, Mrs. R. W. Seymour, W. P. Boright, and W. H. Housman were the advisory board that entertained over 30 bids for construction of a combined grammar and high school. (Courtesy of Jon Meredith.)

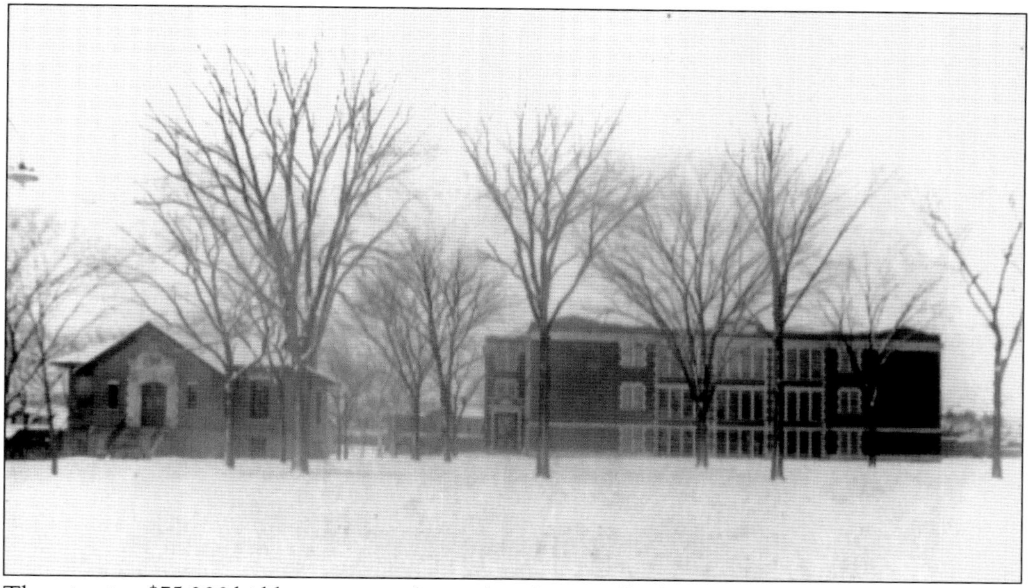

The winning $75,000 bidder contracted to make a fireproof building in 1914 with inside lavatories and adequate ventilation, heating, and lighting. Louis F. Payn provided all the furnishings for the auditorium. (Courtesy of CPL.)

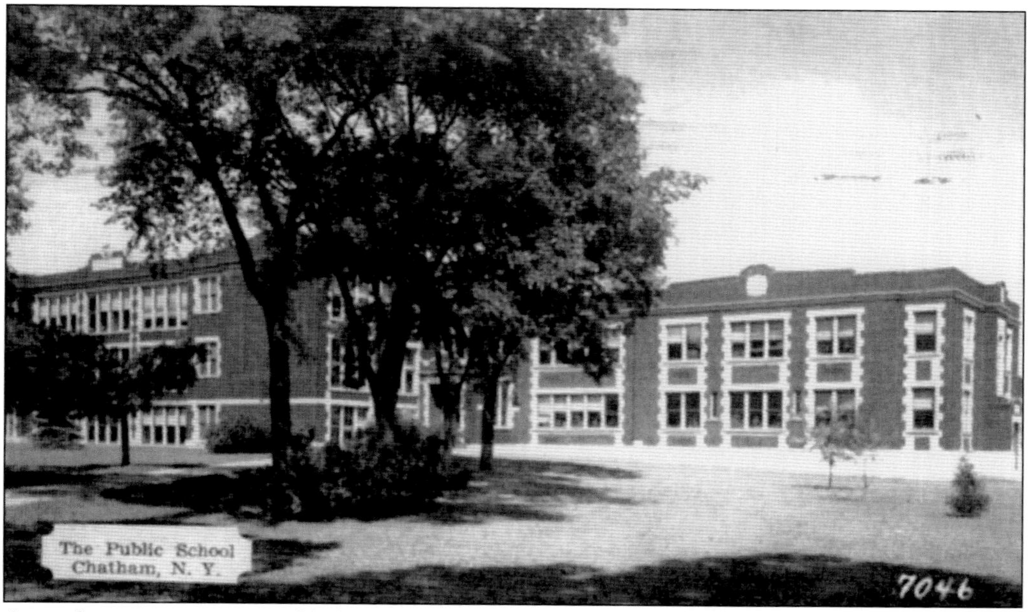

A south wing expansion added a farm shop, a home economics room, an industrial arts shop, and a cafeteria in 1930. Marguerite Chapman attended school there. Her railroad family lived on Hudson Avenue across from Hoffman Avenue. The future film star nearly lost her life coming from school when the car in which she was a passenger stalled on the crossing as an oncoming train approached. (Courtesy of CPL.)

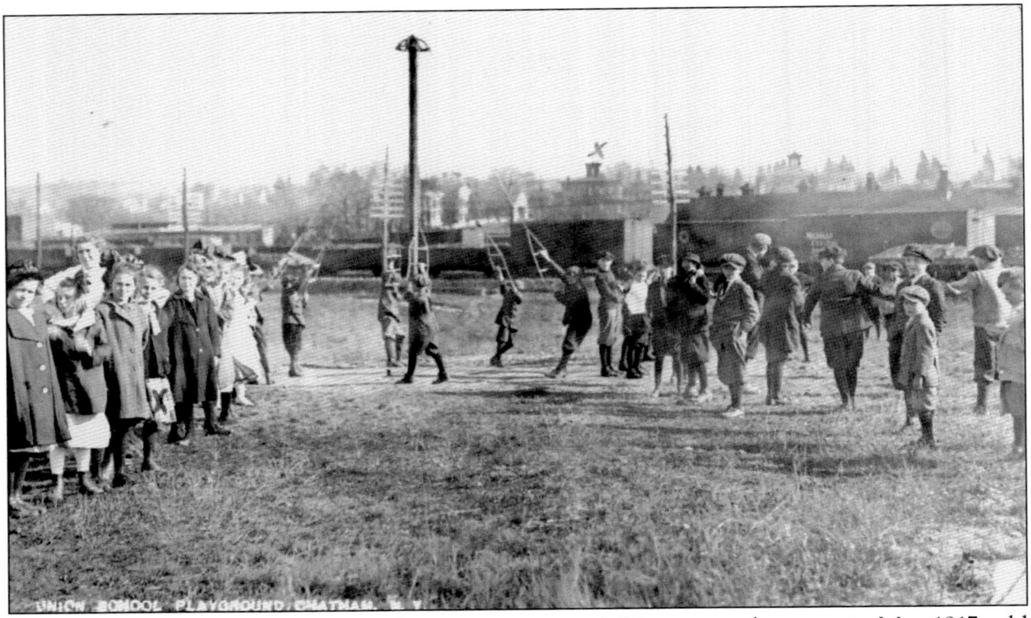

"Florence" put an X on her skirt in this picture postcard. Her note to her aunt in May 1917 told that there were 12 cases of scarlet fever that caused the school to close for one week. The Harlem railroad yard is easily identified behind the school playground. Florence placed a second X over a house on Cemetery Avenue that may have been her home. (Courtesy of Jon Meredith.)

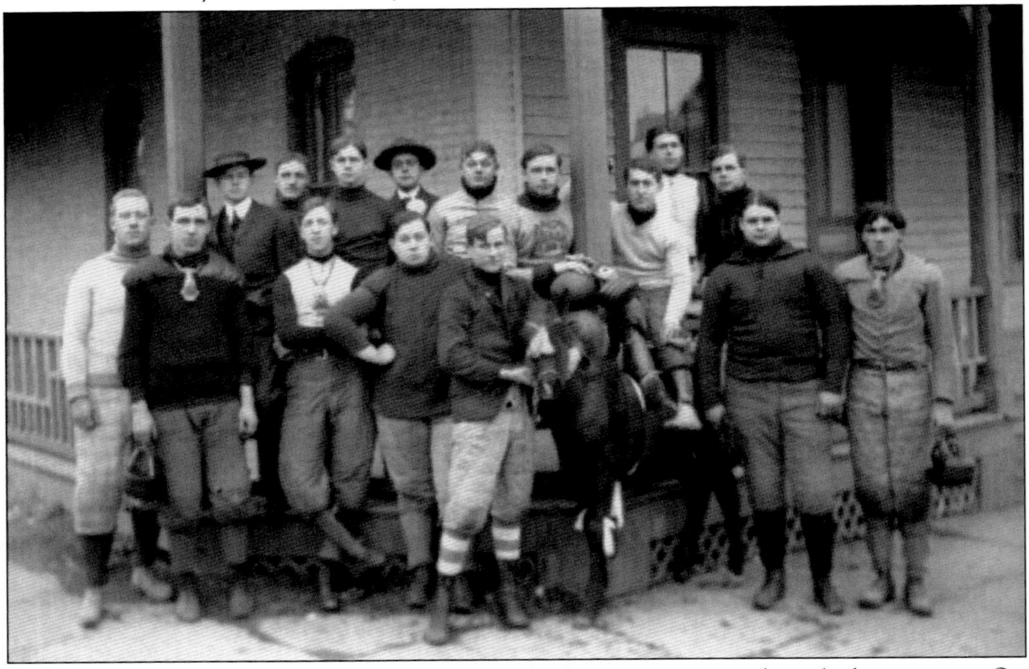

These 1904 football players pose alongside the Chatham House veranda with their mascot. On January 9, 1913, a Gridiron Dinner was held at Cady's Hall honoring Chatham's star football team. An orchestra entertained the ladies and gents whose admission prices were 25¢ and 50¢, respectively. Home field was the Columbia County fairgrounds. (Courtesy of Ike Harvey.)

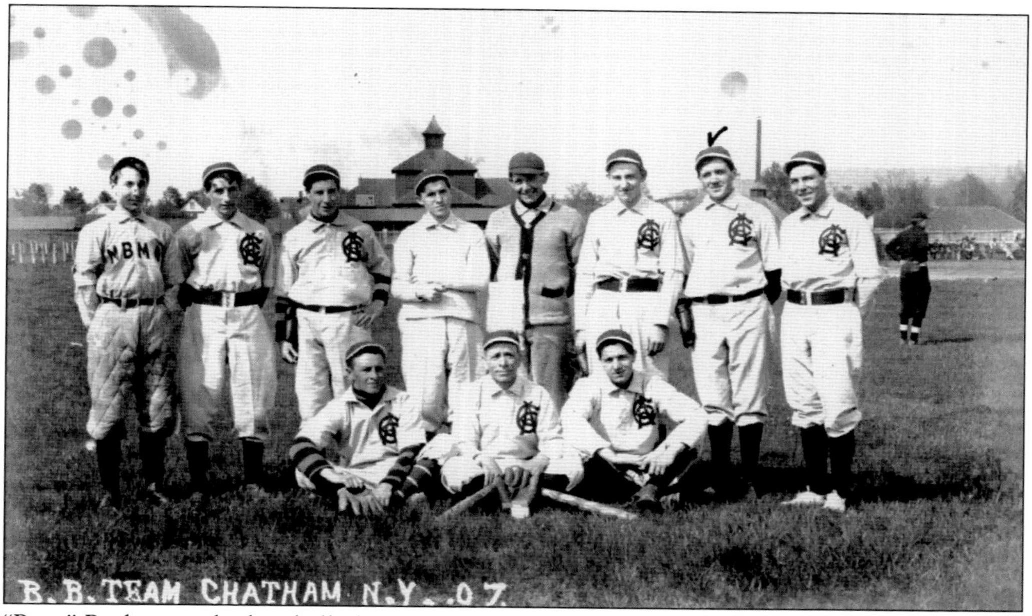

"Bunt" Beebe was the baseball player whom everyone cheered in 1897. George Duggin was on the 1907 team. He had been selected by Ruth Lock as a possible "catch" for her friend Kathy Kuhn, who lived in Spencertown. Floral Hall can be seen in the background behind the baseball team. Besides matchmaking, Ruth Lock had written that she had been to a dance and would be going to moving pictures that March evening. (Courtesy of Jon Meredith.)

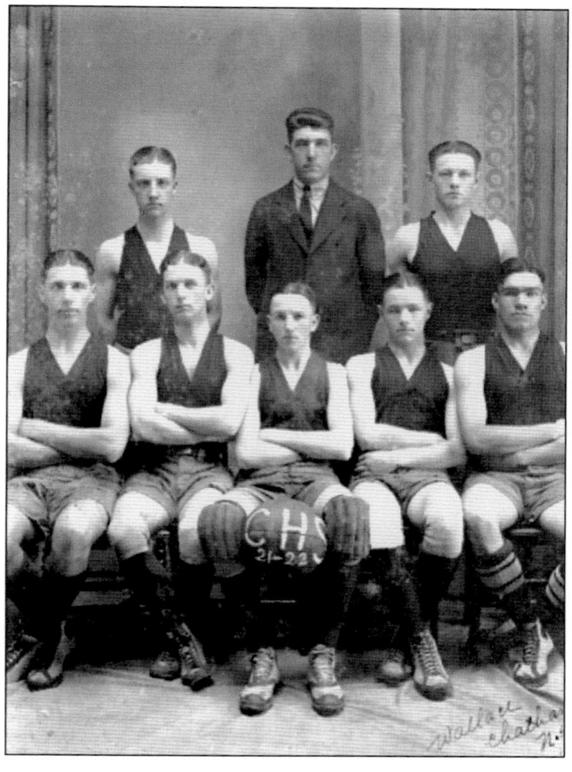

Sports were equally as important as academics throughout the history of the union school. Two members identified on the 1921 basketball team were Jim Broderick, with the basketball, and Salty Wilcox, to his left. Jim Broderick would become a horse trainer, living in the stables on the fairground. He took meals at Helen Strever's Church Street home along with others. Salty Wilcox would become a New York Central Railroad conductor, very popular with the passengers. (Courtesy of CPL, Dardess collection.)

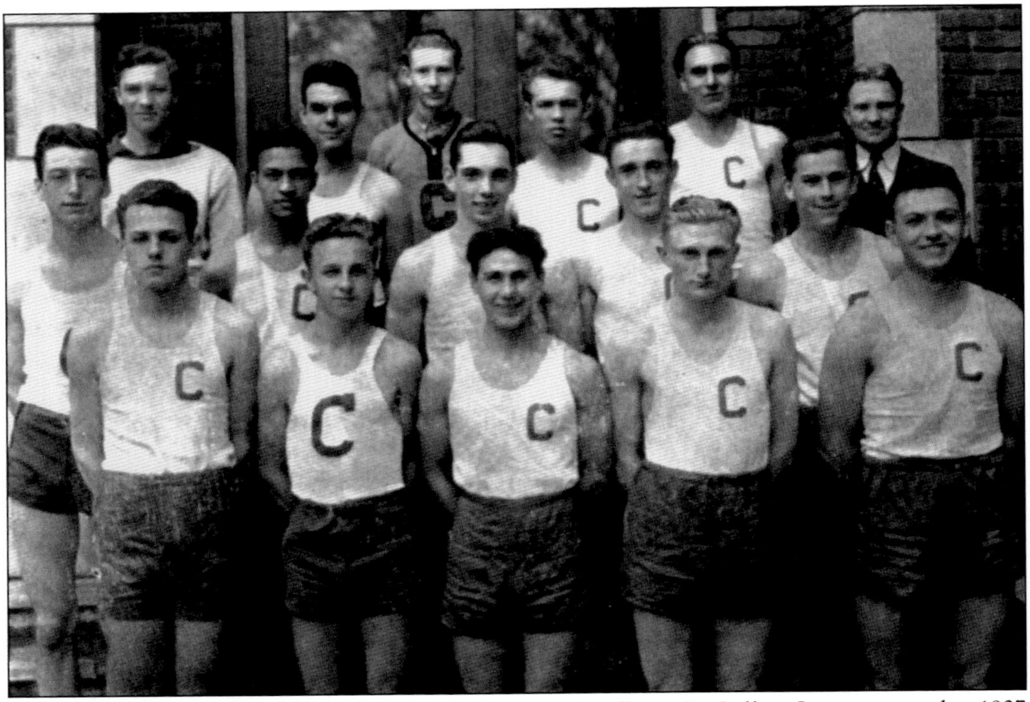

Richard (Dick) Crellin, Howard (Howie) Ploss, and Albert S. Callan Jr. were on the 1937 champion men's track team. All three are pictured here in the first row of the soccer team. Dick's father would start the Crellin Plastics manufacturing company where Dick (on the left) would continue the work. Howie (fourth from left) would work at the Borden milk plant before becoming the village postmaster. His father was a village policeman. Albert Callan Jr. (right) would carry on his father's work as publisher of the *Chatham Courier*. (Courtesy of CPL.)

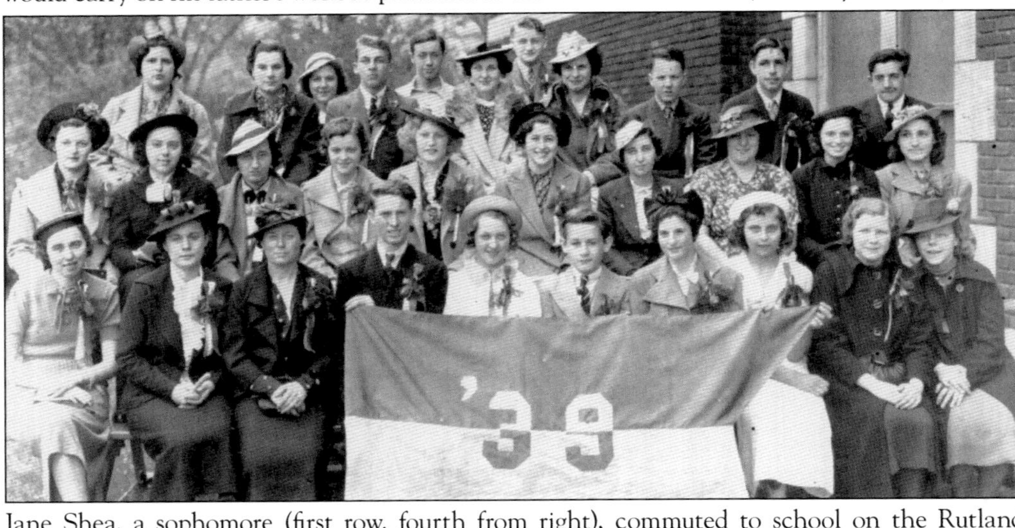

Jane Shea, a sophomore (first row, fourth from right), commuted to school on the Rutland Railroad. She was on the 1937 winning girls' basketball team, the first to win a county title. The class flag was carried for Arbor Day when traditionally there was a formal dress parade, tree planting, athletic competitions, banquet, and dancing into the morning. Arbor Day was a highly anticipated social event. (Courtesy of CPL.)

Nine

THE CHARM

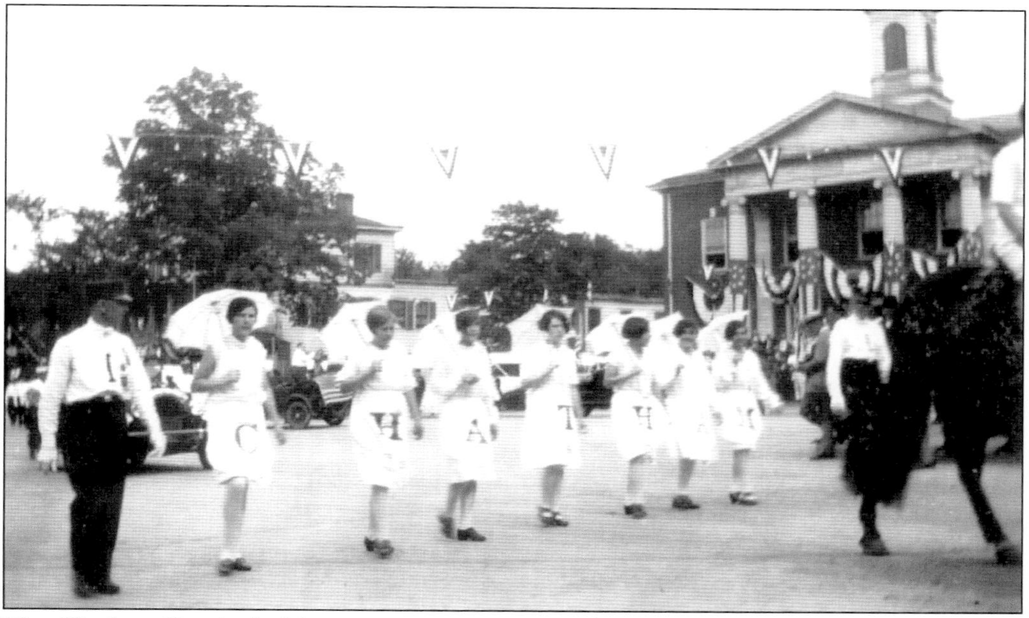

The *Chatham Courier* had become an institution in the community. It reported, "The Tracy Memorial Village Hall, Morris Memorial Community Center, and Louis Payn Memorial Home are gifts. Proof of the village's considerable charm because the bequests were made free and clear 'just because the givers loved the place.' " The parade route crossed the central square in front of the Tracy Village Hall, as viewed in this photograph. (Author's collection.)

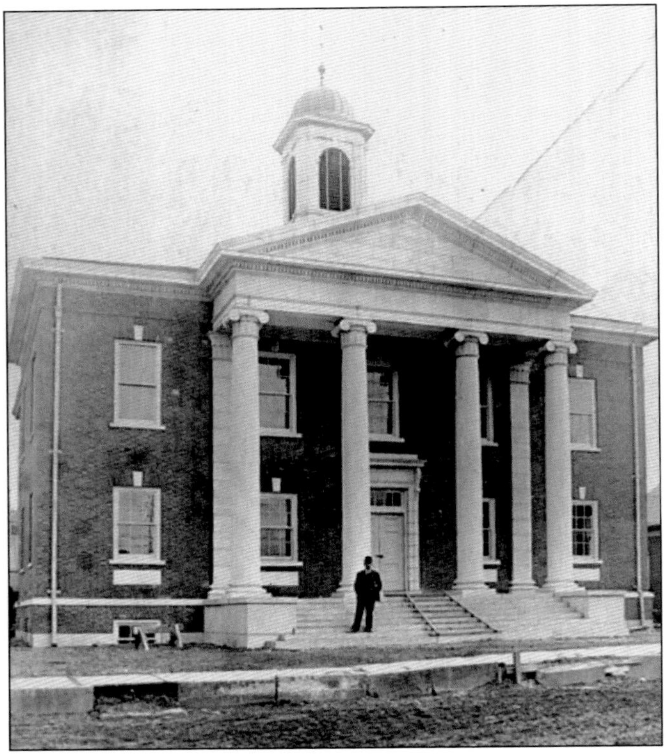

Illness prevented Chatham born and educated Albert E. Tracy from pursuing a college education. In 1880, he served as a postal clerk under postmaster and future congressman George McClellan. Later Judge Hugh W. McClellan would mentor him. He prepared himself to manage the considerable estate he inherited from his father's investments and augmented with local real estate investments. He passed away on August 17, 1910. (Courtesy of Jon Meredith.)

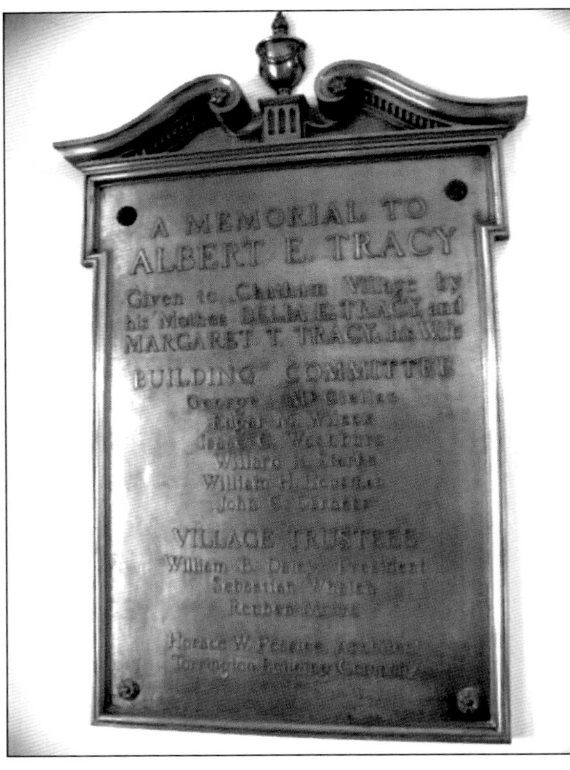

The Albert E. Tracy Memorial dedication was held on a rainy Friday evening, May 23, 1913. The second floor filled to capacity. John C. Dardess, representing Delia Tracy (mother) and Margaret T. Tracy (widow), reminded the crowd of Albert E. Tracy's love for Chatham and his wish to do something for his native village. Architect Horace Peaslee, a Chatham native and graduate, was selected to fulfill Albert's wish. (Author's collection.)

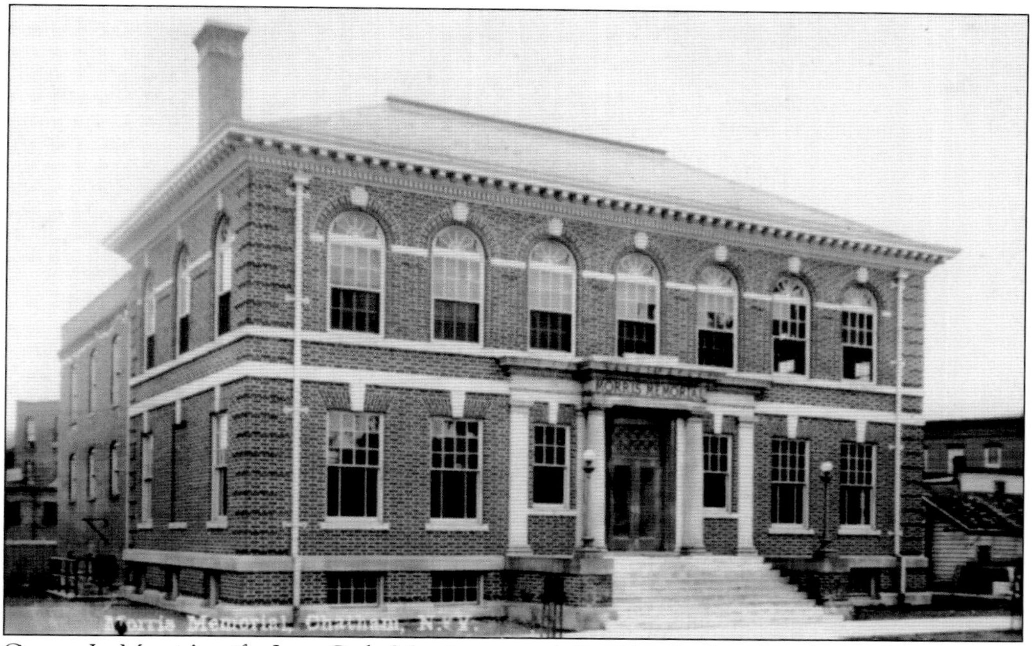

George L. Morris's wife, Jane Cady Morris, memorialized her husband with the donation of a village community center on Park Row. Officers Edward C. White, president; Jerry Browning, treasurer; and Sanford W. Smith, director, were among those charged to improve the conditions under which men and boys lived in Chatham. (Courtesy of Jon Meredith.)

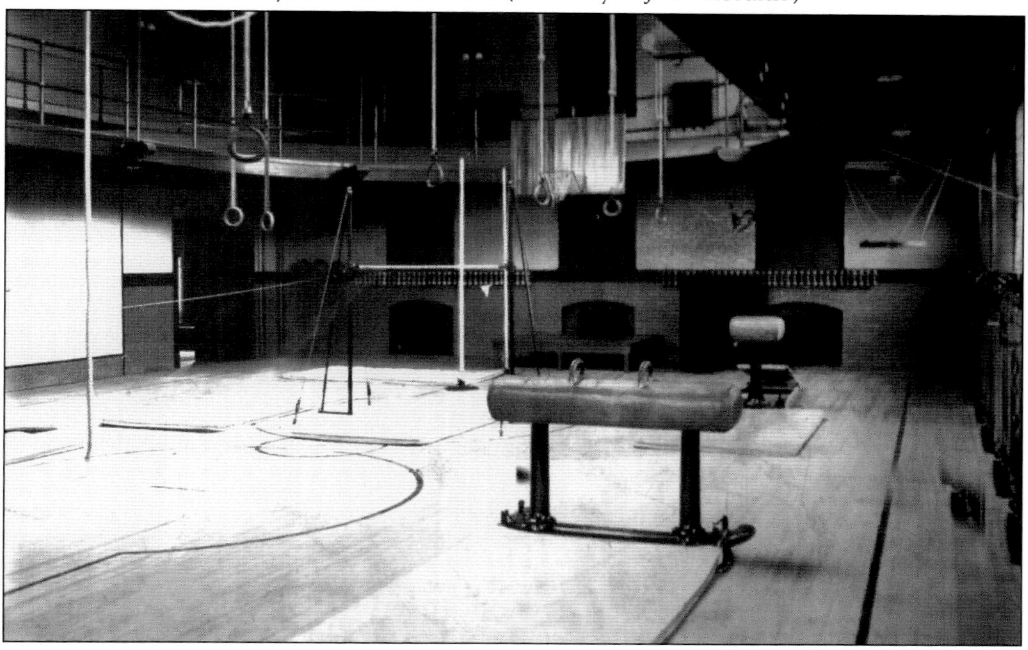

There were dances, minstrels, gym classes, and club meetings. An elevated running track, a basement bowling alley, and pool tables were very popular. This photograph was taken in the gymnasium. Eventually women were allowed access to the Morris Memorial. (Courtesy of Chatham Press.)

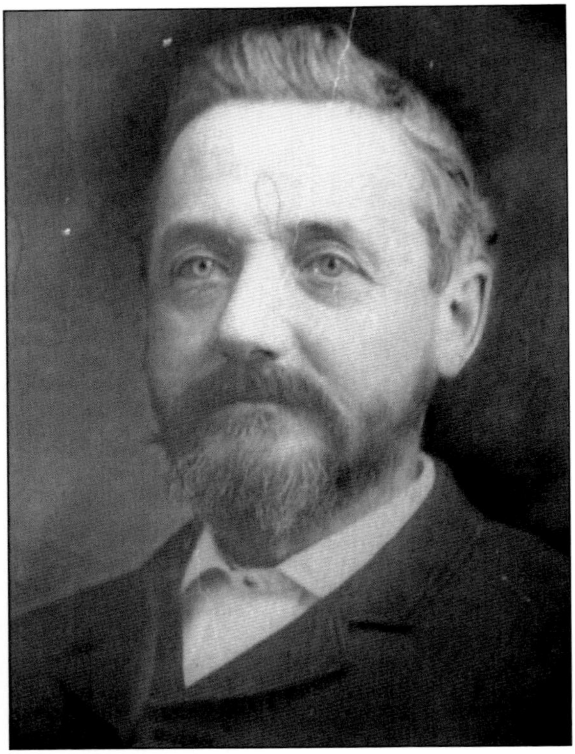

George L. Morris, village tinsmith and hardware store proprietor, became president of the State Bank of Chatham Village on March 8, 1875. T. R. Burrows was vice president. Its first share of stock was issued to John Cadman, attorney. It opened in the residence of W. H. TenBroeck, 31 Kinderhook Street, then expanded into the Masonic building. By 1886, 90 percent of the bank stock was owned by village residents. (Courtesy of CVHS.)

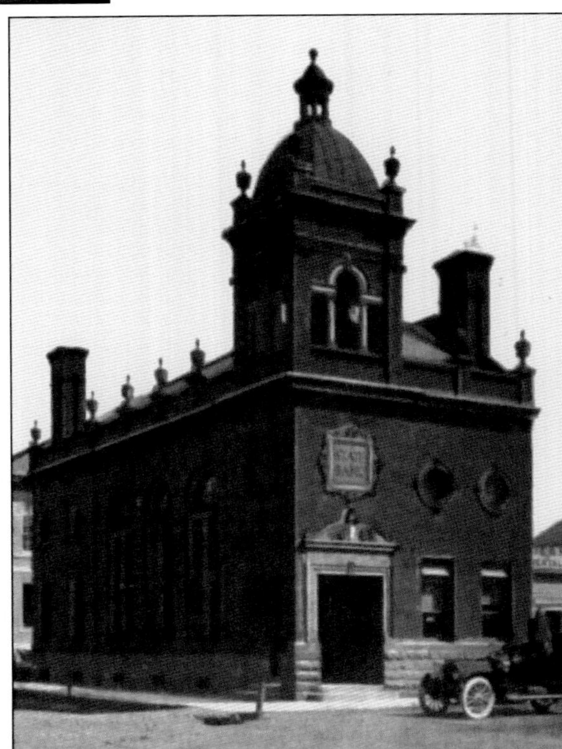

On March 1, 1895, the new bank had been built on the corner of Park Row and Main Street. Amos Starks's son, Dr. Willard Starks, assumed his directorship in 1901. By 1906, safety deposit boxes were offered and foreign exchange was issued. With George L. Morris, bank president, and Dr. J. T. Wheeler, vice president, the bank acquired world credit. Morris remained president until his death in 1909. (Courtesy of CPL.)

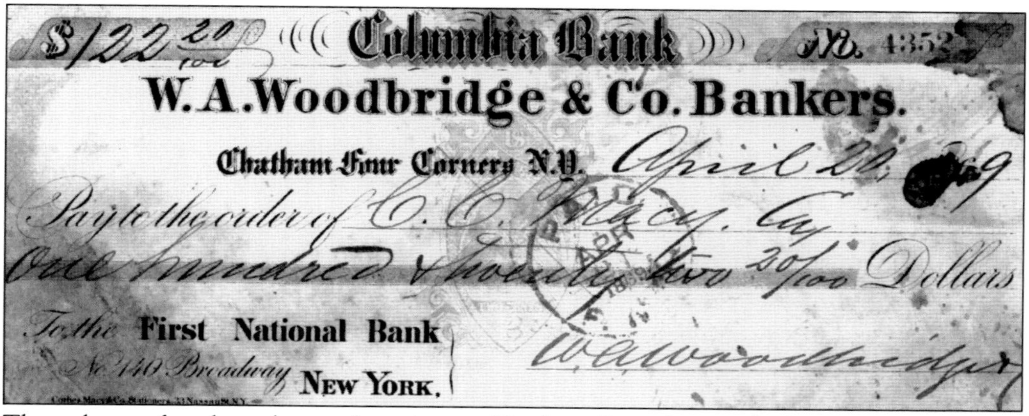

The volume of trade and manufacturing in Chatham Four Corners had created the need for a bank as early as 1859. The Columbia Bank, a state institution, had W. A. Woodbridge as its president. After reorganizing as a private bank from 1867 to 1873, it failed during the panic that hit all industries and financial institutions. Local citizens were without a bank for two years until the State Bank of Chatham Village formed in 1875. (Courtesy of CVHS.)

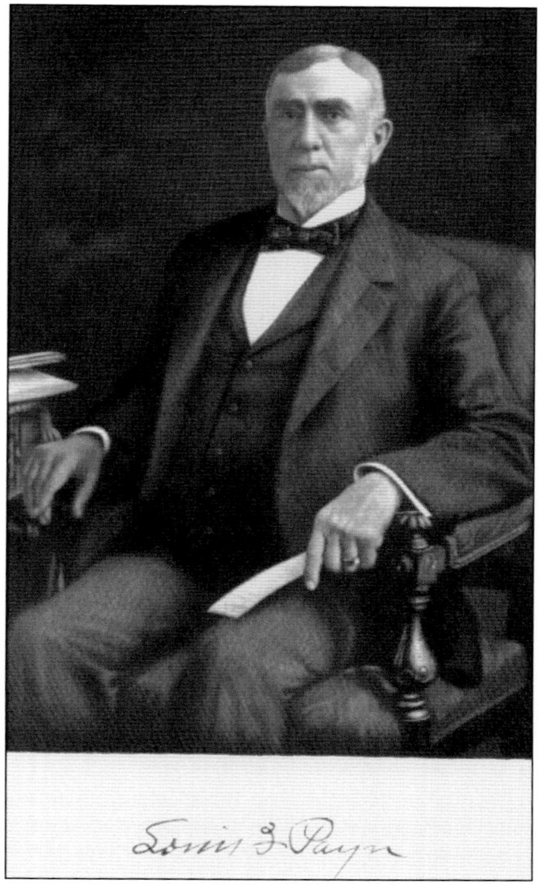

Louis F. Payn, born in 1835 in Ghent to Judge Elijah Payn, moved to Chatham Four Corners eight years later. "Chatham was the dearest spot on earth to him; a hometown man true to himself," according to the 1906 21st anniversary industrial editon of the *Chatham Republican*. Hon. Louis F. Payn was a delegate to every Republican National Convention, superintendent of insurance and under Pres. Ulysses S. Grant, and U.S. marshal for the southern district of New York. (Courtesy of CPL.)

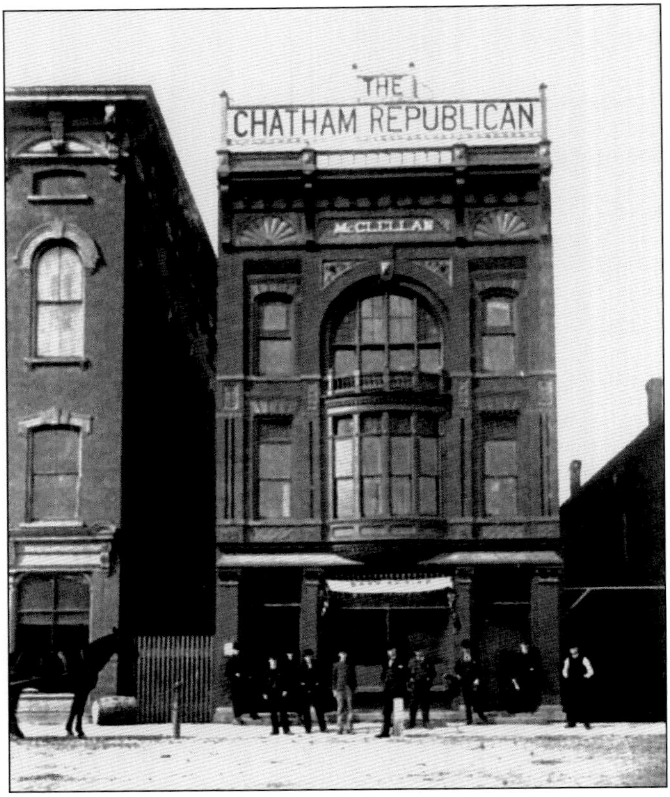

In his hometown Louis F. Payn would edit the *Chatham Republican*, become the founder of Paynville where paper manufacturing employed many locally, and become cofounder of the Chatham Waterworks on Payn Avenue. Despite some setbacks, his nearly completed home burning to the ground and the destruction of the boxboard mills by fire, he retained his label as "one of the rare men of earth who never knew defeat." (Courtesy of CPL.)

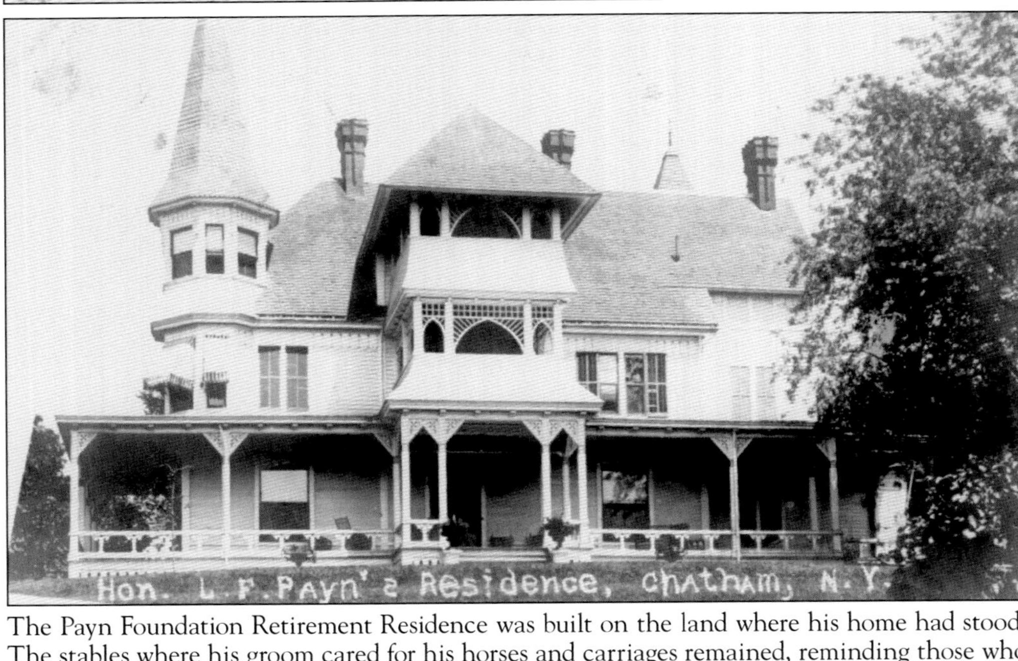

The Payn Foundation Retirement Residence was built on the land where his home had stood. The stables where his groom cared for his horses and carriages remained, reminding those who knew him of the many times he was driven down the village Main Street tossing nickels to the children along the way. (Courtesy of Jon Meredith.)

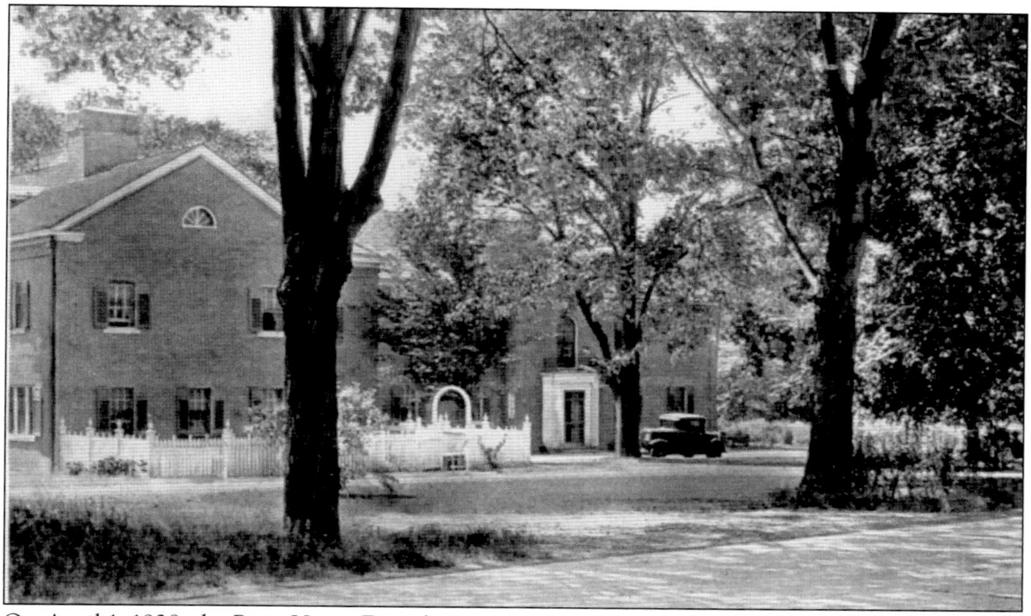

On April 1, 1928, the Payn Home Foundation completed the residence that would be continually occupied from 1929. Speaking at the Payn Home for Aged People, Albert Callan Jr., a journalist and politician himself, would recall when Payn told him he wanted to shake his hand and told him always to remember that he had shaken the hand that shook the hand of Abraham Lincoln. (Courtesy of Jon Meredith.)

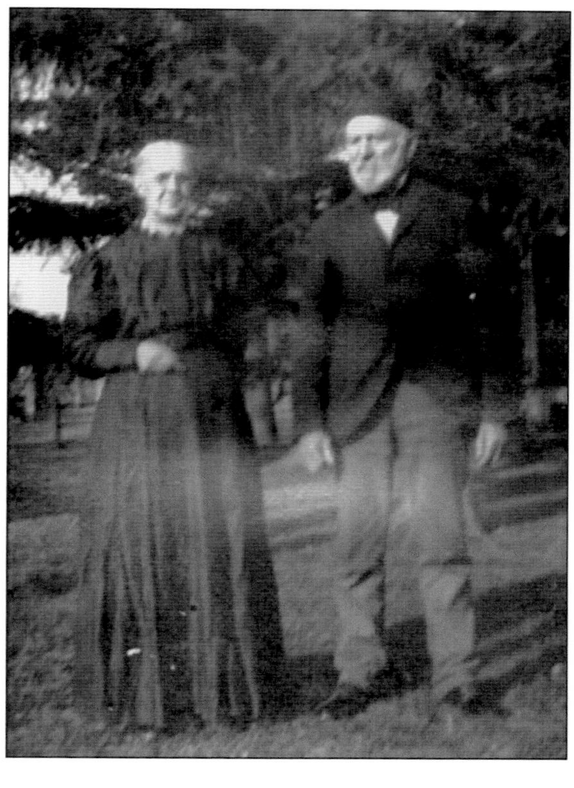

Philo B. Blinn lived in the Hudson Avenue farm built when it was the Union Turnpike (see page 10). His daily record of business dealings trading in horses, cows, sheep, pigs, and even local mortgages is the most extensive record of life in "Chat. 4 Cors" immediately following the Civil War. (Courtesy of CPL, Dardess Collection.)

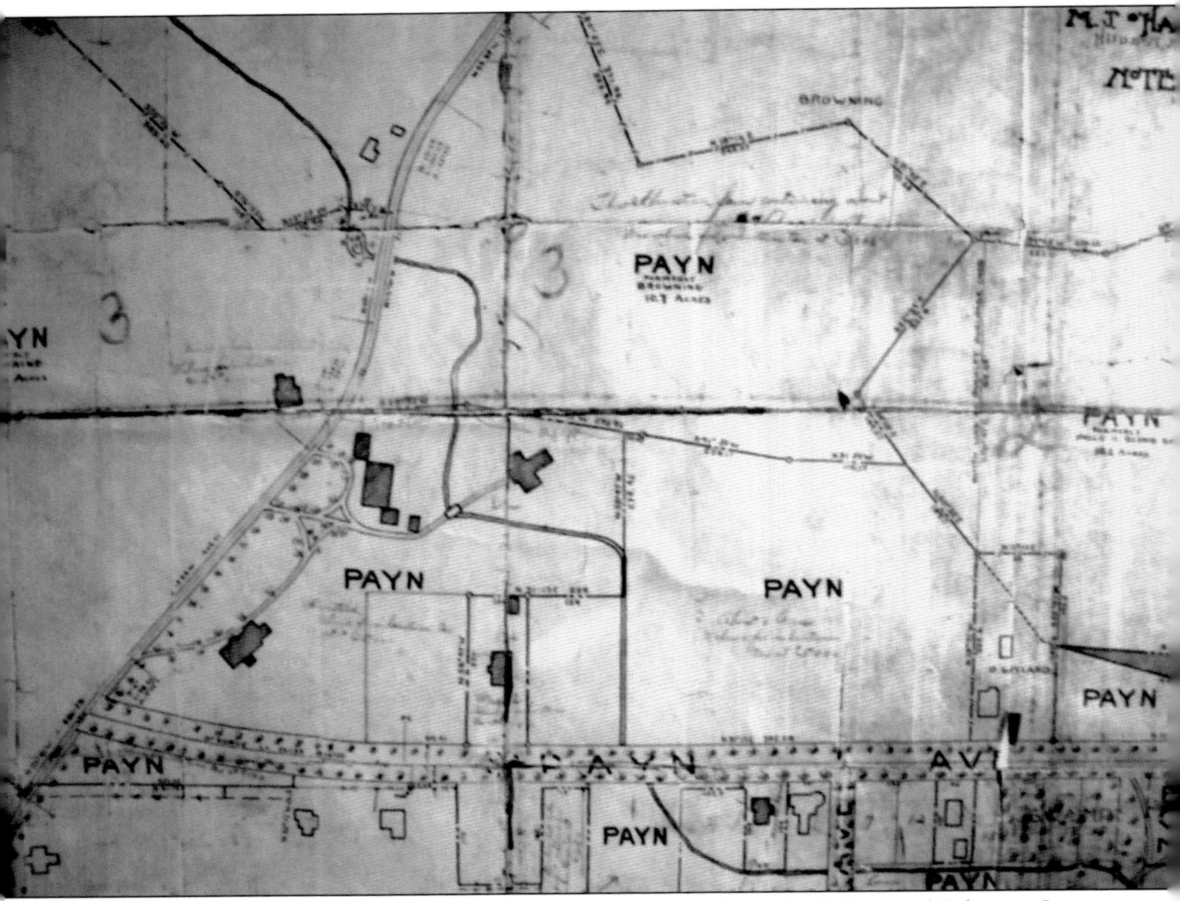

Living on Coleman Street, named for the ancestors of W. C. Coleman (Coleman Lantern manufacturer), the Brownings were primarily milk dealers who partnered with Philo B. Blinn for a period of time. Louis F. Payn owned both the Blinn property and the Browning property at one time. (Courtesy of Payn Foundation.)

Ten

HOMETOWN USA

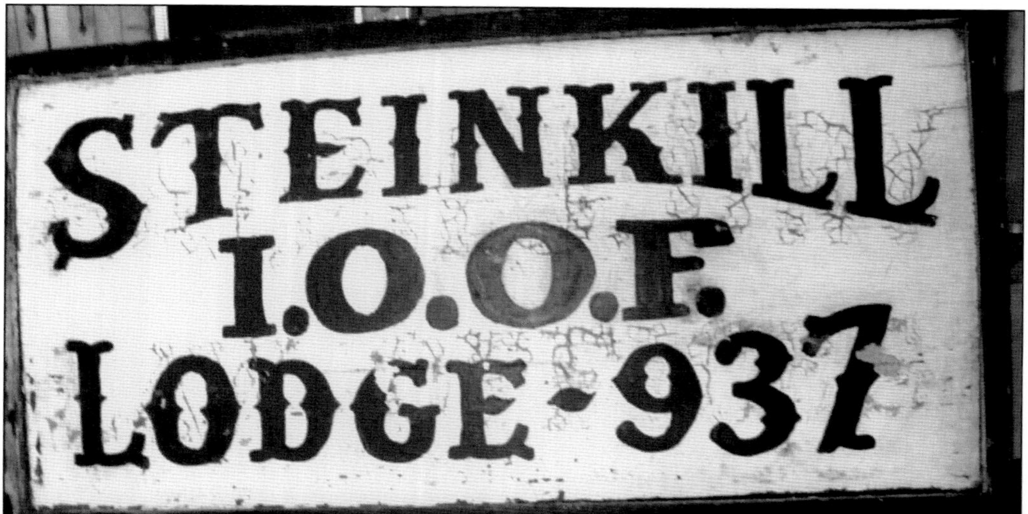

In the 20th century the village of Chatham grew and changed under conscientious guidance from involved citizens. The village sense of community grew stronger during the progressive age transition. Upward of 15 lodges and societies were listed in the village directory. The International Order of Odd Fellows met on Park Avenue. (Courtesy of CVHS.)

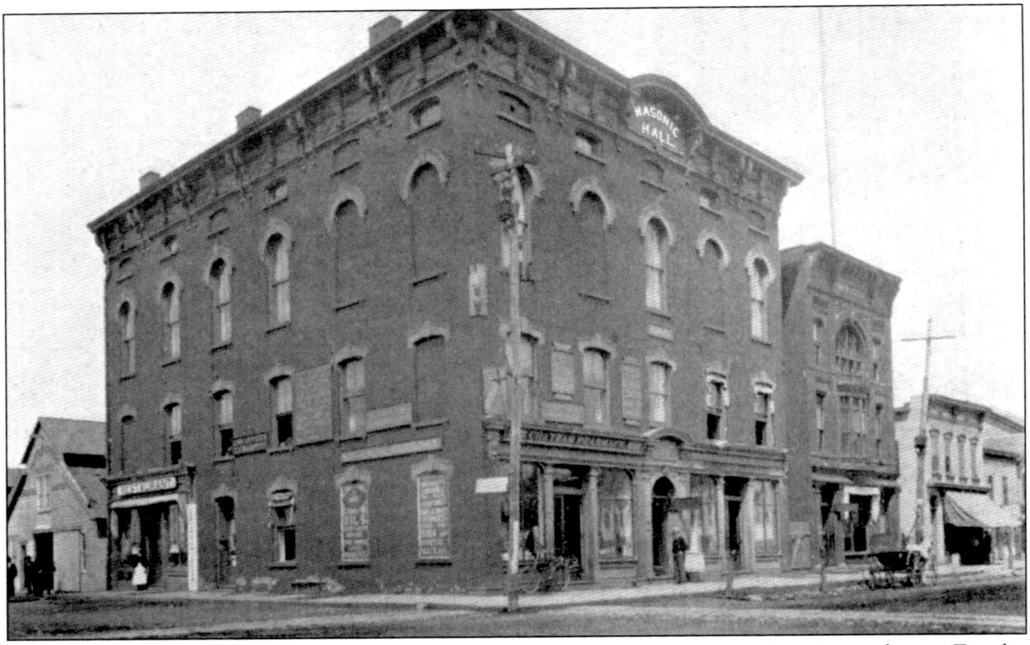

In 1844, Eureka Lodge No. 98 met in Chatham Four Corners at Peter Groat's residence. Eureka Lodge became Columbia Lodge No. 98, Free and Accepted Masons. The Masonic Building Corporation completed its hall at the corner of Park Row and depot square on April 3, 1874, with the largest lodge and dining rooms of all the Columbia County temples. The Payn Foundation Retirement Residence was dedicated by the Masons on November 26, 1929. (Courtesy of CPL.)

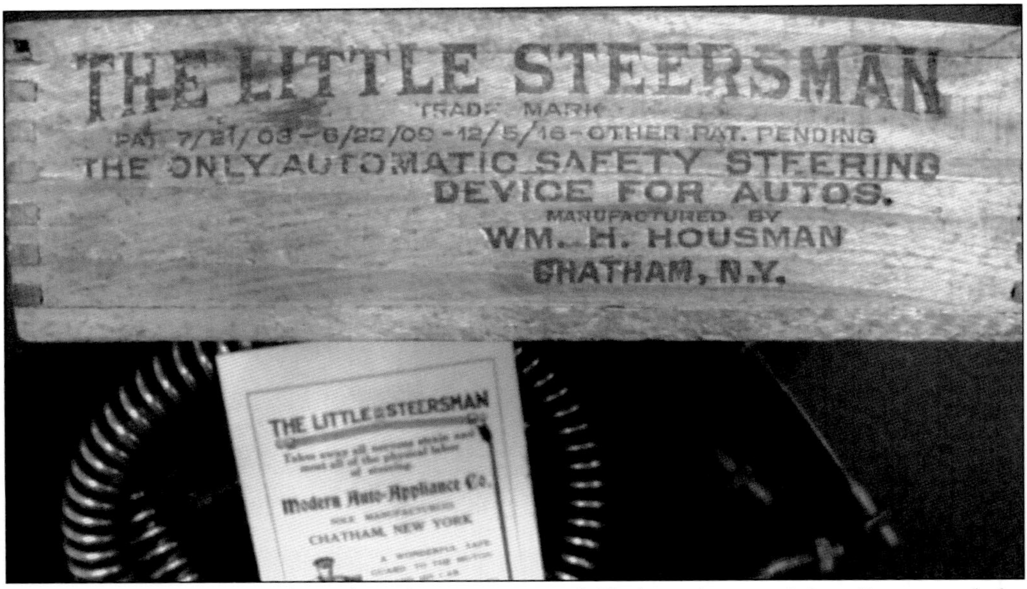

Bituminous macadam and reinforced concrete paved Hudson Avenue, Main Street, and the central square in 1920 for automobiles. The Ladies' Aid water fountain that cooled horses, people, and dogs alike was removed. The Little Steersman, designed and patented at the Vosburgh garage near Woodbridge Avenue, was a coiled spring attached to a car's front axle and advertised "Takes away all nervous strain and most physical labor from steering." (Courtesy of Dwight Sawyer.)

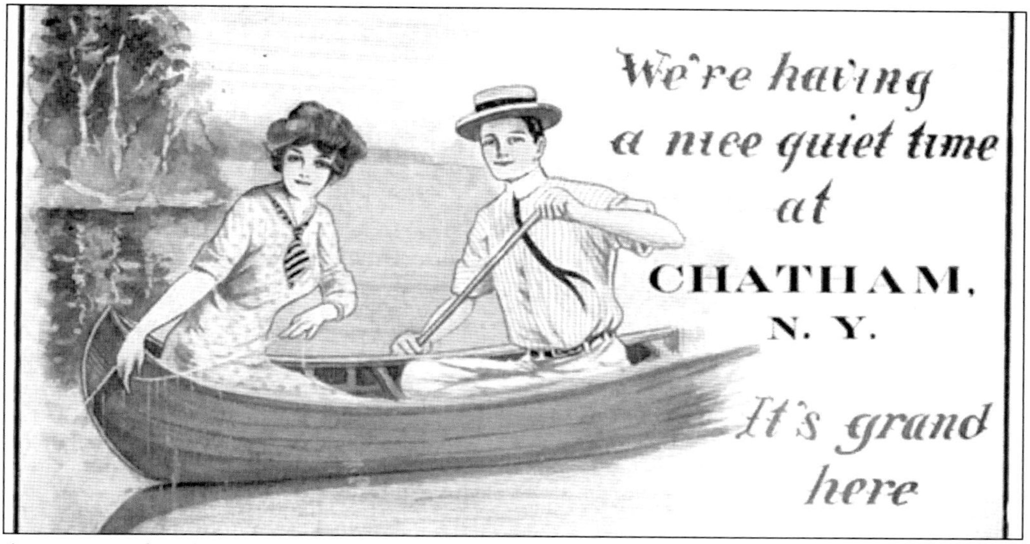

Approximately 25 acres of land was donated by Dr. Willard Starks on Smith's Pond (the old pond) and improved by the Civil Works Administration for Starks Park. Amos Starks, his father, was one of the largest landowners in this section of the village. Dedication ceremonies were held on July 4, 1934. Willard Starks had envisioned footpaths, tennis courts, toboggan slides, picnic areas, and boating facilities. The village moviemakers used the location for movie settings. (Courtesy of CCHS.)

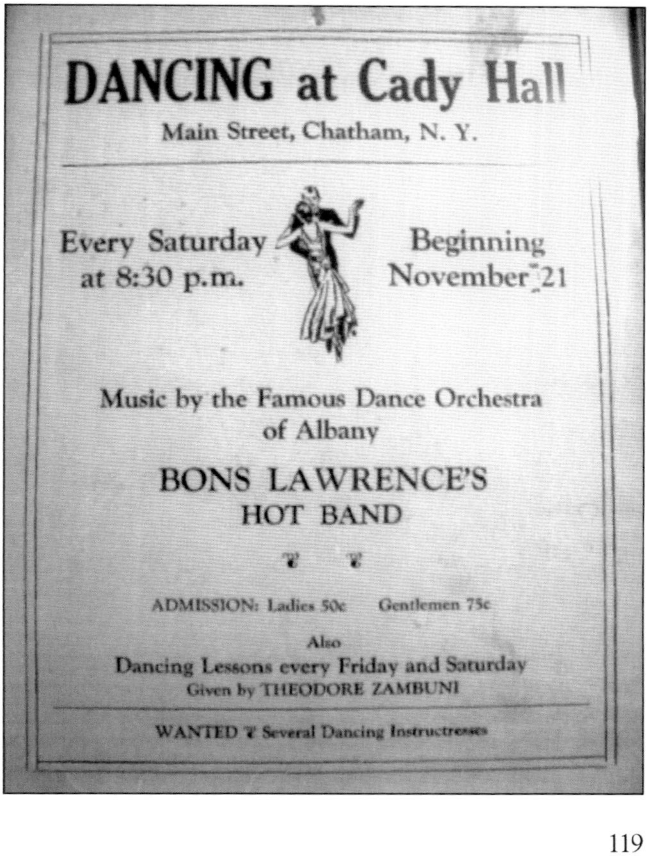

In 1920, the Sphere Motion Picture Corporation auditioned local residents at Cady Hall for *By Man's Law*, filmed on Main Street. Young newcomer Norma Shearer won a part. John C. Dardess, Chatham attorney; Mary Eberle, a local professional actress; and Harry Doty, the editor of the *Chatham Courier* had a role. Chathamite Floyd Buckley would earn a role and become a highly acclaimed Broadway star. (Courtesy of Jon Meredith.)

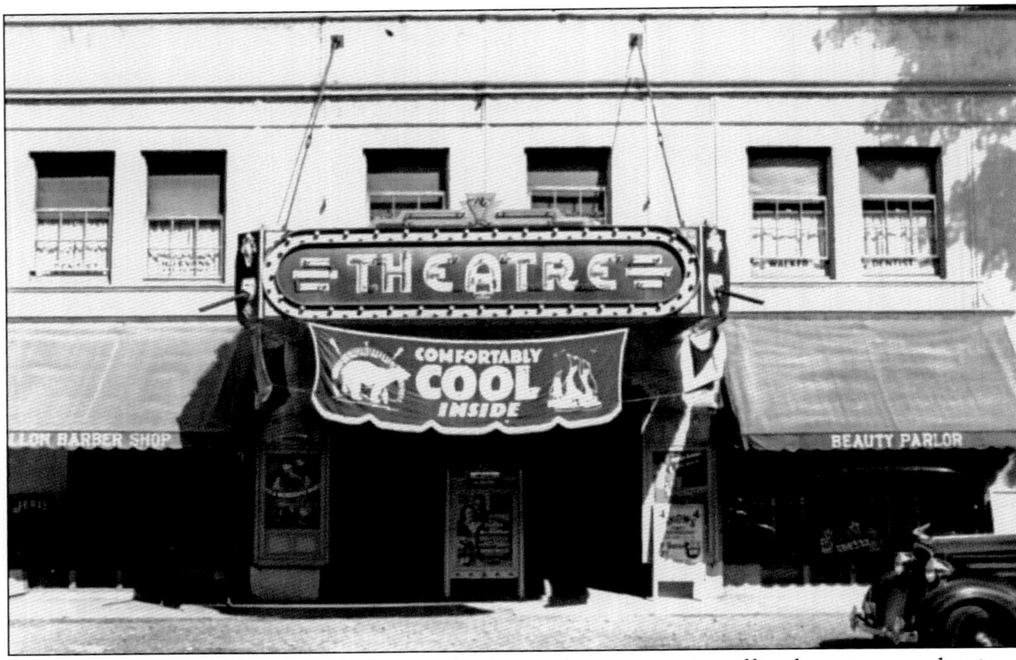

Crandell Theatre, Walter Crandell's contribution to the community, offered amateur productions, moving pictures, plus two storefronts on Main Street. Rose Patlen purchased the Crandell store in the mid-1930s, setting up a dress shop on one side, with a tailor shop run by her husband, Harry, on the other. Her Patlen Smart Shop would continue for decades under the proprietorship of their son, Larry. (Courtesy of Calvin Pitcher.)

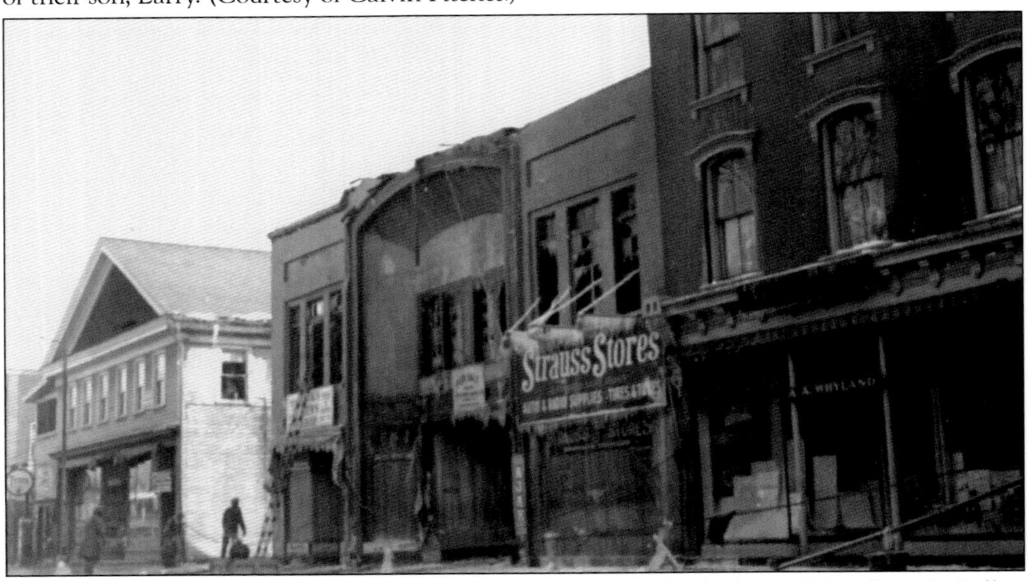

Across the street, another theater was constructed but never finished. In 1930, Albert S. Callan bought and renovated the structure and placed the *Chatham Courier* mechanical and editorial offices at the rear. A major fire erupted in the front clothing store six years later, damaging the *Courier* section, yet the newspaper made its deadline. The A&P store would eventually occupy that building. (Courtesy of Calvin Pitcher.)

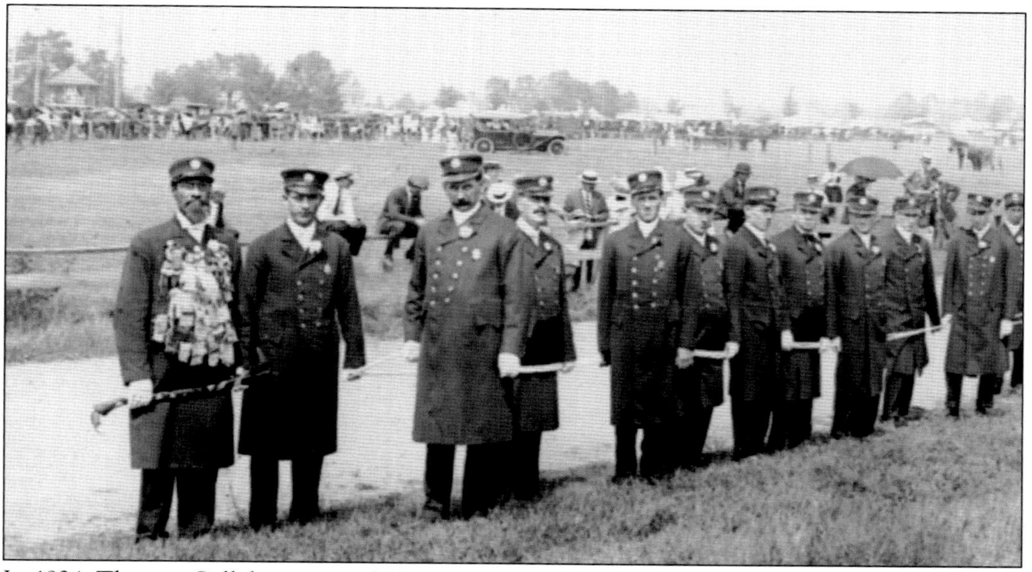

In 1934, Thomas Callahan secured Harry Miner's axe that the village fireman had long carried in parades as part of his highly decorated uniform, to be kept among the company's mementos. In 1930, the Sanford W. Smith Hook and Ladder Company, so named as a tribute to the man who was actively involved in its affairs until his death, joined forces with Ocean Fire Company No. 1. (Courtesy of CCAS.)

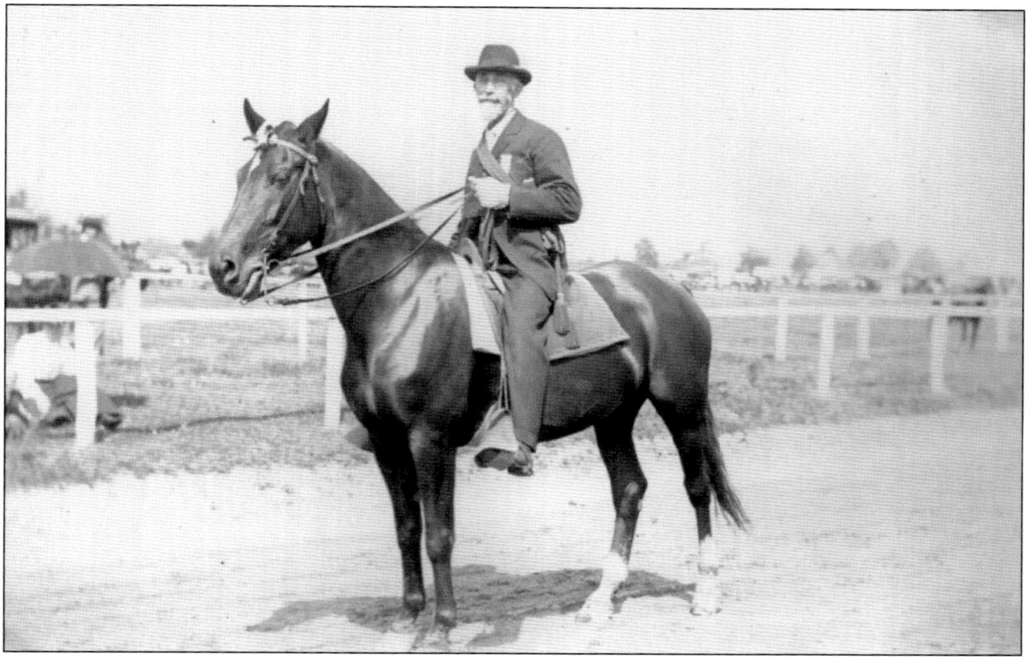

The General Logan Post No. 539 of the GAR had 27 charter members and 42 members in 1906. The post decorated veterans' graves and presented a program of tribute on Decoration Day (Memorial Day) as Civil War soldiers had done since 1885. Congressional Medal of Honor recipient Lt. John Blunt (here in 1903) led the veterans of the GAR in Memorial Day parades. (Courtesy of CCAS.)

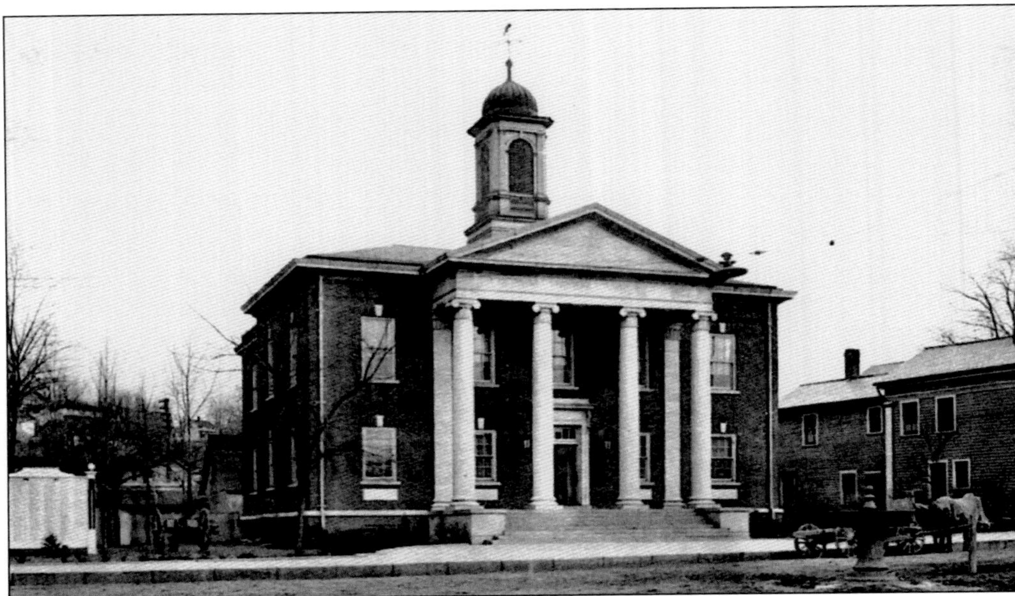

American Legion Post No. 42 assumed General Logan Post No. 539's duties and included Veterans' Day, the 11th day of the 11th month in 1918. Maj. Albert S. Callan Sr. organized the first meeting at the Tracy Memorial. An illuminated honor roll honoring 132 servicemen was presented in front of the Tracy Memorial in 1918 (left in photograph). The Chatham War Memorial on depot square was dedicated on May 30, 1932. (Courtesy of Jon Meredith.)

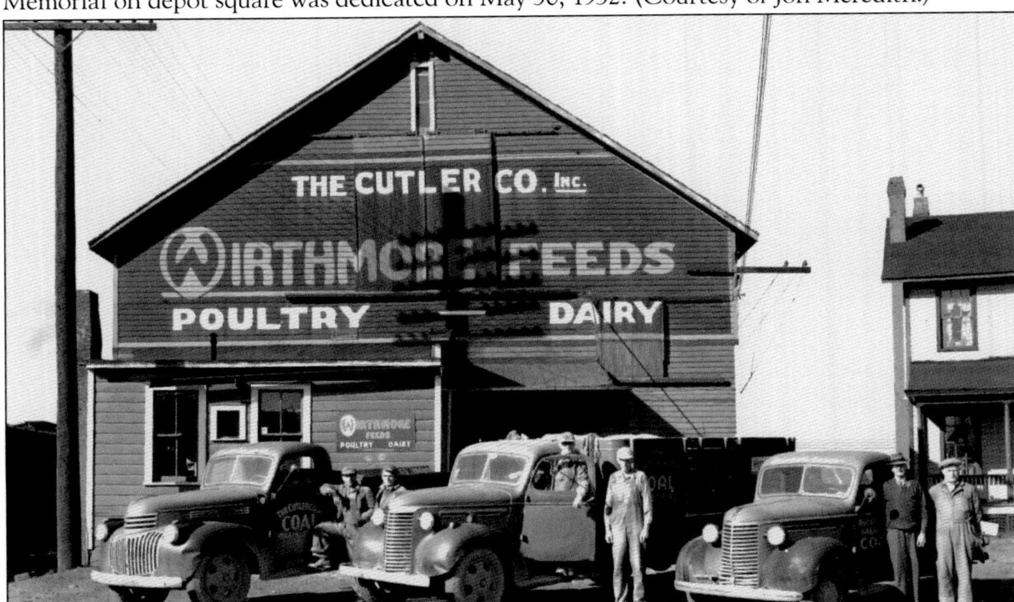

William H. Housman established a 15-carload capacity dry storage plant on Woodbridge Avenue in connection with his feed and grain business by 1906. He also handled Standard Oil Company products. The Cutler Company would eventually rent his place of business. By 1900, his prosperity allowed him the opportunity to offer free land to anyone wishing to start new industry within the village. (Courtesy of Jon Meredith.)

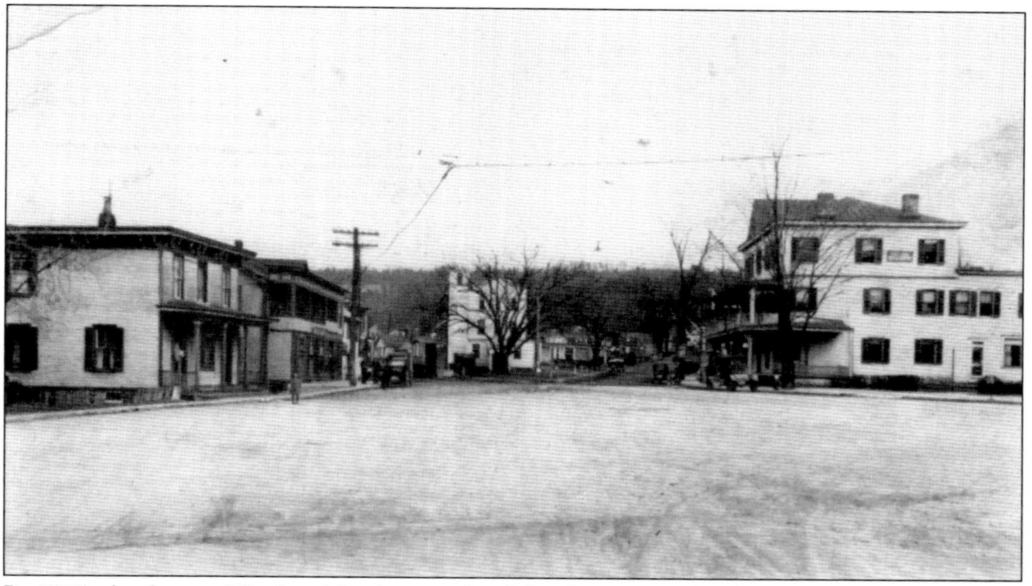

By 1915, the former Windsor Hotel was refitted for the New Columbia Theatre. Patrons sat in curved rows of seats to see Theodore Roosevelt, Harry Houdini, and Norma Shearer. When the New Columbia Theatre closed, the structure (center of photograph) came to be called the Senate Building. William F. Abrams of Abrams and Boright car dealership opened in 1927. (Courtesy of CVHS.)

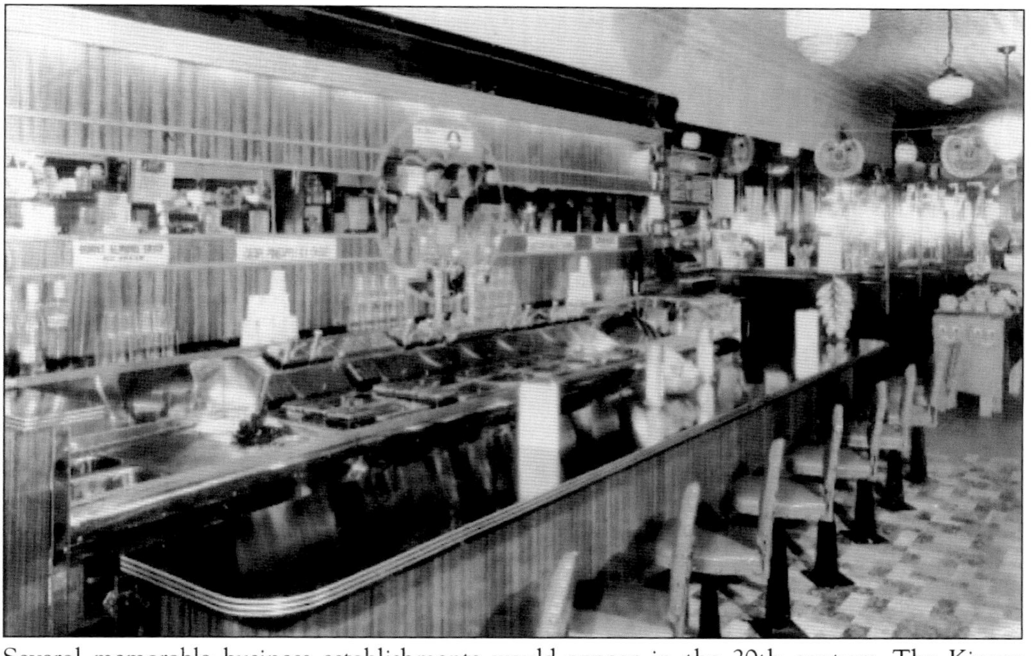

Several memorable business establishments would appear in the 20th century. The Kinum Bakery's brick bread oven extended under the sidewalk. Mr. Kinum lost his life crossing in front of a team of horses on Main Street. Nick Demos and his wife became its proprietors, naming it the Boston Candy Kitchen. The irresistible aroma of homemade candy wafted from this establishment from 1919 to 1962. (Courtesy of Shirley Rosen.)

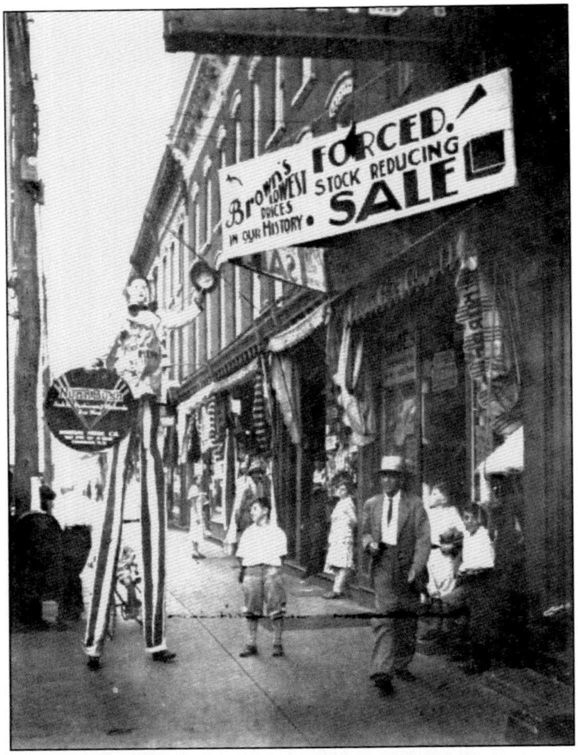

The Brown family fitted Chatham railroad men in work shoes for years at their Albany store. Jules Brown brought the business to Chatham for trainmen and quickly became a civic leader. He teamed with Father Finn, effectively lobbying in Albany to bring the first sewer system to the village. Jules Brown, known for his generosity, made sure every child who needed them had shoes during the lean years of the Great Depression. (Courtesy of Shirley Rosen.)

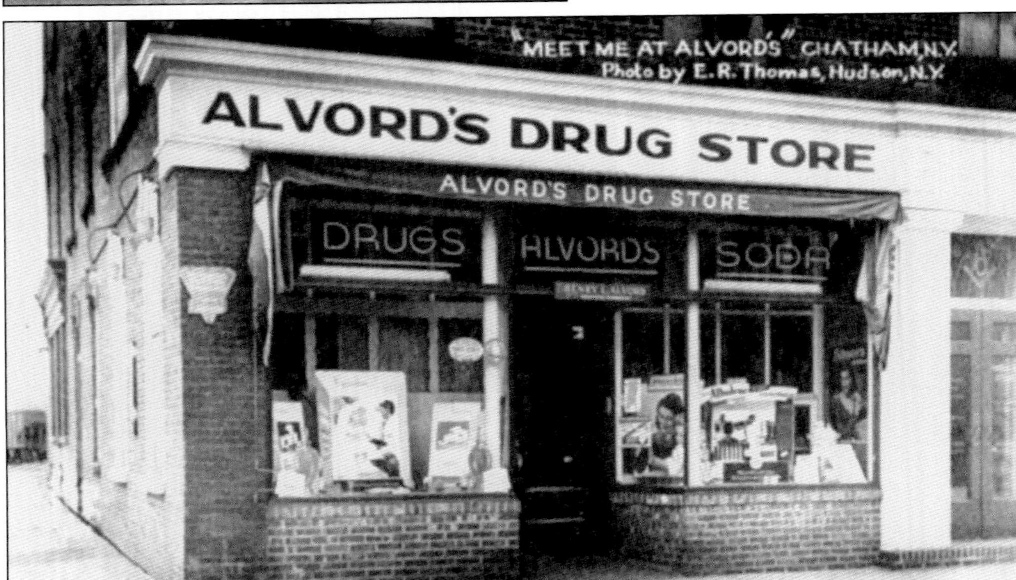

Col. Alvord's Drug Store soda fountain, in the old Fellows Drugstore, was a favorite gathering place for students where ice-cream cones sold for pennies. He contributed generously to the community, working with the rescue squad. L. D. Hess and Son (H. Glenn Hess), butcher shop, occupied what had been Koger's Saloon on the central square. Huge slabs of meat were cut to order right before one's eyes. (Courtesy of Shirley Rosen.)

Homer Crandell's corner of Main Street on the central square would become Hartigan's Busy Corner and then the Shell Gas station pictured here. The Tracy Village Hall is in the background. A banner would hang over the entrance to the Stanwix Hotel. It read, "Stanwix Hotel, Official Stopping Place for Motorists." (Courtesy of CVHS.)

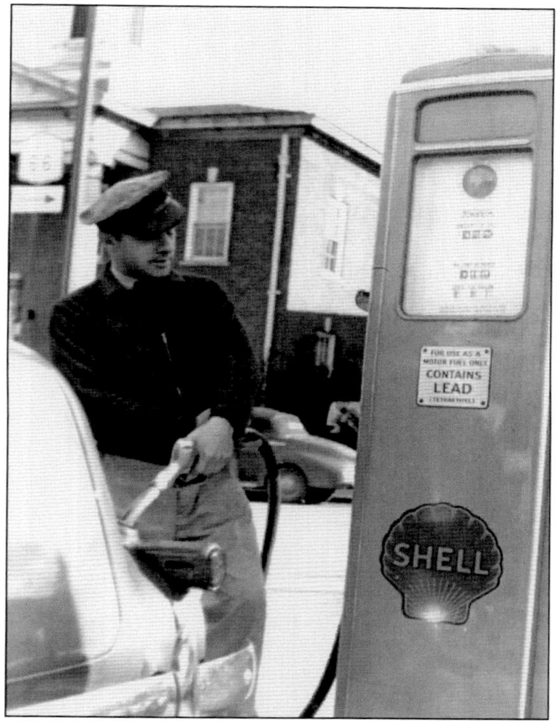

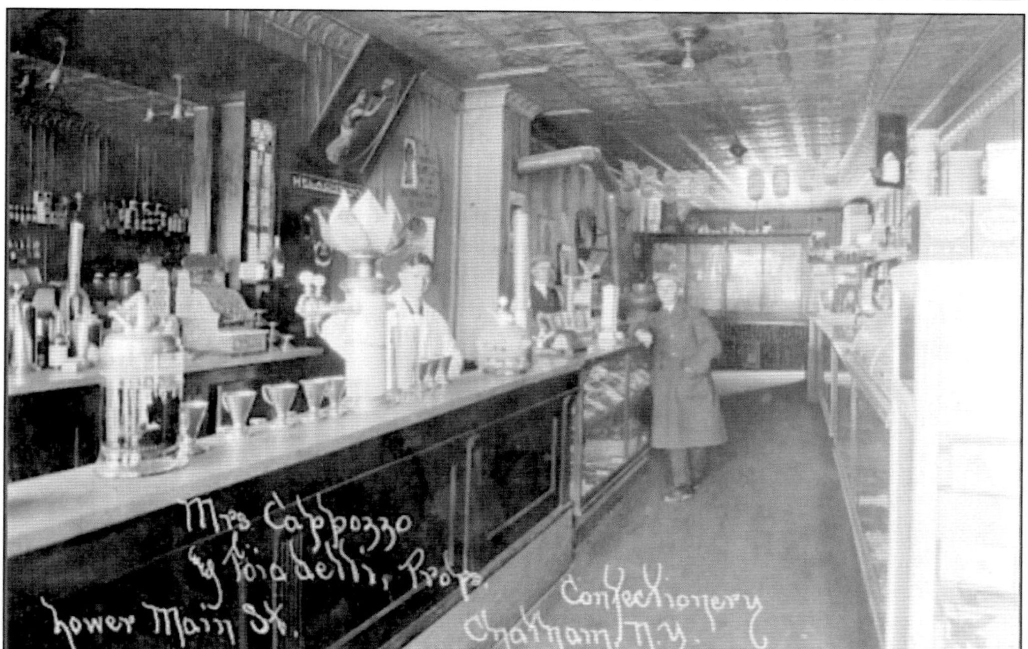

Maddelena was a domestic when she arrived from Italy to America. When she discovered Chatham, she began a confectionery store on Lower Main Street, then officially Hudson Avenue. She first partnered with Mr. Foiadelli, who would marry her sister. Maddelena's husband passed away, and she met and married Fred Cappozzo, also from Italy. (Courtesy of Frank Cappozzo.)

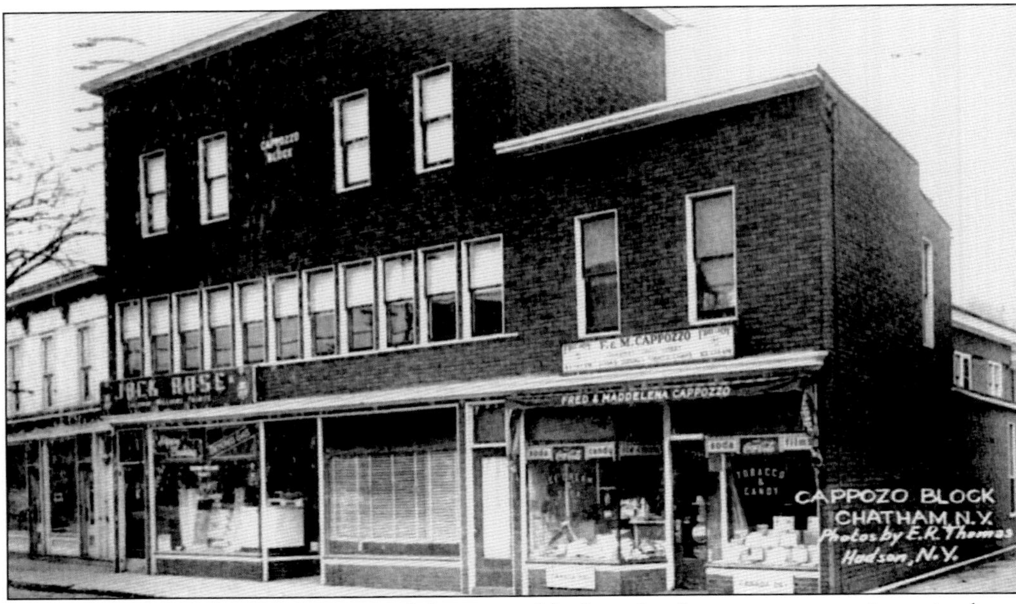

Fred and Maddelena Cappozzo's workday started before the first passenger train arrived and ended after the 11:00 p.m. shift at tower 65 when the tower operator habitually came for a pint of ice cream. The family business expanded to the left section of the building (see page 16). When the upstairs porch was enclosed and the structure resided, Cappozzo Block was lettered on the building. (Courtesy of Frank Cappozzo.)

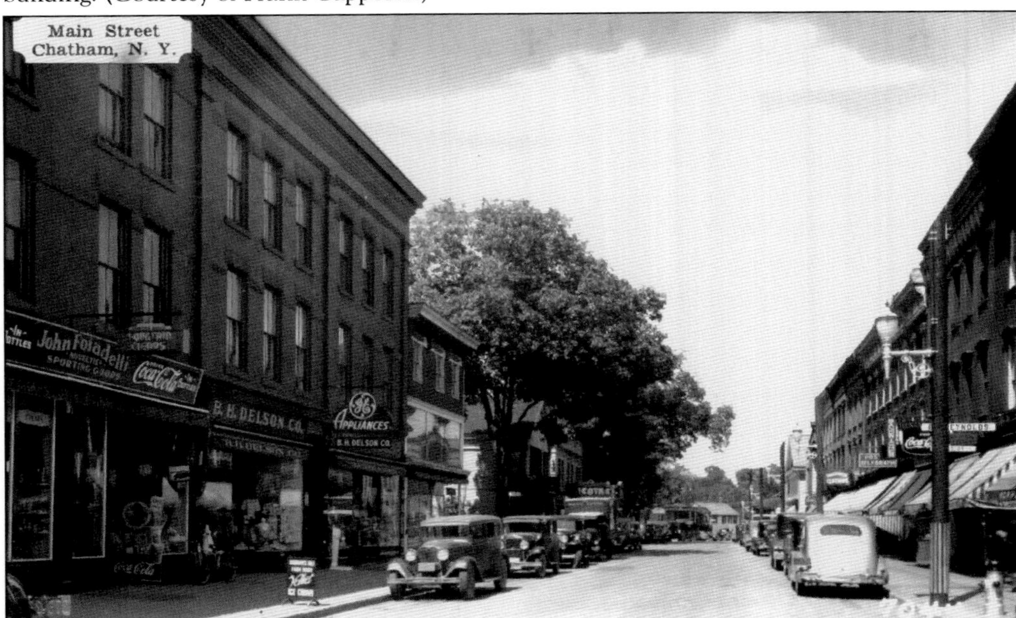

The Delson Company rented a storefront in the Rogowski Building. Mrs. Rogowski would come to collect the rent herself, using her cane as support and to accentuate her opinions. Every child knew the best place in Delson's was down the wide staircase to the basement toy section. John Foiadelli's poolroom in the back was frequented by the adolescents of the day. (Courtesy of Jon Meredith.)

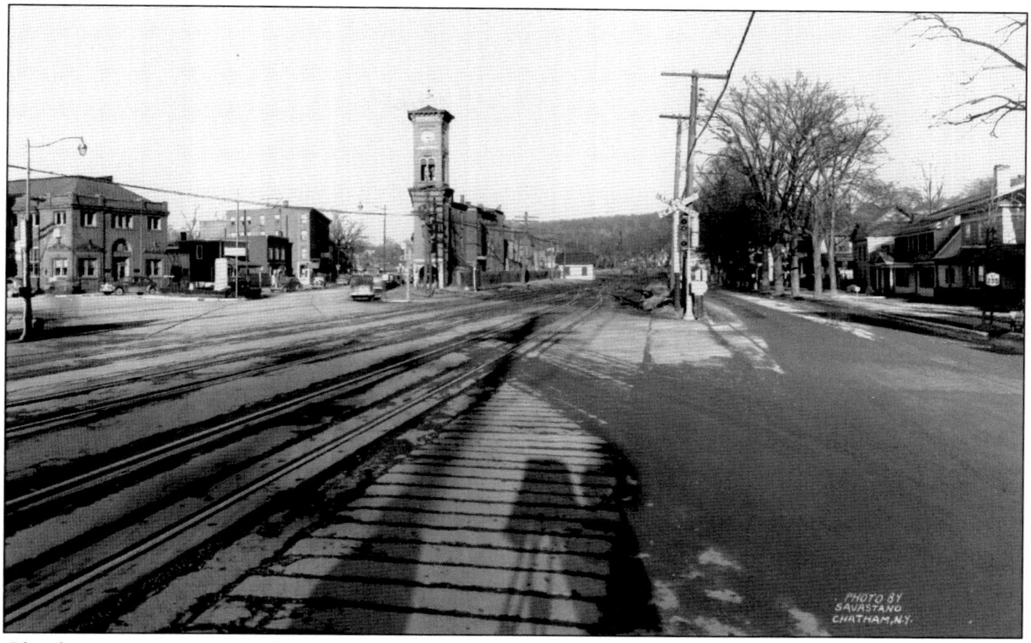

Chatham was recognized as a prosperous major transportation hub. Jennie Horwitz, a shrewd New York City real estate agent, obtained a 116-acre farm near the village for weekend and summer respites. Her boys (stooges Shemp, Moe, and Curly) would perform antics in the village. In 1935, Amelia Earhart campaigned on behalf of Pres. Franklin D. Roosevelt, signing autographs for a huge crowd outside the Chatham Union Station. (Courtesy of CPL.)

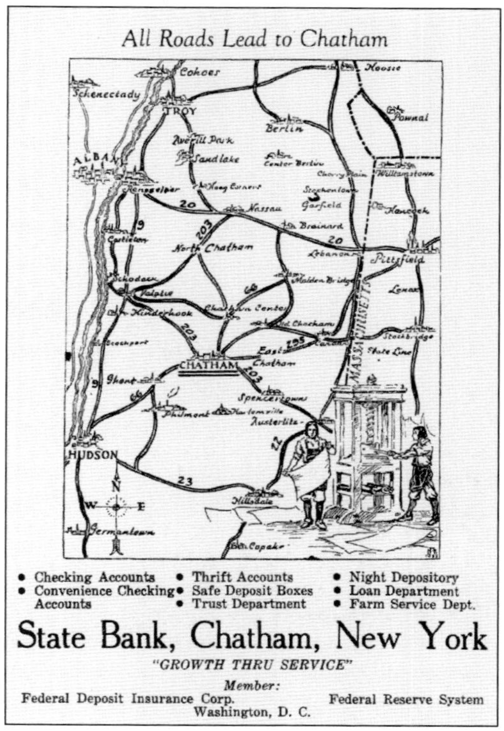

Chatham's hometown charm perpetuated by the pride in its history produced a neighborly atmosphere that continually drew visitors and guests. The village that began as an unidentifiable plot of land in Columbia County would become its agricultural, industrial, and transportation center by the mid-20th century. (Courtesy of Dwight Sawyer.)

DISCOVER THOUSANDS OF LOCAL HISTORY BOOKS FEATURING MILLIONS OF VINTAGE IMAGES

Arcadia Publishing, the leading local history publisher in the United States, is committed to making history accessible and meaningful through publishing books that celebrate and preserve the heritage of America's people and places.

Find more books like this at
www.arcadiapublishing.com

Search for your hometown history, your old stomping grounds, and even your favorite sports team.

Consistent with our mission to preserve history on a local level, this book was printed in South Carolina on American-made paper and manufactured entirely in the United States. Products carrying the accredited Forest Stewardship Council (FSC) label are printed on 100 percent FSC-certified paper.

MADE IN THE USA